Peer-Group Mentoring for Teacher Development

Supporting new teachers is a common challenge globally and the European Commission has recently emphasized the need to promote a lifelong continuum of teachers' professional development by building bridges between pre-service and in-service teacher education.

Peer-Group Mentoring for Teacher Development introduces and contextualizes for an international audience a new model for teachers' professional development: peer–group mentoring (PGM). It is based on the constructivist view of learning, the idea of shared expertise, and the 'model of integrative pedagogy' which emphasizes the integration of different forms of expert knowledge in professional development.

This book explores the theoretical and practical backgrounds for developing the peer-group mentoring model, and provides important contextual information about the Finnish school system in which it was conceptualized, and also about teacher education. It presents several empirical studies on applying the PGM model with primary and secondary school teachers in different school contexts, and outlines future challenges, examining peer–group mentoring in the framework of wider practice architectures of teacher education.

The book is an indispensable reference tool for educationalists and education researchers interested in collaborative and dialogic learning, teacher professional development, and school administration.

Hannu L. T. Heikkinen is a Senior Researcher at the Finnish Institute for Educational Research, University of Jyväskylä, Finland, and Adjunct Professor at the University of Tampere, Finland, and at Charles Sturt University, Australia.

Hannu Jokinen is a Researcher at the Finnish Institute for Educational Research, University of Jyväskylä, Finland.

Päivi Tynjälä is Professor in research on teaching and learning in higher education, at the Finnish Institute of the University of Jyväskylä, Finland.

Peer-Group Mentoring for Teacher Development

Edited by Hannu L.T. Heikkinen, Hannu Jokinen and Päivi Tynjälä

Routledge
Taylor & Francis Group

LONDON AND NEW YORK

First published 2012
by Routledge
2 Park Square, Milton Park, Abingdon, Oxon OX14 4RN

Simultaneously published in the USA and Canada
by Routledge
711 Third Avenue, New York, NY 10017

*Routledge is an imprint of the Taylor & Francis Group, an informa
business*

British Library Cataloguing in Publication Data
A catalogue record for this book is available from the British
Library

Library of Congress Cataloging in Publication Data
Peer-group mentoring for teacher development / edited by Hannu
L. T. Heikkinen, Hannu Jokinen & Päivi Tynjälä.
    p. cm.
    1. Teachers—In-service training—Finland.   2. Mentoring in
    education—Finland.   I. Heikkinen, Hannu L. T. II. Jokinen, Hannu.
    III. Tynjälä, Päivi.
LB1731.P362 2012
370.71'1—dc23
                                                   2011049077

ISBN: 978-0-415-52936-5 (hbk)
ISBN: 978-0-415-52937-2 (pbk)
ISBN: 978-0-203-11592-3 (ebk)

Typeset in Bembo
by RefineCatch Limited, Bungay, Suffolk

Printed and bound in Great Britain by
TJ International Ltd, Padstow, Cornwall

Contents

List of illustrations

Figures

Tables

Preface and acknowledgements

This book introduces a new model for supporting teachers' professional development and well-being: peer-group mentoring. The model was developed in an action research project funded by the Finnish Work Environment Fund 2008–2010 and carried out at the Finnish Institute for Educational Research of the University of Jyväskylä, Finland, in collaboration with the University of Oulu and University of Tampere. We wish to thank all the partners of the project, all the cities and municipalities which made it possible to test this new model, and especially all those enthusiastic teachers who worked as mentors and members of the mentoring groups. We hope that this book will inspire people working with teacher development to exercise the power of collaboration and dialogue for professional learning.

Hannu L.T. Heikkinen, Hannu Jokinen and Päivi Tynjälä

Peer-group mentoring session in the city of Jyväskylä, Finland

Contributors

Minna Ahokas, MEd, made a long career in the hotel and restaurant business before her graduation as a teacher. She has been teaching at the University of Applied Sciences and in vocational education. Currently she is working as a project manager in the Jyväskylä Educational Consortium.

Suvi Alamaa, MEd, has worked as a coordinator of teachers' in-service training in the education department of the city of Kokkola in Finland since 2006. Her job description includes the coordination of teachers' peer-group mentoring processes. Her research and development interests are focused on expanding the successful praxis of peer-group mentoring to other professional groups in the education department and in the entire city organization.

Jessica Aspfors, MEd, is a doctoral student at the Faculty of Education, Åbo Akademi University in Vaasa, Finland. Her research interest focuses on teachers' professional development, especially newly qualified teachers' first years in the profession, and their need for support and mentoring. She is a member of the Supporting Newly Qualified Teachers through Collaborative Mentoring (NQT-COME) network and the coordination group of the Finnish national programme for developing support for new teachers through peer-group mentoring as a representative of Åbo Akademi, which is organizing the support for newly qualified Swedish speaking teachers in Finland.

Eila Estola, PhD, adjunct professor, works as a senior researcher at Faculty of Education, University of Oulu. One of her research interests deals with teachers' narrative identities. She has been developing narrative and action methods for peer groups and used those methods in different courses as well as working as a counsellor in teachers' groups. She is also a representative of the University of Oulu in Osaava Verme programme.

Sven-Erik Hansén, PhD, is Professor of Education at the Faculty of Education at Åbo Akademi University in Vasa, Finland. He is also an affiliated professor at Oslo University, Norway and adjunct professor at the University of Helsinki, Finland. His research interests focus on curriculum development, teachers' professional careers and teacher education. He is also engaged in evaluations of teacher education and educational research. He is a member of the coordination group of the Finnish national programme for developing support for new teachers through peer-group mentoring.

Hannu L. T. Heikkinen, PhD, is a senior researcher at the Finnish Institute for Educational Research. He is also an adjunct professor at the University of Tampere, University of Jyväskylä, Åbo Akademi and Charles Sturt University, Australia. He is responsible for the Finnish Network for Teacher Induction, Osaava Verme, a national programme for developing support for new teachers through peer-group mentoring. He has also contributed to international networks related to early career teachers, such as Supporting Newly Qualified Teachers through Collaborative Mentoring (NQT-COME).

Anu Hiltula, MEd, graduated from a nursery school teacher college in Oulu in 1992. After that she worked as a nursery school teacher and has worked elsewhere in the Educational Department in Ranua. In 2008 she started studying to become a class teacher in the University Consortium Chydenius in Kokkola, from where she graduated in 2010. In her Master's thesis she studied the group mentoring programme in Kokkola with Anu Oksakari.

Leena Isosomppi, PhD, is a senior lecturer at Kokkola University Consortium Chydenius of the University of Jyväskylä. She works with students in a teacher education programme for adults. Her research interests include teacher education, teachers' professional development and teaching practice. She has also published articles and books on mentoring and supervision of student teachers in teaching practicum.

Peter Johnson, PhD, works as Director of Education in the city of Kokkola in Finland. He worked as a teacher for ten years, and for eighteen years as principal before he started in his current post in 2008. During 2003–2006 he was a member of a research group at the Finnish Institute for Educational Research of the University of Jyväskylä. He defended his doctoral thesis in 2006 in the field of school development. His research interests are the sociology of education, school leadership and sustainable development of education.

Hannu Jokinen, MEd, is a researcher at the Finnish Institute for Educational Research of the University of Jyväskylä. His research focuses on supporting newly qualified teachers through mentoring during the induction phase. Hannu Jokinen serves as a researcher in the national Osaava Verme programme which aims at developing support for new teachers through peer-group mentoring. He has actively contributed to the development of the PGM model. Jokinen is one of the founders of the Newly Qualified Teachers in Northern Europe (NQTNE) network and the NQT-COME network.

Saara-Leena Kaunisto, MEd, is a doctoral student at the Faculty of Education, University of Oulu, Finland. Her research interest focuses on how a peer group can support teachers in their work. As a psychodrama leader, she has worked with different groups and in mentoring-related projects where she has also been developing narrative and action methods based on peer support and psychodrama.

Stephen Kemmis, PhD, is Professor of Education at Charles Sturt University, Wagga Wagga, New South Wales, Australia and a member of the CSU's Research Institute for Professional Practice, Learning and Education. A key aspect of his work since the late 1970s has been in developing the theory and practice of educational action research as a participatory form of research and evaluation which embodies the aspirations of a critical science of education. He has also written extensively on educational research and evaluation, and, most recently, practice theory.

Maria Lahdenmaa, MEd, graduated in 2010 from the University of Jyväskylä. Currently she is working as a primary school teacher in Kauhajoen koulukeskus, Kauhajoki, Finland. In her Master's thesis, she studied homogeneous and heterogeneous peer-mentoring groups.

Tuuli Maunu, MEd, graduated from the University of Oulu in 2009. She is a qualified primary school teacher and is also qualified to teach Swedish in secondary school. She works as a teacher in a Swedish early total language immersion class in Helsinki. She wrote her Master's thesis about newly qualified teachers' experiences of their first years in the field.

Päivi Mäki, MA, works as development manager in the Department of Education of the City of Oulu, Finland. She is the head of the Centre for Learning and Resources which provides support services and in-service training for teaching staff. She works in the Finnish national programme for developing support for early career teachers through peer-group mentoring and in the network Newly Qualified Teachers through Collaborative Mentoring (NQT-COME). Her research activity focuses on promoting educators' professional development and well-being at work through peer-group mentoring.

Raimo Niemistö, Licentiate of Psychology, TEP (trainer, educator and practitioner in psychodrama, sociometry and group psychotherapy), has worked for many years in the fields of rehabilitation and work communities. Currently he works as a psychotherapist and work counsellor. He has researched group phenomena and worked as a trainer of group leading and psychodrama methods.

Anu Oksakari, MEd, is a teacher in Vaasa, Finland. In her Master's thesis with Anu Hiltula, she focused on headmasters' experiences and teachers' professional development through peer-group mentoring.

Helena Rajakaltio, PhD, is a project manager at the School of Education, University of Tampere. Her research and work are related to teachers' professional learning as a continuum covering basic and continuing teacher education. Her main interests include educational policy, school change and school as a professional community. She has been actively involved in developing peer-group mentoring both nationally and in the network Newly Qualified Teachers in Northern Europe (NQTNE).

Leena Syrjälä, PhD, is Professor of Education at the Faculty of Education, University of Oulu. For years she has been interested in narrative research on teachers. She has been a leader of the research group 'Living Story', in which narrative and multidisciplinary approaches have been used in research on teachers' identities and well-being and in the practice of teacher education.

Eija Syrjäläinen, PhD, is Professor in Teacher Education at the University of Tampere. She is also an adjunct professor of Didactics at the University of Helsinki. Her research interests have been gender issues and active citizenship in teacher education. Her current research project deals with students' and teachers' well-being and safety experiences in school life.

Sini Teerikorpi, MEd, graduated in 2012 from the University of Jyväskylä. In her Bachelor's thesis, she analysed the elements which make a peer-mentoring group successful. In her Master's thesis she studied the education of PGM mentors within the theoretical framework of integrative pedagogy. She has also been working as a research assistant in the national project for developing PGM mentoring at the Finnish Institute for Educational Research.

Päivi Tynjälä, PhD, is Professor in Research on Teaching and Learning in Higher Education at the Finnish Institute for Educational Research of the University of Jyväskylä. Currently she serves as an editor-in-chief of the *Educational Research Review*. She is also an editorial board member of *Vocations and Learning – Studies in Vocational and Professional Education*. She has published widely both nationally and internationally especially on constructivist learning environments, workplace learning and teachers' professional development, and she is one of the developers of the peer-group mentoring model.

Jouni Välijärvi, PhD, is a Leader of the Finnish Institute for Educational Research and Professor in Educational Research and Development. He represents Finland in the IEA (International Association for the Evaluation of Educational Achievement) and is the national project manager of the OECD PISA study in Finland. He has headed a series of national research projects on curriculum, school assessment, teacher education and well-being of students, served in a number of national and international expert groups, for example for the OECD and EU, and has published widely in his field.

Peer-group mentoring in a nutshell

Peer-group mentoring (PGM) is a new model of supporting professional development. It can be organized among a variety of professions but here we focus on teachers. PGM differs from the traditional mentoring model in the following ways:

- The main idea in traditional mentoring is that a senior and more experienced worker transfers knowledge to a younger colleague, whereas PGM is based on the idea that the relationship between the mentor and the mentee is reciprocal and both parties have something to give to each other.
- While traditional mentoring takes place in one-to-one discussions PGM is implemented in groups that consist of both novice teachers and their more experienced counterparts. The ideal size of the group varies between five and ten members.
- The concept of learning in traditional mentoring can be characterized as traditional: it is assumed that knowledge can be transferred from one person to another. Peer-group mentoring, in contrast, is based on the constructivist view of learning. Constructivism maintains that knowledge as such cannot be transferred between individuals because we always interpret new knowledge on the basis of our prior knowledge, conceptions, experiences and beliefs. This is why the same thing can be interpreted and understood in different ways. Therefore discussion is an essential element in creating shared understanding. Knowledge is thus not transferred as such; instead we all form our personal conceptions in social interaction.

Peer-group mentoring is an activity involving teachers sharing and reflecting on their experiences, discussing problems and challenges they meet in their work, listening, encouraging one another, and, above all, learning from each other, and learning together. This kind of group activity always raises ethical questions, and therefore it is important to keep in mind the following ethical principles or rules:

- The members of the group are equal participants. Everyone's voice will be heard, and nobody will dominate the discussion.
- What is shared in a group will not be shared outside.

Part 1

Peer-group mentoring and work-based learning in the teaching profession

This part of the book introduces the theoretical basis of the peer–group mentoring model as a form of work-based learning combining both informal and formal learning experiences.

For understanding the basic tenets of the peer–group mentoring model it is important to understand the context in which the model has been developed: the education system in Finland. As a result, the Finnish culture of teacher education and teacher development is also described.

Dear reader

In this book we shall invite you to reflect on your experiences and ideas related to work-based learning. The book also includes reflection tasks that will hopefully encourage you to embark on a conceptual journey and explore your own history of work-based learning.

We hope that you will first identify where exactly you have learned the skills and competences that you currently apply to your work. How much of your professional competence comes from education? Here you can take into account both degree-awarding education and potential additional qualifications and continuing education. How much do you think that you have learned outside formal educational environments? Have you, for example, learned something essential for your work while reading a newspaper or through a discussion with your colleague? How much have you learned by simply performing your tasks, through personal experience?

Write down your estimates rounded to the nearest 10 per cent. Do not think too long; trust your first instinct. No one will ask you to report on your estimates, just as no one will be able to perform a precise measurement of the amount of learning. It is enough if you try to be honest with yourself.

Based on my experience, I estimate that *through education* I have acquired approximately _____ % of the knowledge and competence that I use in my job.

Based on my experience, I estimate that *outside education* I have acquired approximately _____ % of the knowledge and competence that I use in my job.

Chapter 1

Teacher education and development as lifelong and lifewide learning

Hannu L. T. Heikkinen, Hannu Jokinen and Päivi Tynjälä

It is common for teachers to acquire part of their core professional skills outside of formal education. We have often posed the questions on p. 2 to teachers who are beginning their mentoring studies, and their answers are typically distributed as Fig. 1.1 shows.

When teachers have been asked how – apart from education – they feel they have developed the knowledge and skills essential for their profession, the following have been typical answers:

- through own life experiences
- through own school experiences
- from pupils' parents
- from pupils' feedback
- from their own children and family
- from an experienced teacher – and from younger teachers
- from colleagues
- from different informal teacher groups
- from the Internet
- through hobbies
- through school board activities.

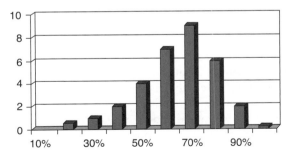

Figure 1.1 Experienced teachers' estimates of the amount of their learning outside teacher education

We have noticed that when teachers (or other professionals) are asked where they have learnt the most important skills they need in their job, about 70 per cent of the respondents tend to report having learnt those skills at work or somewhere else outside the formal education system (e.g. Tynjälä, Slotte et al., 2006; Heikkinen et al., 2010).

Our findings are in line with international research results. Numerous studies have shown that as a rule as much as 70 to 80 per cent of relevant know-how at work is based on informal and nonformal learning (Fullan, 2001, p. 107; Marsick & Watkins, 1990, pp. 46–48; Kim et al., 2004, p. 40; Pesonen, 2011, pp. 18–19). Merriam et al. (2007) have noted that upwards of 90 per cent of adults are engaged in hundreds of hours of informal learning. This is something that newly qualified teachers do not necessarily recognize. Therefore, it has been suggested that new teachers should be helped to value and utilize the informal learning opportunities that their work offers (Williams, 2003). Similarly, the current trend of emphasizing practice as the crux of teacher preparation (Cochran-Smith & Power, 2010) recognizes the power of learning in authentic work contexts.

The results described above clearly indicate that teaching professionals develop some of their core competences in varying contexts. This is currently a common phenomenon in many other fields as well. People make significant gains in learning in various life situations, not merely within education. Therefore, we usually speak about lifewide learning, which means that learning takes place widely in different life contexts, such as work, free time, and training. In addition to being lifewide, learning is also lifelong. In other words, learning is not restricted to school during childhood and adolescence, but instead continues throughout life. The concept of lifelong learning thus refers to vertical learning that takes place gradually over the course of time. Lifewide learning, in contrast, refers to horizontal learning in different activity contexts.

Learning has often been classified into three types (European Commission, 2001; Merriam et al., 2007, pp. 29–30; Tynjälä & Heikkinen, 2011):

1   *Formal learning* takes place in educational institutions and is intentional in nature. It is highly institutionalized, often even bureaucratic, curriculum-driven, and formally recognized with grades, diplomas, or certificates.
2   *Nonformal learning* is organized outside of the formal educational system, for example, in the workplace. Learning is also intentional but does not lead to formal certification. This kind of education tends to be short-term, voluntary, and have few if any prerequisites. However, it typically has a curriculum and often a facilitator.
3   *Informal learning* is usually unintentional and takes place as a side effect of other activities, such as work, in everyday settings.

It is often difficult to distinguish between the above types of learning. For example, success in many jobs requires active information retrieval, which is why the media and the Internet have become increasingly crucial tools of learning in working life. Formal education includes practical training periods in workplaces, and the informal learning experiences gained in this way are utilized in formal learning. This sort of integration of formal and nonformal learning is not new as such – in various versions it has been implemented in all education leading to a profession.

We sometimes hear people claim that theories are of no use at work, with practical competence instead being the decisive factor. However, the division between theory and practice is problematic and to some extent even deceptive. It creates the illusion that theory and practice are two separate entities, even though the study of expertise actually confirms that, in skilled activities, theory and practice are both parts of one entity. This merger of theory and practice is crystallized in Kurt Lewin's famous phrase: 'Nothing is as practical as a good theory!'

In light of the aforementioned definitions, reflect on your own learning path for a moment.

- My most memorable experiences of informal learning have been . . .
- I have experienced nonformal learning . . .

Informalization and formalization of learning

Formal education frequently applies methods that resemble informal learning. For instance, training events include pair or group discussions through which people can better link their everyday or work-life experiences to the phenomena being addressed. It is also increasingly common to integrate work-based learning, projects, and portfolio work into formal education. Formal learning is consequently enriched by new forms that resemble daily work or a collegial exchange of ideas. In recent years, we have witnessed a trend in formal learning towards a kind of *informalization* of learning, that is, a move to more nonformal and informal forms of learning. The mushrooming of work-based learning, introduction of 'lifeplace learning' (Harris & Chisholm, 2011), and the increasing use of social media (see e.g. Huber, 2010) are examples of this trend of utilizing informal learning also in the context of formal learning.

In quite a few workplaces, the content of work as such equals learning. Today it is not even a question of having to keep up to date in order to manage in one's job, but rather that the actual tasks change to encompass a larger amount of information processing, and consequently also learning. This kind of work, based on the processing of concepts and symbols, is called symbolic–analytical work. Tasks like this have become more frequent in the information society, in which a teacher's work has also moved closer to the work of a 'symbolic analyst'.

One important task of teachers today is to provide the learners with symbolic-analytical skills; for example, those related to information retrieval, its critical analysis, and processing through words and symbols.

The development of social media has also changed the forms of learning and contributed to the blurring of formal learning boundaries. For example, it is common for university course participants to form a functioning, informal social media group on Facebook, Ning, or LinkedIn. The communication is often very casual, but it also includes a broad exchange of ideas relevant to learning on the course. With respect to these discussion groups, it is often quite difficult to distinguish what is learning that complies with the course curriculum, and what is something else.

The informalization of learning is a reflection of a major pedagogical trend in our time, constructivism, which is based on the idea that learners construct their knowledge on the basis of their prior views, knowledge, and experiences. In education, it is important to 'activate' people's preconceptions and experiences, so that they can better be linked to the information at hand. The aim is for education to offer such learning situations in which informal and nonformal knowledge are better connected to formal knowledge, through general theories or conceptual models, for example. This is how the information offered through formal learning better meets people's previous ideas and background experiences, which will promote the learning process and enhance its profundity.

At the same time, there is a trend towards the *formalization* of informal learning taking place in everyday situations. Methods that enable the recognition of prior learning are being promoted in formal education; they also serve to demonstrate what people have learned in their work and everyday lives. For this purpose we use, for example, skills demonstrations and portfolios. The recognition of different forms of learning has actually become an international trend: the recognition of prior learning as well as the development of tools for systematizing, documenting, and assessing informal and non-formal learning are parts of this trend. This was the leading theme, for example, at the Copenhagen conference of 2008, which was a continuation of the Bologna process that aims to create a common European Higher Education Area (EHEA). One of the main goals of this European process, which started in the 1990s, has been to establish closer links between education and working life.

Two opposite processes thus seem to be taking place at the moment, which are sometimes difficult to distinguish from each other: first, the formalization of informal and nonformal learning; and second, the informalization of formal learning. As a joint consequence of these interconnected and parallel processes, formal, informal, and nonformal types of learning are verging on each other (see Fig. 1.2).

The trends of formalization and informalization can be seen in teachers' professional learning as well as in other professional fields. While earlier it was typical to distinguish between formal in-service training and informal job-embedded learning, it is now recognized that the organization of teachers'

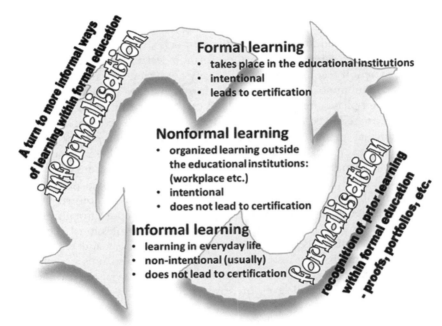

Figure 1.2 The dialectics of formalisation and informalisation of learning

Sources: European Commission, 2001, pp. 32–33; Tuschling & Engemann, 2006.

informal professional learning communities is becoming increasingly structured and formalized, and – at the same time – the formal forms of learning are often integrated with informal learning taking place in teachers' everyday work (Wei et al., 2009; Siivonen, 2010).

From the viewpoint of what we know about the nature of professional expertise, the trend of blurring the boundaries between formal and informal learning is a welcome one. High-level expertise requires integration between the three basic elements of expertise: formal theoretical or conceptual knowledge; more informal experiential or practical knowledge; and self-regulative knowledge (e.g. Tynjälä, Slotte et al., 2006; Tynjälä, 2008; Heikkinen et al., 2011). Utilizing informal work-related learning in formal training and combining them promotes the integration of the components of expert knowledge. The findings by Wei et al. (2009) suggest that this approach to teacher development is positively reflected in student achievement. They made a comparison of countries that participated in the OECD PISA studies and found a number of common features characterizing professional development practices in the high-achieving countries. These features included extensive opportunities for both formal and informal in-service development; time for professional learning and collaboration built into teachers' working hours; professional development activities that are embedded in teaching contexts;

school governance structures that support teacher involvement in decisions regarding curriculum and instructional practice; teacher induction programmes for new teachers; and formal training for mentors.

In developing teacher education, these forms of learning have been taken into account as action recommendations in many countries. The aim is to create a seamless continuum of teacher education, in which degree-awarding education, the induction phase after graduation, and career-long continuing professional development are linked to one another. In all of these phases, formal, informal, and nonformal learning opportunities are utilized. In addition, the aim is to bring together teaching professionals who are currently in these various phases, and to make them meet each other in different learning situations.

The key idea of this book's topic, peer-group mentoring, relies on the integration of formal, informal, and nonformal learning, with constructivism as its core principle. Peer-group mentoring resembles learning through informal conversation, in which the participants acquire relevant professional knowledge and develop their skills on the basis of their prior ideas and experiences. However, the group is not just chatting over coffee, as it also aims at explicating what has been experienced and learned; in other words, at raising learning to a conscious and conceptual level. Increased understanding of the challenging situations included in teachers' work helps one face new situations and develop new solutions. Learning through peer-group mentoring is thus realized through the interaction of practical work and reflective discussions addressing it.

High-quality expertise in any field is not just about individual knowledge and competence (Tynjälä, 2008). For example, in order to be a skilled teacher, it is certainly important to be familiar with teaching methods, curricula, the facilitation of learning, learning theories, and so on. But it is also important for a teacher to recognize knowledge embedded in the operating environment and socially shared practices of the workplace. A significant part of this contextual and collaborative competence implies so-called tacit knowledge, which is not easy to express in words. Mastering this nonverbal social knowledge is a crucial part of teachers' expertise, which is addressed in peer-group mentoring with the help of joint reflection and discussion.

Induction phase as a challenge in the teaching profession

- What were your feelings when you arrived at your first workplace?
- How were you received?
- How did you learn the practices of the workplace?

The transitional stage from studies to working life is always a challenge, but for teachers it is even more radical than in many other professions. As a rule, careers progress gradually to take on tasks of ever-increasing responsibility, and the employee has time to get accustomed to new challenges over the course of time. Teaching, on the contrary, usually implies the adoption of full juridical and pedagogical responsibility right after graduation. Teaching has, in fact, sometimes been described as a profession with an 'early career plateau': teachers face great challenges right at the beginning of their career, but these challenges do not significantly increase later, so long as they do not change career orientation and become, for example, head teachers.

Teachers' legal responsibilities and rights are usually the same from beginning to end, and their social esteem, i.e. professional status, does not significantly rise. In several other fields, instead, the growth of professional status is symbolically demonstrated through stepwise changing job titles. It is true that a teacher's salary gradually increases, and experienced teachers are often appreciated precisely because of their experience; still, this has no direct impact on professional status: as a rule, all teachers' job titles read 'teacher'.

Teachers have generally experienced the induction phase to be quite challenging. A direct transition from studies to a high professional status often leads to a sort of need to prove oneself: young teachers must stake their position and show others that they can master their tasks. This is also emphasized by the individualistic tradition of teaching: teachers have undertaken their work quite independently and solitarily. Only recently have there been signs of schools beginning to adopt more collaborative work methods. Nonetheless, a very traditional working culture still dominates in many schools: teaching takes place both symbolically and concretely behind closed doors. When young teachers have to manage their duties without support from more experienced colleagues, the heaviness and loneliness of the induction phase are emphasized.

Instead of supporting new teachers, the tacit teaching culture sometimes advocates a 'sink or swim' mentality: a large or even excessive burden may be placed on a novice teacher during the first years (Howe, 2006, pp. 289–291). The induction phase includes many practical issues unfamiliar to the new teacher – teacher education does not address a variety of things related to, for example, pupils, curricula, and the school community. The induction phase introduces teachers to the school community, its working culture, and the teaching environment and conditions. Indeed, new teachers think that teacher education should be brought closer to the everyday of 'ordinary' schools. They point out that there are significant differences between universities' own teacher training schools, in which teaching practice is carried out, and other 'ordinary' schools with regard to such things as group size, equipment, and financial resources. Furthermore, student teachers do not become genuine members of the teacher training school's work community, but rather identify with the specific role of teacher trainee, which includes features of both teacher and student roles. Moreover, formal teaching practice offers few opportunities to meet pupils' parents, or to cooperate with other experts (Jokinen & Välijärvi, 2006).

The need to support new teachers seems to be a common challenge in many countries, even at the global level (European Commission, 2010). The methods used to support novice teachers include mentoring, orientation, workshops, distribution of written materials, classroom observation, internship, reduced workload, and time given for reflection and collaboration with colleagues. The most common component of the induction programmes is to assign a suitable mentor to the new teacher (Alhija & Fresko, 2010; Howe, 2006; Ingersoll & Smith, 2004; Wong, 2004).

In the US there is considerable interest in mentorship and internship. The number of states implementing reforms to teacher induction has risen, and in some states all teachers must complete a programme of induction. In Germany, a two-step model into the profession has been developed, including mentoring and other support from more experienced colleagues, reduced teaching load, formal learning opportunities with theoretical seminars, and informal learning through gradual introduction to teaching with explicit feedback (Bickmore & Bickmore, 2010; Fransson & Gustafsson, 2008; Howe, 2006; Lohmar & Eckhardt, 2010). In the UK the induction year includes a 10 per cent reduction of teaching load, regular meetings with a named induction tutor, and an individualized programme of support and monitoring, half-termly observations of their teaching, a termly assessment meeting; and a job description in which the demands must be 'reasonable' (Williams, 2003; Jones, 2006). In the Nordic countries, the classical one-to-one mentoring model seems to be the most common solution (Fransson & Gustafsson, 2008). The various web-based forms such as e-mentoring and social media have lately become more popular tools for supporting teachers in their career (e.g. Huber, 2010).

Due to the hardship of the induction phase, teachers may end up considering a career change. In many countries, young teachers consequently leave the profession after a few years' practice. Teacher attrition, particularly during the early years of teachers' careers, is a serious problem in many Western societies (e.g. Marvel et al., 2007; Scheopner, 2010). For example, in the US up to 50 per cent of teachers leave their jobs within five years of induction (Ingersoll, 2003). However, an OECD report (2005) indicates that there are a lot of differences between the countries in teacher attrition, in general, and among newly qualified teachers, in particular. In some countries (e.g. Italy, Japan and Korea), the rates reported for teachers leaving their profession were lower than 3 per cent. In Finland the rate is still small, but it seems to be increasing within the Helsinki capital region (Almiala, 2008, p. 6). In the US there are also remarkable differences in the rates of teacher attrition between districts, depending on different social and economic factors such as district salary schedules and social circumstances (Bickmore & Bickmore, 2010, p. 1006).

Teachers' career changes have traditionally followed economic trends: during boom periods, teachers are tempted to move to the private sector due to its higher salaries and more favourable benefits, whereas during recessions they appreciate the security of the teaching profession. Nevertheless, economic fluctuations cannot explain teacher attrition as much as previously. One reason for this seems to be the fact that not even teaching is as solid and sustainable a profession as it used to be. In particular, young teachers' employment relations are short and uncertain. In addition, teaching is commonly experienced as hard work mentally. The popularity of job alternation leave and early retirement pensions indicates how much of a strain teaching can be.

Even if transfer from one field to another can be regarded as natural job market mobility, from the viewpoint of teaching it still causes concern about the availability of competent teachers. From the perspective of national economy, it is questionable to educate qualified professionals who will not remain in the field. A wide variety of solutions is needed, including the improvement of payment and terms of employment. Above all, in order to support teachers in their work, effective forms of professional support are also needed to promote the development of professional competence and occupational well-being.

Mentoring as a tool for professional development: the Finnish case

> • For what kinds of issues do you need support or a listener in your work?
> • What could you offer teachers who are just now starting their careers?

In a wide variety of fields, mentoring has been proven to be a good tool for the guidance of new employees. As the applications of mentoring can vary widely, we should examine and analyse mentoring within the local school context, as well as look for practical implementations that meet the needs of schools and new teachers. On the basis of various experiments, we have arrived at the conclusion that the most functional solution for the Finnish school system is the organization of mentoring in groups. Such *peer-group mentoring* (PGM) aims at supporting both teachers' coping with work and their professional learning.

Supporting young teachers in their work is a topic highlighted both in the European Commission communication (European Commission, 2007) and in the development report of Finnish teacher education, Opetusministeriö (2007). The European Commission communication aims at broadly enhancing the appreciation for and appeal of the teaching profession, highlighting the special problems young teachers encounter along the continuum of teachers' lifelong learning. In compliance with the European Commission's view, all teachers in all European countries should participate in a support programme at the induction phase. Finland's efforts to develop mentoring are thus in line with the aspirations of the rest of Europe.

The aforementioned Finnish teacher education report strongly highlights the importance of supporting young teachers in their work. The report emphasizes the continuity of teacher education from basic education to continuing education, in line with the European Commission document. The support provided to young teachers is addressed as a special question between basic teacher education and continuing professional education:

> Teacher education must be reformed so that it will form a continuum in which basic education, so-called induction phase training, and continuing education form a consistent entity that promotes the continuous development of teachers' expertise . . . The right to participate in induction phase training must be guaranteed to all teachers . . . Mentoring must be developed as the central method used in the induction phase.
>
> (Opetusministeriö, 2007, pp. 46–47)

The idea of teacher education as a lifelong continuum, which appears both in European and Finnish teacher education policies, is the foundation of peer-group mentoring. Teachers' professional development is seen as a lifelong and lifewide process. The basic idea here is to provide teachers of different ages with the opportunity to share in groups their competence as well as the problems encountered at work.

Who are you and where do you come from, mentor?

Please explore your own mental images related to mentoring through analogies or metaphors.

- What is your first association when you hear the word 'mentor'?
- Analogy: The mentor is like . . .
- Metaphor: The mentor is . . .

We have posed the preceding question to experienced teachers who attended mentor training, asking them to paraphrase their associations, analogies, or metaphors related to the word 'mentor'. The request brought to their minds the following terminology:

- listener
- mind expander
- confidence builder
- the one who cares
- armchair (in which one can think without disturbances)
- support person
- professional shoulder
- flashlight (helps people who wander in darkness, but its batteries are not everlasting).

These mental images speak volumes about mentoring and the mentor. They highlight the mentor's role as a professional helper and support person. Analogies, metaphors, and associations can reveal to us significant new dimensions of a concept – which could hardly be discovered simply through dictionary definitions.

According to the classical definition, mentoring is a professional guidance relationship in which an experienced, intellectually and socially valued mentor acts as adviser for a less experienced employee and helps this 'mentee' develop her/his work. This relation resembles the medieval guild institution, in which masters taught their skills to journeymen and apprentices. The etymological background of the concept supports the idea that a mentor possesses solid competence and a high social status. In classical Greek mythology, Mentor was King Odysseus' friend who brought up the king's son Telemachus while the king was away during and after the Trojan War. However, it was actually the goddess Pallas Athena who was disguised as Mentor, which explains Mentor's divine wisdom as an educator. On the basis of this legend, it is natural that the mentor figure has been associated with remarkable wisdom and authority of even divine origin (Murray, 2001, p. xiii).

It is consequently common to associate mentoring with a more experienced mentor who guides and supports a less experienced mentee (Roberts, 2000). However, there are currently various interpretations of mentoring, and mentoring is used in order to achieve different goals. Mentoring seems to have become the global mantra within teacher education (Sundli, 2007); in other professional fields its use has become widespread as well (e.g. Vuorinen, 2004; Tunkkari-Eskelinen, 2005).

Conceptual change in mentoring

The concept of mentoring has undergone a transformation over the past years during which mentoring has increased in popularity. On the basis of international research literature, a conceptual change seems to be going on at two different levels (Heikkinen, Jokinen et al., 2008). First, the concept's range of usage seems to be continuously broadening – and blurring – in teacher education: mentoring has more and more frequently also been understood as a synonym for the supervision of teaching practicum (Sundli, 2007).

Second, a conceptual change has taken place towards mentoring being associated with collaboration, collegiality, and interaction. This interpretation is not based on the concept's 'cosmogony', in which authority and experience are emphasized. According to the traditional view, a mentor is experienced and, in this sense, transcendent – usually a senior, socially and professionally recognized person.

Research has demonstrated that young employees are not the only ones who benefit from mentoring: experienced employees can also find new perspectives on their work through mentoring. Mentors themselves have reported that they learn from the group discussions and the opinions presented by teachers (Jokinen, Heikkinen et al., 2006; Jokinen & Välijärvi, 2006; Jokinen & Sarja, 2006). These remarks suggest that mentoring avails both the mentor and the mentee.

The applications of mentoring do not only support new teachers' induction periods but also the professional dialogue between teachers of different ages, in which both the novices and the experienced teachers learn something new. Mentors do not 'transfer' the correct view or knowledge through dialogue but rather construct meanings and interpretations together with others. In a dialogic relationship, no one has a better or more valid vision of reality, as all of the participants in the discussion understand that their visions are incomplete (Heikkinen & Huttunen, 2008).

A dialogue is an interactive relation that generates new information. Dialogue means motion: a dynamic flow forward. It is like a game that the players never thoroughly master. A genuine game proceeds on its own terms, and none of the participants can fully control its progress (Huttunen, 2003, pp. 132–133; Gadamer, 1975, pp. 97–98). According to the dialogic view, mentoring refers to a reciprocal exchange of ideas and joint construction of knowledge, from which both parties learn. In a mentoring dialogue, both parties participate in verbalizing their conceptions, experiences, and mindsets. In international research literature, the interactive character of mentoring is highlighted through such expressions as co-mentoring, mutual mentoring, collaborative mentoring, peer collabora-tion, critical constructivist mentoring, dialogic mentoring, and peer mentoring (Bokeno & Vernon, 2000; Musanti, 2004; Le Cornu, 2005).

Emphasizing interaction and collaboration has also implied that, in addition to classical bilateral dialogue, mentoring is to an increasing extent also applied to group activities. So we talk about peer-to-peer mentoring and peer-group mentoring. Peer-to-peer mentoring has provided good experiences, for example, in supporting nurses' professional development (Glass & Walter, 2000) and young teachers' work (Boreen & Niday, 2000). The group is used as a social learning platform, in which experiential practical competence is combined with theoretical knowledge (Cross, 1998; Kutilek & Earnest, 2001; Angelique et al., 2002).

Mentoring practices seem to be shifting in the same direction as the conceptions of knowledge and learning. Teaching has been shifting towards constructivism: the learner's own experiences and conceptions are regarded as the point of departure for the knowledge construction process; learning is understood as the gradual alteration of these conceptions. Learning is thus not understood as knowledge transfer but rather as the encounter of different conceptions and testing of preconceptions on the basis of new information. Therefore, it is natural that mentoring is no more regarded as one-way guidance but as conversation, discussion, or dialogue. The collaborative forms of mentoring have been so far removed from the classical, bilateral relationship between an experienced expert and a novice that the modern interpretation cannot even be considered to be an updated version of traditional mentoring (Chaliès et al.,

2008, p. 562). As philosopher Pierre Hadot (1995) says, the history of Hellenistic philosophy is full of these kinds of reinterpretations of historical concepts, many of which can even be called misinterpretations. However, Hadot thinks that these misinterpretations are mostly creative misunderstandings that contribute to advancing thinking.

How did peer-group mentoring come about?

This book provides a description of peer-group mentoring, abbreviated as PGM. This new approach to mentoring has evolved to its present form only over the course of the last decade. The development has been contributed to by European and national strategies and programmes, as well as by international research collaboration and interaction between researchers and teacher educators. Moreover, the formation of PGM has been impacted by numerous research and development projects implemented through inter-university cooperation, which are grounded in ideas concerning constructivist work-based learning and the construction of professional identity through narratives.

Traditional mentoring – with the mentor and mentee meeting each other on a one-to-one basis – has also been tested in the teaching context in Finland. One of the first concrete mentoring development projects was implemented in Helsinki in the early 2000s. In this project the mentor was an experienced teacher and the counterpart a novice in the field. The mentors and mentees met each other approximately once a month for one academic year, agreeing independently on the venue. In the spring semester, some of these meetings became less regular or ended altogether. Ultimately, this classical way of organizing mentoring did not prove to be viable in teaching, and failed primarily due to issues related to working time and financing. The school administrators were too busy to search for mentors to all potential mentees and the mentors were not always motivated to provide guidance without payment, so this classical one-to-one mentoring project faded away in the mid-2000s (Heikkinen, Jokinen et al., 2008).

These experiences were taken into account in the development of peer-group mentoring. First, group mentoring was adopted because it enables more extensive social learning, as the topics addressed in the groups are handled from more variable perspectives. Second, group mentoring is more cost-effective than pair mentoring since the requisite number of mentors is much smaller than in pair mentoring. Third, the ease of organization is a strength of group mentoring: one mentor leads a group of several teachers, which means that organizing the activities is more flexible than when pairs are formed. In accordance with international concepts, the action model was given the name peer-group mentoring. Teachers of different ages and at different stages of career were included in the groups – not only those new to the profession.

Systematic training for mentors was started in 2008 to support group mentoring, and it has been implemented since then collaboratively with cities and municipalities all over Finland. Training takes one academic year and it is organized in five two-day seminars. The instructional design of training is based on the model called 'integrative pedagogy' (e.g. Tynjälä, 2008; Heikkinen et al., 2011) described later on in this book. The basic idea is that during training each participant leads a peer-group mentoring group and that training provides participants with conceptual tools and theoretical models for sharing and reflecting their experiences as mentors. Narrative and group working methods are applied in training.

Since autumn 2010, PGM has been applied and further developed within the Finnish Network for Teacher Induction, 'Osaava Verme' ('Skilful PGM') project, funded by the Finnish Ministry of Education and Culture. It is part of the national Osaava programme, which aims at enhancing teachers' professional competence by developing new forms of in-service training and professional development tools. Within this programme Osaava Verme develops peer-group mentoring through collaboration between universities' teacher education departments and vocational teacher education colleges.

Principles of peer-group mentoring

The core of activities is the peer-mentoring group, which meets six to eight times in an academic year, for about 1.5 to 2 hours at a time. The group devises a plan of action in its first meeting. The group can choose a common broad theme for the entire period, such as multiculturalism, curriculum work, or teaching method development in a specific discipline. The mentor is the leader of the group and responsible for the group's schedule. The mentor also directs discussion, trying to allot discussion time equally among participants. The mentor can also propose themes to be addressed and stimulate discussion through different narrative and action-based exercises.

The group first makes an *agreement upon action*. All the agreements must include two basic principles: confidentiality and discussion ethics. The principle of confidentiality means that everything spoken in the group stays in the group; in other words, disclosures made within the group are not shared outside the group. The ethical discussion principle means that the group's purpose is not to be a rumour mill, wherein other employees' or pupils' personal affairs are debated. That is why the group agrees to avoid mentioning by name or stigmatizing in any way people who are not part of the group. The group activities are naturally also subject to teachers' professional ethics principles and statutory confidentiality obligations.

For example, one group made the following agreement upon action:

- The group only addresses issues relevant to teaching.
- The issues addressed in the group are confidential.
- Each group member chooses a level of handling professional issues that suits him/her personally.

- Topics for the following meeting can also be sent via e-mail. Only neutral or encouraging messages are sent via e-mail.
- Subsequent meetings are agreed upon in group meetings.
- If a meeting includes themes that arouse negative feelings, they should be addressed collectively before the meeting ends.
- Our aim is to support well-being at work and to discover joy in the everyday.

Autonomy and equality as background ideas

In the Finnish school context, the idea of equality is particularly suitable for mentoring relationships, as we still tend to regard teaching as a very autonomous profession. The Finns seem to build on a culture of responsibility and trust that values teachers' professional autonomy (Sahlberg, 2010, p. 11). 'Autonomy' literally means operating 'according to laws that one has made for oneself' (Greek *auto nomos*). A high level of autonomy does not necessarily mean that teachers can do whatever they wish though. As the concepts of autonomy and individualism are often misunderstood, it is worth taking a look at the origins of the word. Etymologically, the concept of autonomy comes from the Greek words *auto* and *nomos*. The word *auto* means *self* and *nomos* means *law* or *rules*. In ancient Greece this expression was used for a town-state (*polis*) that instituted its own laws. In an autonomous *polis*, the laws were discussed and established by the citizens of that particular *polis*. In the opposite case, the town was ruled by laws that had been constituted by another *polis*, and in that case the town or village was described by the words *hetero nomos*, which literally means that someone else (another *polis*) had instituted the laws. This is the origin of the word *heteronomy*, which is the opposite of *autonomy*. The concept of autonomy thus emphasizes interaction and collective will-formation in a social sphere, whereas individualism refers to action based on the will of a particular individual (Aspfors et al., 2011).

Finnish peer-group mentoring draws on the idea of professional autonomy as collective meaning-making and will-formation. This approach to mentoring can be understood as a continuum of the rather high level of autonomy of the teaching profession in Finland. Compared to many of their international counterparts, Finnish teachers are self-directed and seem to be less regulated. With reference to the Greek meaning, teachers constitute a *polis*, an independent community that acts in compliance with the laws it has made for itself. Finland represents a Nordic, rather liberal democracy, in which administration is based on trust instead of control, and equality between people is emphasized. In addition, Finnish teachers are highly educated – a Master's degree is a basic qualification for all teachers – which is why no external quality standards (except the teachers' qualifications) have been adopted.

In this sense, the Finnish school system seems to differ considerably from the educational systems in many other countries. The Finnish educational system has remained quite unreceptive to what is often called the *global education reform movement* (GERM), which has been adopted as an official agenda or accepted as educational orthodoxy within many education reforms throughout the world, including the US, the UK, and Germany. Today it is very common to define standards for education, as well as the competences to be achieved through it, in order to be able to evaluate teachers' and schools' activities (Sahlberg, 2010). This standard- or competence-based system has probably been developed the most in the movement's country of origin, England. The system was created during Margaret Thatcher's term of office in the late 1970s, but it continued under Labour rule (Whitty, 2008). This standardization of schools and teaching, common in Western industrialized countries, seems to be spreading elsewhere as well.

In several countries, the development of mentoring has started from the point of departure of standardization and control, which then makes the mentor the young teacher's supervisor and 'quality assurer'. Nevertheless, there is no evidence of the standard-based system yielding the best results. According to Sahlberg (2010), quite the contrary has happened: increasing external control of schools and on teachers has led to a weakening of teachers' work ethics and contributed to skilled teachers' retreat from teaching. Finnish teachers' pedagogical freedom is still extensive when compared at the international level, and Finnish pupils' good performance has been attributed to teachers' high professional skills (Sahlberg, 2010; Välijärvi, 2007, pp. 59–60).

High professional autonomy enhances teachers' work motivation, commitment to developing the school, and the status of the profession. This has led to a positive spiral: school leavers then see teaching as a meaningful career choice. There is a logical connection between good learning outcomes and teacher autonomy. Learning motivation research has shown that autonomous teachers also guide their pupils towards being autonomous learners, whereas teachers who get used to being controlled become controllers. In the latter case, pupils do not develop an internal motivation for knowledge formation but only see the extrinsic value of studying. Self-directed teachers, instead, steer their pupils towards self-directed learning (Roth et al., 2007).

Another logical connection, based on which teachers' autonomy enhances the quality of teaching, is related to the meaningfulness of teachers' work and teachers' coping therein. In the US, where teacher attrition is a growing problem, a connection has been discovered between a lost sense of autonomy and attrition. The US National Center for Education Statistics interviewed 7,000 teachers, some of whom were still teaching and some of whom had moved to other fields. Of those who had left teaching, 64 per cent experienced an increase in their professional autonomy after the career change. Thus, it seems that a high degree of control over teachers leads to a situation in which most independent, courageous, and skilled individuals seek employment outside the teaching profession (Palmer, 2007). Even though a Finnish teachers' position is still regarded as fairly autonomous, teachers themselves have experienced a weakening of their autonomy and some even report that it has disappeared altogether (Lapinoja, 2006). This could be a more general trend: autonomy is presently experienced as having narrower boundaries in a number of traditional professions (Välijärvi, 2007, p. 60).

It has been common to see teachers as civil servants who, subject to official liability, perform their civil servant duty. Over the recent decade this servant metaphor has gradually been replaced with neoliberal metaphors. Teachers are seen as servants of production and economy, who produce for the market workers, consumers, (inner) entrepreneurs, and actors who adapt to market trends. The servant metaphors share one feature: teachers serve an external party which exploits teachers, education, and upbringing as a medium – in other words, teachers act heteronomously. However, the idea behind peer-group mentoring as related to teachers' autonomy is based on the view that teachers are not in the service of any ideology, any political system, or any other external party. Teachers serve, above all else, growing children or young people, and their ultimate goal is to promote these learners' opportunities to lead a good life.

Affordances and constraints of equality

Even if the basic starting point of peer-group mentoring is equality between the participants and respect for autonomy, this equality does have its own constraints. If these boundary conditions of parity are not taken into account, the group can encounter problems in its activities. In any case, the mentor is in charge of steering the group's activities. Furthermore, parity cannot mean that everyone would be equal in terms of their knowledge and experiences: interaction is enriching precisely due to diversity.

When examining parity, we should distinguish from each other parity

1   as human beings, i.e. at the existential level;
2   associated with competence and knowledge, i.e. at the epistemic level; and
3   associated with responsibilities and duties, i.e. at the juridical level.

Existential parity refers to the equality of all human beings. From a humanistic perspective, each individual's life has equal value in its uniqueness, irrespective of whom we are dealing with. For instance, the dignity provided by social status has no importance in the existential sense: everyone is on the same page in terms of the fundamental issues related to life and death. The value of a human life is great, special, and immeasurably precious, irrespective of a person's achievements and social esteem. At the existential level, we can thus basically presume that the relation between the participants in a peer-mentoring group is symmetrical.

The epistemic level is about knowing or about being able to do something. At this level it is easy to say that some people have more competence than others. It is thus natural that, epistemically, people are not at the same level.

However, in a mentoring relation it is essential to consider the context in which competence is examined. With regard to professional competence, a more experienced participant, the mentor, has more knowledge and experience. But it is likely that in other areas of life the younger participants have competence and know-how that can also be significant and feasible for success in teaching. This knowledge may be informal. As a case in point, younger teachers are often better in touch with youth culture than their professionally more experienced senior colleagues, and this competence capital can also be utilized at work. Similarly, young people are often more experienced in applying IT, such as the Internet, in teaching. As a consequence, the equality of competence capital can vary: in certain areas the mentor's competence and knowledge are supreme, whereas the young teacher may master other things better. At the epistemic level, equality does not exist, because one or the other always has more experience and competence in a particular area.

Sociologist Pierre Bourdieu's (1986) theory of the fields of knowledge and forms of capital provides our examination of parity at the epistemic level with an even more interesting perspective. By adapting Bourdieu's theory, we can say, for example, that the mastery of IT comprises a field of its own, and that art history or moped repairing skills constitute their own fields. In each field the initial capital starts to grow additional value. Capital attracts capital, in the same way as in the economic theories. The more one knows and masters in a specific field, the better the possibilities of acquiring additional competence within the same field.

According to Bourdieu, life is a struggle for capital in different fields of knowledge. A field is a socially constructed space in which individuals struggle in order to acquire more and more capital. One strategy in this struggle implies changing the boundaries and structures of the field: one's own position is enhanced by changing the rules of the field. This is typically done by employees who boost their careers by emphasizing the role of their own competence area in the organization's strategy. In other words, changing the structures of a field contributes to increasing the importance of a specific form of capital (Bourdieu, 1986).

Bourdieu's concepts of field and capital make it easier to understand not only peer-group mentoring but also more generally the appreciation differences between the forms of competence essential in the field of teaching. However, Bourdieu's theory has its own particular emphasis which, as such, is not suitable for peer-group mentoring: it stresses the individuals' competitive positions and the aspiration to achieve a position in the field at the cost of others, 'one's competitors'. In PGM, on the contrary, we do not emphasize monopolistic or competitive positions, but rather apply the concepts of field and capital with less battle spirit. In fact, in a peer-mentoring group, capital is not vied for but rather – if we apply an economic metaphor – invested in a joint investment fund, in which each investor's profit grows in accordance with the volume of the different forms of capital brought to the joint investment fund. Capital growing in a shared investment fund, i.e. the peer-mentoring group, thus best contributes to each participant's individual competence development.

The concepts of field and capital also elucidate the possibility that in certain areas young employees may have the kind of experience that makes them superior to their more experienced co-workers. Epistemic parity thus offers various options – a relationship can be in a variety of ways asymmetric, in favour of either the mentor or the mentee. This can also be consciously utilized in the relation between the mentor and the mentee: both have the opportunity to learn from each other and jointly accumulate capital instead of vying against each other.

At the juridical level, parity is explored with regard to the officially and formally defined division of responsibilities, duties, and rights. For instance, the teaching practice that is included in teacher education resembles, to some extent, mentoring: the student teaches pupils, but it is the actual teacher or supervisor who has juridical responsibility. This juridical position is concretized in situations such as the teacher trainee going on a cycling trip with pupils. In case of an accident, the supervising teacher or sometimes the head teacher assumes juridical responsibility. In terms of responsibilities and duties, the student teacher and supervising teacher are not equal. On the other hand, the rights are not shared equally either: student teachers are not usually paid for teaching, as this work is formally recognized as credits, through which it is constituted as judicially defined teacher qualifications. The capital accrued by the students is in fact symbolic capital that is transformed both into money and judicially recognized qualifications later.

In mentoring relationships, it is usually the mentor who bears the main responsibility. The relationship between the mentor and the mentee is thus often judicially 'off balance' or asymmetric, as the mentor has to assume more legal responsibility than the mentee. In a peer-mentoring group, however, young and experienced employees basically share the same legal position, except for the responsibilities that derive directly from the roles defined within the peer-mentoring group. Due to the mentoring task, the person appointed as the team leader has certain responsibilities and rights that the other group members do not have.

All things considered, parity in a mentoring group is a highly complex phenomenon. In order to understand it, all of the previously described levels must be considered, as well as the various opportunities for symmetrical and asymmetrical relations residing therein. These levels of and opportunities for parity can be summarized in the following:

1 EXISTENTIAL EQUITY – existence and human worth
   - Symmetry M = m
      the mentor and mentee are equal at the existential level
2 EPISTEMIC EQUITY – knowledge and expertise
   - in the field of his/her expertise, the mentor is superior:

- Asymmetry M > m
  the mentor has more capital
- in a different field, the mentee can be superior:
  - Asymmetry M < m
    the mentee has more capital
3 JURIDICAL-ETHICAL EQUITY – responsibilities, rights, and duties
  - Asymmetry M > m
    the mentor bears more responsibility

In your work, studies, or work community activities, have you encountered symmetry or asymmetry between people:

- at the existential level
- at the epistemic level
- at the juridical level?

How has the symmetry or asymmetry been manifested?

Mentoring as knowledge construction

The change in mentoring has also been described as a transition towards constructivism. Learning is increasingly seen as joint knowledge construction, the process in which the learners construct knowledge in social interaction on the basis of their previous experiences and knowledge. Jian Wang and Sandra Odell (2002, 2007) have identified three perspectives in the mentoring programmes: a humanistic perspective, a situated apprentice perspective, and a critical constructivist perspective.

Mentoring with a humanistic perspective focuses on helping early career teachers solve and anticipate their personal problems, as well as on promoting their well-being within the profession. A close and trusting relationship between the mentor and the mentee is essential in the humanistic approach. The mentor is expected to meet the young teacher's emotional needs. The aim is to foster novice teachers' confidence and abilities, which is believed to contribute to success in teaching. Educational contents and practices are not central, and neither is the social dimension of school; focus is on the teacher's personal development. In the humanistic approach, the mentor is primarily expected to be warm, easy to approach, trust-inspiring, and safe (Schmidt, 2008; Wang & Odell, 2007, p. 476).

Mentoring with a situated apprentice perspective focuses on helping new teachers adapt to the existing culture and pedagogical norms by supporting their coping skills. The aim is to assist them in finding work methods that are suitable to the situations they encounter. Development into teachership is seen from a community perspective: it is gradual socialization into the 'tribe' of teachers. It is the mentors' task to promote new teachers' orientation to school culture, to support them as they look for their own meaningful place. In this approach the mentor is primarily expected to have strong local, practical experience (Wang & Odell, 2007, p. 476). The perspective of situated apprentice thus underlines transfer of school tradition and tacit knowledge. The support and learning environment offered to a new teacher by the school community depend on inter-teacher personal, cultural, moral, professional, political, and occasionally temporal or spatial distances, which are determined by the teachers' experiences, competence, and position (Hargreaves, 2001a).

The traditional image of mentoring follows assumptions related to the two aforementioned approaches: the humanistic and situated apprentice perspective. This traditional model underlines the knowledge transfer metaphor (Roehrig et al., 2008, p. 686). Traditional mentoring, in Piagetian terms, implies the assimilation of knowledge to meet established schemata rather than a change taking place in old schemata, i.e. accommodation.

The critical constructivist perspective challenges the aforementioned traditional approach. It is based on two theoretical mindsets. One of them is critical theory, according to which the goal is to learn to deconstruct, that is, to question existing knowledge. Based on this, after critical analysis, we can reconstruct a more conscious conception in which social structures are seen as products of power. We thus try to evaluate prevailing conceptions and practices from the viewpoint of the exercise of power: the ultimate purpose is to recognize prevailing hegemonies; that is, the belief systems regarded as self-evident which uphold the ruling groups' privileges. The aim is to become emancipated through critical thinking, awareness, and discussion; in other words, to liberate ourselves from these axiomatic belief systems (Carr & Kemmis, 1984; Wang & Odell, 2007).

The second theoretical background idea of critical constructivism is the basic hypothesis of constructivism, according to which knowledge is actively constructed by drawing upon prior knowledge and experiences. Learning refers to these conceptions being accommodated through social interaction. This conceptual change often takes place slowly, partly even unconsciously; but sometimes it happens quickly and radically. If critical theory is combined with constructivism, the focus will be on accommodating old conceptions, which will result in the reshaping and change of the learners' original ideas and assumptions. From a Piagetian perspective, this implies that new kinds of schemata are discovered in teachers' pedagogical thinking. In practice, the critical constructivist perspective in mentoring means that new teachers are encouraged to pose questions, challenge existing teaching practices, and alter the way of acting as a teacher. The mentor's role is described by Wang and Odell as that of an agent of change (Wang & Odell, 2007, p. 477).

Mentoring helps teachers integrate into everyday practice the theories and theoretical concepts they have learned in teacher education. The critical constructivist approach allows the examination of teaching- and learning-related notions and conceptions supported by the mentor. This challenges teachers to look for new outlooks and practices. Mentoring is not only the young teacher's process of learning to teach but also an opportunity for mentors to learn (Schmidt, 2008, p. 646; Wang & Odell, 2002, 2007). In addition, group mentoring allows different-aged teachers with different experiences and backgrounds to meet each other, so that both the more experienced and the novice teachers can benefit from each other's knowledge and experience base. When peer-group mentoring is based on a critical constructivist perspective, elements of the humanistic and situated apprentice perspectives can also be utilized in the process of new knowledge creation: learning takes place in a warm and respectful interactive relationship that promotes growth in all of the parties (humanistic perspective). At the same time, something is learned about the common culture and ways of work (the situated apprentice perspective). However, the aim is not to transfer existing practices as such but to examine them critically and renew them, instead. This is how peer-group mentoring can utilize all of the aforementioned theoretical foundations of mentoring.

From a constructivist perspective, peer-group mentoring means exchange of ideas and joint knowledge construction, in which all parties learn. It implements the idea of integrative pedagogy, in which practical and theoretical knowledge are integrated in order to enable the teacher to better direct his/her own activities. The model of integrative pedagogy will be presented in the following chapter.

> How are the humanistic, situated apprentice and critical constructivist perspectives manifested in the mentoring group's activities?

Integrative pedagogy in teacher education

The ideas of formal, nonformal and informal learning, as well as parity and constructivism, provide the basis for a model of expertise development called integrative pedagogy (Tynjälä, 2007, 2008). This model (see Fig. 1.3), which can also more generally be regarded as the teacher education ideal, is applied in peer-group mentoring. The point of departure for the integrative pedagogy model is that expertise is constituted by the following four basic elements (see, Bereiter, 2002; Bereiter & Scardamalia, 1993; Eraut, 2004; Le Maistre & Paré, 2006; Tynjälä, 2009):

1   theoretical and conceptual knowledge;
2   practical and experiential knowledge;
3   self-regulative knowledge; and
4   socio-cultural knowledge.

Theoretical knowledge is formal in nature and easy to express explicitly. It is knowledge that is learned, for instance, through texts, figures, discussions, or

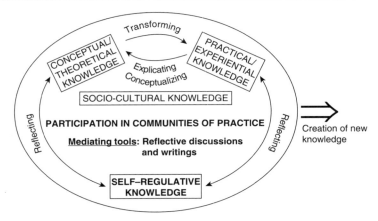

Figure 1.3 Model of integrative pedagogy in peer-group mentoring

Sources: Heikkinen et al., 2010, 2011; Tynjälä et al., 2006; Tynjälä, 2008, 2009; Tynjälä & Kallio, 2009.

lectures. It is abstracted or conceptual knowledge evolving as a result of a conscious and conceptual thought process. After all, theoretical knowledge is not enough for the development of profound expertise; it also needs to be complemented with practical and experiential knowledge. This knowledge is not learned from books – it develops through practical experience. That is why it often remains implicit, tacit, or inarticulate – and informal – knowledge.

Practical knowledge has also been called procedural knowledge, i.e. knowledge of how specific things are done. The terms 'know-how' or simply 'skills' also refer to this kind of practical competence. This competence is often intuitive in nature. Intuition refers to spontaneous knowing, in which the knowledge is obtained directly. Intuitive knowledge is the opposite of abstracted knowledge: it is neither conceptual nor analytic in nature but is based on a presentiment or a guess instead. Some studies have shown, for example, that leaders rely on intuitive decision-making in difficult situations (Burke & Miller, 1999; Sinclair & Ashkanasy, 2002). In the same way, mentors often have to solve complex social situations using their intuition. Experience helps them make the right decisions even when relying on intuition. However, experienced professionals in general are not aware of their intuition and cannot explain afterwards precisely why they solved the problem as they did. Scientific thinking is also often based on intuition: researchers first get an intuition about the solution and only afterwards generate a conceptual theory. Referred to as abductive reasoning, this relies on an intuitive thought process in which the solution is first generated by itself, after which its correctness is verified through the process of logical and analytical reasoning.

The third central element of expertise – self-regulative knowledge – includes metacognitive and reflective knowledge and skills. A typical feature of high-level expertise is strong self-regulation, which refers to the reflective evaluation of one's own activities, awareness of one's own strengths and weaknesses, and development of competence. An example of self-regulative knowledge in skilled managers' activities is how they, through discussion and reflection, learn to find reasons for having solved a difficult situation in a certain way. On the basis of this knowledge, the managers may also regulate and change their own activities. Likewise, mentors as group leaders may arrive at a solution through self-regulative knowledge, as a result of which their ways of action change. In addition to the regulation of one's own activities, the concept of self-regulation can be broadened to include the reflective examination of activities in the entire work community or professional field. In this case, we use the term 'regulative knowledge' (Bereiter, 2002).

While theoretical, practical, and self-regulative knowledge represent personal expert knowledge, the fourth component of expertise, socio-cultural knowledge, refers to knowledge that is embedded in social practices and cultures. Every workplace and social community has its own ways of action and practices which can be learnt only through participating in them.

Even though these four components of expertise can be analytically distinguished from one another, it is typical of high-level expertise that these forms of knowledge are closely integrated with one another. Experts do not need to consider separately which theory the solution is based on when solving practical problems, as their theoretical knowledge is so strongly intertwined with practical experience that solutions are flexibly generated.

According to Bereiter and Scardamalia (1993), formal theoretical knowledge is transformed into expert informal knowledge when it is applied to solving practical problems. Respectively, when the conceptual tools offered by theoretical knowledge are applied in solving practical problems, the actor's understanding of the problem increases. In terms of expertise and competence development, it is actually important, on the one hand, to adapt theoretical knowledge to a form in which it can be utilized in practical problem-solving and, on the other hand, to explicate and conceptualize the tacit knowledge generated through practical experience. In other words, theories should be examined in light of practice, and practical experience in light of theories and conceptual knowledge. The third component of expertise – self-regulative knowledge – develops through reflective activity, as the individual critically reflects on his/her own actions and experiences. During this reflection, theoretical concepts or models serve as tools for understanding one's own experiences as parts of more general phenomena. For ideal development of expertise, all this takes place in authentic communities of practice where personal expert knowledge meets socio-cultural knowledge and practices.

In order to establish the aforementioned interaction between theoretical, practical, self-regulative, and socio-cultural knowledge, we need tools to reflect on our own experiences in light of conceptual knowledge. These tools can include analytical writing assignments, learning diaries, small-group discussions, guidance and mentoring discussions, and practically all the methods that allow us to reflect on and conceptualize experiential knowledge, as well as to examine conceptual knowledge in light of experience. Indeed, the basic idea of integrative pedagogy is to combine theoretical, practical, self-regulative, and socio-cultural knowledge in learning situations. In addition to the various components of expertise, integrative pedagogy integrates other elements of learning and expertise: it encompasses informal and formal learning, thinking, and action; learning and work; professional skills and so-called general/transferable skills (e.g. communication skills); scientific thought and concrete action; individual and collaborative learning; and potentially also contents from various disciplines.

The idea of integrative pedagogy has been implemented in training of mentors as follows:

1   The introductions by experts provide the participants with conceptual tools that help them understand and piece together the phenomena central to mentoring. The key concepts include, for example, dialogue, interaction, parity, formal and informal learning, and the very concept of integrative pedagogy.
2   Narrative and action-based methods, as well as discussions and small-group tasks are employed in the training sessions, in which the participants reflect on their own experiences with the help of conceptual tools.
3   Between the training sessions, the participants are given writing assignments, in which they discuss and analyse questions related to the preceding session's theme. In addition, they complete assignments to highlight experiential knowledge with regard to the following training session's theme.

On the basis of the participants' feedback, these methods broadened their understanding and inspired them.

- How do you reflect on your own work?
- Which theoretical concepts have you found useful in understanding your work-related problems?
- Have you ever started to wonder about things regarded as routine?
- Have you tried to change these habits?
- What were the consequences?

Applying integrative pedagogy to peer-group mentoring

The conscious aim of PGM groups is to integrate informal knowledge with formal knowledge. Mentoring is traditionally quite an informal, unstructured form of professional development support, in which a more experienced colleague is offered as a discussion partner to a less experienced one. In peer-group mentoring, informal interaction is also implemented between more experienced colleagues, and younger colleagues can support older ones.

Informal interaction mainly includes two forms of knowledge: practical, experiential knowledge and self-regulative knowledge (see Fig. 1.3). In contrast, a third component of expertise – theoretical and conceptual knowledge – is usually scarce in informal mentoring discussions. The challenge for group mentoring is particularly how to include the theoretical element in the integrative knowledge construction process.

On the other hand, the power of mentoring is embedded precisely in the informal nature of activities. Teachers experience group sessions as empowering largely because within the group they can share their experiences and thoughts without performance pressure. That is why many of them prefer mentoring groups to more formal continuing professional education events.

However, theoretical knowledge provides conceptual tools that contribute to a better understanding of practical problems. Theoretical concepts describe a phenomenon in a more abstract way than an individual's practical experiences, which is why they can be used to examine things at a more general level. Conceptual knowledge and theoretical concepts can thus add depth to the understanding of everyday phenomena and problems. It would not be possible to achieve this just through discussion at the level of personal experiences.

In terms of competence development, formal education is in fact problematic because its theoretical knowledge, which is usually distributed through formal education, is not linked to the teachers' experiential and self-regulative knowledge. Theoretical knowledge and concepts consequently remain disconnected, and no integration of the key components of expertise takes place. In PGM groups, however, it is possible to create forms of professional development that combine the best elements of formal and informal learning: the conceptual tools of formal education and the processing of experiential and self-regulative knowledge, enabled by informal interaction.

In practice, how can we then integrate the basic elements of expertise, that is, theoretical, practical, self-regulative, and socio-cultural knowledge, in peer-group mentoring without generating performance pressure for teachers, and without transforming the group sessions into heavy lectures or formal study circles? In other words, how can we include in mentoring discussions such theoretical concepts or models that enhance understanding – and still maintain the informal learning atmosphere typical of mentoring? For example, the following stimuli can be utilized in the groups in order to introduce theoretical knowledge into peer discussions:

- When a problem requiring more understanding arises in discussion, an article on the topic is provided and read as a basis for the next discussion. In order to avoid performance pressure, reading the article is voluntary. There are usually some people in the group who like reading and sharing their reading experiences with the others, which is enough to introduce the topic for discussion. It is essential to find in the text some concepts or models that go beyond the everyday experience and contribute to a better understanding of the phenomenon at hand.

- An educational TV programme is chosen, perhaps from the archives, and is watched in order to stimulate discussion. These programmes usually offer conceptual tools that can be examined in light of everyday experiences and personal activities.
- Knowledge is searched for on the Internet (e.g. Wikipedia, blogs, research articles). This is sometimes a fairly quick medium for finding views, concepts, or theoretical models that can be linked easily to everyday experiences. Access to the Internet during the mentoring session can help the participants collaboratively find new theoretical dimensions to bring to the conversation.
- An expert or researcher is invited to visit the mentoring group. The expert can be asked to take part in the discussion and to provide an outsider's view on the topic at hand, or he/she can be asked to provide a brief introduction.

It is essential in all of these alternatives that, while reflecting on their experiences and activities, the participants may utilize not only their own experiential knowledge but also theoretical concepts or models. When one's own experiences are examined with conceptual tools, the elements of expertise are integrated and expertise becomes more profound.

Mentor training

The activities of peer-mentoring groups are supported by mentor training, which introduces the theoretical background of PGM as well as the working methods used in the groups. For example, the mentor training programme implemented in Central Finland lasts one academic year and comprises 10 ECTS study points (ECTS = European Credit Transfer System). The training follows the principles of integrative pedagogy described above. Thus, the conceptual frameworks and the methods used in training are applied to practice and developed further in the peer-mentoring groups. The mentors are trained to utilize interactive and constructive learning methods so as to promote social learning in the group. The mentor training programme consists of five seminars, of two days each, and learning assignments on a web-based learning platform. During the one-year study module, the mentors focus on issues such as interaction and dialogue in the working community, well-being in schools, constructivism and collegiality in learning, tacit knowledge and reflection, social change in education, supporting professional identity through narrative work, and studies in professional ethics in education.

Of course the educational themes we have mentioned are not the only possible ones though they have gradually been crystallized as central themes in our mentor training. When implementing training, themes that are topical or otherwise prove to be important to specific situations and individual training groups are also taken up. According to the principles of integrative pedagogy, it is essential for the mentors in the training to simultaneously examine and reflect on their own experiences of leading the group. The one-year mentor training is actually completed while leading one's own group. Learning about mentoring is enhanced by sharing experiences with other mentors. The mentor training participants are divided into small groups, which serve as venues for sharing experiences. These 'home groups' are permanent, which is why they constitute an experience approximately parallel to operating in a one-year peer group.

However, mentor training is not restricted to this one-year course: the participants are also provided with the opportunity for experience-sharing regarding mentoring afterwards. The mentor community thus constitutes a peer community that, in terms of methodology and content, mirrors the activities of peer-mentoring groups.

Chapter 2

Peer-group mentoring and the culture of teacher education in Finland

Jouni Välijärvi and Hannu L.T. Heikkinen

In many ways the peer-group mentoring (PGM) model in Finland seems to be a special way of organizing support for new teachers which differs from the practices of many other countries. What are the reasons behind Finland's practice of supporting new teachers through peer-group mentoring? Why not support new teachers through a different approach? This chapter takes a closer look at Finnish educational traditions and culture to better understand PGM.

The practices of induction are situated within a context of political and educational *metapractices* (see chapter 14 in this book). This is one of the reasons why models of induction cannot be directly transferred from one educational and political system to another. No model of mentoring as such can be haphazardly transferred elsewhere, as that would require transferring an entire mindset and operating culture. In the European Union there seems to be a growing trend to disseminate rather similar practices of teacher induction throughout Europe. These practices are transplanted from one national context to another through EU projects. It is perhaps questionable whether national contexts and characteristics are always appropriately taken into account.

The Finnish solution for supporting new teachers, the PGM model, has been developed within a specific educational context and at a particular historical time. One of the most visible things in Finnish education from an international perspective has been that Finns have achieved excellent results in international student achievement tests (PISA) for more than a decade. The outcomes of international comparative studies on student achievement in mathematics, science and language have been repeatedly excellent. The Finnish educational system has also been celebrated elsewhere: for example, in 2010 *Newsweek* declared Finland to be the best country to live in in the world. One of the key components of a good life, according to *Newsweek*, is education. In Finland eduation was ranked best in the world in this universal comparison. The *Newsweek* article was based on a survey focused on five categories of national well-being: education, health, quality of life, economic competitiveness and political environment. This special survey took several months to be completed by the *Newsweek* team supported by an advisory board consisting of internationally acknowledged university professors and directors of international research institutes (Foroohar, 2010, p. 33).

It is possible to understand the success of the Finnish educational system as part of a historical continuum drawing back to the European traditions of education and social and political development in Scandinavia. In Finland and the Nordic countries, the European tradition of 'Bildung' (Ax & Ponte, 2008) has been adopted and developed along with the Scandinavian welfare state, based on strong values of democracy, equity and solidarity (Rönnerman et al., 2008). This process, also called 'the folk enlightenment movement', has been a mainstay of Nordic democracy and society (Kemmis, 2008, p. xi). Educational practices in Finland can be understood within this social, political, cultural, and material–economic context. Education has always been seen as important in the Nordic countries. Parents still regard education as the best policy to ensure a positive future for their children. Moreover, in Finland parental trust in education is less dependent on their social status than in many older industrialized countries. Admittedly, however, educational aspiration and academic achievement are connected with the family's economic status and the parents' educational level in Finland as well as in many other countries. From a historical perspective, relatively positive attitudes towards education have been, nonetheless, characteristic of the working class and rural population as well.

In parallel with the situation in the other Nordic countries, education has been identified as an essential part of the development of the nation and national identity. Teachers have always played an important and respected role in society. Such high respect is still apparent today, for instance, in national surveys on public ratings for various professions and occupations. According to such surveys, in people's minds the status of a teacher is largely comparable to that of a lawyer or a doctor. The teaching profession has also remained a popular choice among young people. Among secondary school leavers, teaching has always been high on the list of favourites and an indicator of the high appreciation of teaching is the willingness of young people to apply for teacher education.

In Finland, we may see a 'positive circle of recognition' (Heikkinen, 2003) taking place in recruitment to the teaching profession. Finnish teachers have been recognized as excellent professionals by comparative international studies, such as the above-mentioned PISA and *Newsweek* surveys, and as a result the status of the profession has become even higher. This means that many young people consider becoming a teacher, and the number of applicants is high. This enables universities to select the best students for these programmes in terms of their previous academic achievement. The people chosen to participate in teacher education have excellent academic skills and are highly motivated to study. As a result, Finland gets good teachers who in turn achieve good results, and the cycle continues. This creates a circle of positive recognition of teachers which seems to be exceptional from a global perspective (Heikkinen, 2003; Honneth, 1995).

In many countries, the number of applicants for teacher education has decreased, and the circle of recognition is negative: the less teachers are appreciated, the less young people are interested in the job and the greater are the numbers of teacher resignations. Finnish teacher education has not faced any serious problems in attracting applicants, with the exception of mathematics and some foreign languages. Class teacher education, special-needs teacher education and student counsellor education are examples of fields where the number of applicants is far greater than the number of student places available. For example, for the approximately 800 student places offered in teacher training programmes there are annually about 5000 applicants.

A brief history of teacher education in Finland

Teacher education is currently provided by eleven universities and five vocational teacher education institutions in Finland. In terms of qualification, both offer the general pedagogical qualification which is required to work as a teacher in Finnish primary and secondary schools. In the following, we concentrate on teacher education provided in universities and the development of this teacher education.

Teacher training in Finland has taken shape gradually and separately for each school type and even for each individual type of teaching assignment. The bisection of the education system into folk school (*folkskola*) and secondary school (*gymnasium*) which took place in the nineteenth century also determined that teacher training was divided into two main streams: teachers for folk schools graduated from teacher training colleges (*seminariums*), whereas secondary school teachers were trained at universities.

Prior to the comprehensive school reform of the 1970s, the issue of teacher training was the subject of many major controversies. The issues to be solved included the unification of teacher training and the implementation of the principle of a single degree, the transfer of training from teacher training colleges to institutions of higher education and the harmonization of theoretical and practical training, on the one hand, and pedagogy and other disciplines, on the other. These topics were addressed by several different committees and the final decisions did not satisfy all interested parties.

One of the turning points in the development of teacher education was the Teacher Education Act ratified in December 1971. It resulted in the final transfer of training for primary and secondary school teachers to university level. The main purpose of the Act was to unify the education of primary and secondary school teachers and to develop programmes of an academically high standard for training all new teachers. The training for primary school teachers replaced the training for folk school teachers, and the upper secondary school matriculation examination became the basic educational requirement for all applicants. New teacher training objectives were drawn up, according to which training was divided into primary school teacher training (i.e. 'class teacher training' (grades 1–6) and subject teacher training (grades 7–9 in lower secondary and upper secondary classes in ten to twelve school years). This division still applies today (Niemi, 2002; Linnakylä, 2004).

A new decree in 1978 led to the creation of degree programmes for primary school teachers, lower and upper secondary school subject teachers, and educational planners, as well as programmes for special needs teachers and student counsellors, which could be characterized as postgraduate studies. The decree included provisions to guarantee the national uniformity of teacher training.

Maintaining the sense of status and respect associated with the teaching profession was one of the main reasons for transferring teacher education to universities in the 1970s. In order to strengthen the academic basis of teaching, a Master's degree was established as the basic level for qualified teacher status. Familiarizing teaching students with the latest research and training them for carrying out research became integral components of that degree.

The latest teacher education reform has been influenced by the European Bologna Process, which was aimed at harmonizing higher education. The main purpose of the Bologna Process is the creation of the European Higher Education Area (EHEA) by making academic degree standards and quality assurance standards more comparable and compatible throughout Europe. The Finnish universities revised their curricula on teacher education following the guidelines set up by the Bologna Process in 2006. According to the national framework for curricula the basic idea of Finnish teacher training is to educate competent teachers for society's educational system and to develop adequate professional qualities to ensure a lifelong teaching career.

The new Finnish reform based on the Bologna Process aims further to reinforce the academic basis of the teaching profession. The new curricula of teacher education emphasize the readiness of teachers to apply research-based knowledge to their daily work. To promote this, all students are required to conduct a study of their own (Jakku-Sihvonen & Niemi, 2005). The purpose of strengthening the research capabilities of new teachers is to enable them to develop their own work while working in school. In this development, we may find clear influence of the traditions of the international 'action research' or 'teacher as researcher' movements.

Finnish research-based teacher education leans on the ideas typical of these movements. The main aim is to support professional teacher development as a process that continues throughout a teacher's working career. The personal involvement of student teachers in research activities provides a basis for this. For this aim to be successful, however, the education of teachers must integrate research with the everyday problems encountered in teachers' work.

A central aim of teacher training, which spans across a teacher's entire career, is to support their individual professional development. On the other hand, it is also increasingly important that both pre-service and in-service training support teachers' capabilities as regards working together with other teachers, experts in other fields, and various stakeholders outside the school. At the same time competency requirements in society are increasing with families' growing social problems. This is changing the content of teachers' work in many ways and may become a threat to their well-being.

It is also important that the in-service training of teachers is closely interlinked with the pre-service training provided by universities. In-service training should enable integration between fundamental research-based knowledge about teachers' work as acquired in the university, and practical competencies gained in daily school life. This notion highlights the responsibility of universities in the organization of in-service training for teachers (Niemi, 2000). Today, this connection is being strengthened by the peer-group mentoring model disseminated by the Osaava Verme ('Skilled PGM') network including all the teacher education departments of universities and vocational teacher education colleges in Finland.

Teacher training in the universities

The teacher education system in the universities is twofold: part of the responsibility for training lies with the faculties of education, while another part is carried out in co-operation with the faculties of different teaching subjects. Studies conforming to the decrees governing teacher education and degrees in education can be completed at eight universities. In addition, art academies have their own system for teacher education. The general objectives of teacher education emphasize teachers' professional competency to work as independent experts and to develop their work through their whole career (Niemi, 2000).

When primary school teacher training was transferred to universities, at first there were some mixed feelings about this reform. On the one hand, the reform was supported by arguments concerning the increasing professional demands on teachers' knowledge and competence as a consequence of changes that have made society increasingly reliant on the application of knowledge and the production of new knowledge. Higher and higher competencies were being required at the workplace and more capable teachers were needed to provide them. Teachers were expected to have more and more elaborate pedagogical skills and the ability to utilize the latest knowledge in their work.

On the other hand, those in favour of the old system (seminaries) pointed out that the teaching profession is, after all, very practical in nature. Teacher preparation should therefore be based on the acquisition of concrete skills practised in real school life. The theories underlying various pedagogic applications were not considered important to teachers, although for teacher educators such knowledge might be of some use. As for prospective teachers, a connection to research was seen as secondary to versatile and authentic experience. According to this line of thinking, particularly the idea of completing a Master's thesis as part of teacher studies was vigorously rejected. Many students also doubted the relevance of a Master's thesis in developing practical competencies for teachers' work (Niemi, 2000).

The main subject in *primary school teacher* education is education. This provides the theoretical foundation for taking charge of teaching duties. A further objective of the educational studies is to lead students into scientific thinking and research. The scope of the Master's degree in education is 300 credits in the European Credit Transfer System (ECTS), and students with the degree are eligible for postgraduate studies in education. The popularity of such postgraduate studies aiming at a doctoral degree has increased steadily in recent years. Some universities have also introduced separate programmes for teacher graduates in order to support their postgraduate studies.

Students may choose their secondary subject studies fairly freely. For example, a student may concentrate on a comprehensive school subject and study it for the whole 60 credits, so as to get a qualification to teach this subject for grades 7–9 as well. Optionally, students may choose to specialize in primary education, special-needs education or in a subject taught at the lower grades. Alternatively, the secondary subject studies may include modules of philosophy, social sciences, humanities, or any other faculty in the student's own or another university. Each student is required to complete a Master's thesis as part of their advanced studies in education. Class teacher graduates are eligible to go on with postgraduate studies heading to a doctorate in education.

Subject teacher education includes studies in one, two or three teaching subjects and the teacher's pedagogical studies as part of a Master's degree. Subject teacher training is regulated by field-specific decrees. In terms of other subject teacher training, students are admitted to the faculties or degree programmes representing different subjects and some of them are usually only selected for subject teacher training later. In some universities, however, students apply directly for subject teacher training (such as training for subject teachers in English, in mathematics, physics and chemistry, or in religion). It is also possible to graduate as a subject teacher by separately doing teachers' pedagogical studies once a university degree has been completed.

A teaching subject means a subject included in the curriculum of lower or upper secondary school or another educational institution. Teaching subject studies consist of advanced studies in one subject, with a minimum scope of 80–90 credits, and intermediate studies in a second and possible third subject, with a minimum scope of 50–60 credits in each. According to the new curriculum, subject teacher qualification calls for 60 credits of pedagogic studies.

The pedagogic studies for subject teachers are divided into two components. *Basic studies in education* deal with the fundamentals of growth and learning (15 credits) and also comprise practical training under supervisors' guidance (10 credits). *Intermediate pedagogic studies* extend subject teachers' competencies especially for communication, educational ethics, and the methodologies of educational research (20 credits). Nearly as great a share of the pedagogic studies (15 credits) is allocated for practice teaching in classrooms. This practice first takes place under close supervision but becomes more independent with individual work in the classroom towards the end of the programme.

Interest in teacher education and training, in mathematics and natural sciences in particular, clearly increased after student selection procedures were changed to enable students to opt directly for a programme specializing in subject teacher education. It is clear that universities need to make more extensive use of similar direct student selection procedures in other fields as well. Research findings on student selection procedures for teacher education and training indicate that teacher graduates' commitment to teaching work is more permanent when the selection procedures have been sufficiently sensitive to applicants' aptitude for the field and to their conscious career choices. In the future, it is also advisable to develop selection models for teacher education and training, which will enable a more flexible transition from other occupations into teaching positions.

Pedagogical studies as a core component of teacher education

Pedagogical studies make up an obligatory component common to all teacher qualifications, including vocational teacher degrees. These studies are in essence intermediate studies in education, which emphasize teachers' pedagogical thinking and pedagogical research, and include teaching practice. The studies may be oriented towards teaching assignments in comprehensive or upper secondary schools, in vocational institutions or in adult education.

The pedagogical studies build on a scientific analysis of teachers' work and the knowledge to be mediated in the work. When describing this starting point, different researchers use different terms, such as 'research-based teacher education' (Kansanen, 1999a), 'evidence-based teacher education' (Niemi, 2000), 'action research' or 'teacher as a researcher' (Heikkinen, 2001). What is common to all these definitions is that they each emphasize research knowledge as the basis for all teacher education. Approaches and methods typical of research should be present in all education. A teacher educator's task is to find ways to fit this demand to the theme and contents being studied, as well as to the students' current competencies.

The nature of a teacher's work is much like the activities of a practitioner-researcher. Reflection is one way to gain knowledge about interaction in the teaching-studying-learning process. Kansanen (1999b) points out that reflection calls for a certain distance in order to focus properly on one's own decisions and their role in practice. In this process, the teacher may use his/her knowledge about research-based thinking skills. This refers also to the practice of reading articles in professional journals and research reports. The aim of research-based teacher education is the ability to make decisions based on rational argumentation, in addition to tacit knowledge or intuitional argumentation. The aim is that teachers internalize a research-oriented attitude towards their work. This means that teachers learn to take an analytical and open-minded approach to their work and are ready to learn new methods for their professional practice. The aim is that they can see their profession as an intellectually, socially and morally challenging career.

In research-based teacher education the practical aspects and theoretical basis of teachers' work are seen as complementary, not as opposites. This is clearly indicated in the 'model of integrative pedagogy' discussed in detail elsewhere in this book. The curricula accordingly emphasize the dynamic and collaborative nature of scientific knowledge and learning. According to this line of thought, teacher educators and teacher students are researchers of teachers' work and searching for new understanding. Hence, the curricular emphasis on process goals rather than the contents to be learnt or on objectives related to students' post-training behaviour. Along with making progress with their studies, teacher students should take greater responsibility for their own learning. Ultimately, teacher training should yield experts of pedagogic practice, who are willing and capable to develop their own professional skills in a continuing process throughout their work careers.

In the new curriculum for teacher education, a dialogical and constructivist approach is emphasized. The notion of dialogue accentuates interaction between different approaches and lines of thinking in the quest for a deeper understanding of learning. A teacher should be able critically to evaluate different ways of working with children as well as continuously to question his or her own thinking patterns. Teachers need to be ready to listen to other people and also able to argue for their own views. This applies to teacher students as well as to their educators.

When teachers' professional development is defined as a process continuing throughout their working careers, integration between pre-service and in-service education becomes a crucial issue. This is also the challenge which the peer-goup mentoring model seeks to address. Today, the responsibility for teacher's pre-service training rests with the universities and vocational teacher education institutes, whereas in-service training for teachers is provided by many private as well as publicly funded organizations. Teacher associations also provide plenty of such training services. In general, the provision for in-service training is poorly coordinated and the quality of services varies to a great extent. There are national efforts to coordinate and enhance in-service teacher educa-tion through the national programme *Osaava Ohjelma* ('Skilled Programme') 2010–2016, which aims at furthering the continuing professional development of teachers. One of the key elements of this national programme is the peer-group mentoring model.

Teachers as autonomous professionals

The idea of an autonomous teacher who is able to think and act independently and justify his/her own educational decisions presupposes readiness to read professional texts such as research reports and journals. Therefore, important aspects of professional literacy include an ability to choose and critically evaluate the texts for one's own use. Everyday intuitive thinking, with justifications from one's own experiences and discussions with colleagues, attracts rational arguments. Although pedagogical thinking is mainly mixed with intuitional and rational arguments, a research-based attitude makes it possible to steer this thinking systematically towards rational educational decisions.

The high autonomy of Finnish teachers is also interrelated with the teacher role in school-based decision-making in Finland. In the light of PISA surveys (Välijärvi et al., 2002; Välijärvi, 2005b) Finnish teachers have a significant amount of power when it comes to deciding on essential points concerning the operational contents and policies of the school. In most other countries teachers play a more minor role in decision making, while the principal, school board, and outside administrators have a greater say in directing the school activities.

In Finnish schools teachers play a central role as regards decisions on course provision (courses to offer) and on course contents. In more than 80 per cent of Finnish schools decisions on these matters are essentially based on teacher expertise, whereas across the OECD countries, on average, in only one-third of the schools do teachers have a major role in deciding upon course provision, and only half of the teachers have any greater influence on course contents. In Finland the choice of textbooks is also largely based on teacher expertise in most (89 per cent) schools, whereas on average in OECD countries only two-thirds of schools rely on their teacher views when selecting textbooks.

Finnish schools also rely heavily on their teachers' expertise when establishing disciplinary policies and assessment policies for schoolwork. In Finland 90 per cent of schools define their assessment policies on the basis of teacher views, whereas in other countries about 40 per cent of schools, on average, often leave teacher expertise aside in these matters. In the same vein, nearly 80 per cent of Finnish schools base their disciplinary policies essentially on teacher views, whereas in less than half, on average, of the schools in other countries teachers are involved in such decision making.

Considering all OECD countries, teachers rarely hold a major role in deciding upon student admission, teacher selection, or expenditure and budget allocations. In comparison to other countries on average, Finnish teachers still have clearly greater influence on school budgets and the allocation of resources within the school. In 23 per cent of the Finnish schools teacher views play an essential role in the resource allocations within the school, while the corresponding average percentage across all OECD countries is only 14 per cent.

The devolution of decision-making powers closer to schools and teachers has been characteristic of Finnish education policy since the 1980s. This trend became particularly strong in the 1990s. The aim in increasing the decision-making powers of schools has been to enhance the abilities of schools to respond to the needs of their surrounding communities. This is in line with the general principle of bringing decision making as close as possible to those affected by the decisions made. This has increased opportunities for teachers to influence their own work as well as the policies of all educational institutions. In many other countries such decentralization trends have not reached teachers but shifted decision-making powers to school principals, school boards and local authorities instead.

Decentralization brings up the issue of decision making within schools. The high-level research-based education and broad-based expertise of Finnish teachers provide a good basis for democratic decision making founded on the equity of members of the school community. Effective utilization of teacher expertise for the benefit of the whole community is also a challenge to school management. According to Lapinoja (2006) and Välijärvi (2007), Finnish teachers consider that they do have some say and influence in their working communities.

One problem with strong teacher autonomy is that it has sometimes been misinterpreted as individualism. In actual fact, autonomy is not individualism; in contrast, autonomous professionalism is based on collective social meaning-making processes and professional ethics. As an outcome of individualistic practices, the teachers have still sometimes been reluctant to open their classes to their colleagues or parents. An obvious challenge to Finnish schools and teachers is how to open classrooms, more than is the case today, to cooperation with colleagues, parents and other experts involved in students' lives. Nevertheless, the high expertise of the teachers, yielded by their education, the high social status of the profession, and their strong influence in school-based decision making, provides a good basis for the development of the teaching profession towards more collaborative approaches (Luukkainen, 2005a; Välijärvi, 2000).

Trust and openness are cornerstones in the development of the teaching profession. Society in general and parents in particular need to be able to trust schools and teachers in that each child must be provided with equal high-level learning opportunities irrespective of their place of residence or their family's social background. Teachers, for their part, need to be able to trust that they will be allowed to work, just as other highly educated experts, as autonomous pedagogical professionals, in a way that takes full advantage of their potential. This Finnish model of the teacher's role, based on trust, seems to be yielding excellent results in international comparisons. Maintaining and further increasing the respect for the teaching profession and the sense of trust in teachers' professional competence are therefore cornerstones for the development of teacher education as well.

The PGM model is a clear recognition of the high professional autonomy of teachers. It is based on the assumption that teachers are competent professionals with high expertise in their area, and the starting point for peer group mentoring is that the teachers are able to study their work collaboratively in groups. The aims and study plans are determined by the group itself, leading to highly self-directed learning, utilizing the personal competencies and interests of the group members. The PGM model owes much to the European and Nordic tradition of *Bildung*, based on strong values of democracy, equity and solidarity.

Part II

Empirical studies on peer-group mentoring

The second part of this book presents empirical evidence on the feasibility of the peer-group mentoring model. All the studies described were conducted as part of the project 'Peer Group Mentoring for Teachers' Professional Development and Well-Being' financed by the Finnish Work Environment Fund 2008–2010.

The tapestry of the studies reflects the diverse contexts in which the peer-group mentoring model has been experimented with in the Finnish school system. Mentoring groups have been organized for different groups of teaching professionals, from newly qualified teachers to head teachers and to heterogeneous groups of teachers. The studies also describe peer-group mentoring from different perspectives, from individual learning to the school development point of view. Altogether, the studies show that peer-group mentoring provides a working tool for professional development.

Chapter 3

The first years as a teacher

Eila Estola, Leena Syrjälä and Tuuli Maunu

When I imagine a classroom full of thirty little individuals, each with their individual demands, I can feel a tension in my stomach. I should be able to 'comprehensively develop their personalities', as I have read so many times in pedagogical literature. I feel relieved when realizing that I am actually not a qualified teacher yet. Will I be ready for teaching when I'm holding in my hand that shiny piece of paper with 'Master of Education' written under my name?

(Maunu, 2008, p. 3)

This is how Tuuli Maunu, one of the authors of this chapter, described her sentiments shortly prior to her graduation. The quotation is an extract from her Master's thesis (Maunu, 2008), on which this chapter is based.

The research data were collected between November 2008 and February 2009 in four peer-group mentoring meetings intended for newly graduated teachers, i.e. teachers who had graduated within the past five years of the data collection. The group was led by a primary school teacher who participated in the mentor training during autumn 2008 and spring 2009. Even though the group leader had leader's duties and responsibilities, she was also a member of the group as well as a participant. In addition to her, the group included five members working within basic education: four females and one male. All of them had a subject teacher qualification, and two of them a class teacher qualification as well. Three of these teachers worked in the same school. The average age of the participating teachers was twenty-eight years. Tuuli Maunu took part in the meetings both as a researcher and as a group member.

The main data were based on participatory observation. The researcher made short notes during the meetings but mainly focused on participation in the activities. After the meetings, she wrote a detailed description of each meeting, also reflecting on them. The meetings included various kinds of writing assignments, which also served as research data. At the end of each meeting, the participants wrote and reflected on their experiences of the session in question. These anonymous essays were also used as research material. Furthermore, all of the sessions were recorded on video, so that the researcher could return to them afterwards and complement her observations and notes. The analysis was inductive. The stories that were constructed in the group meetings were analysed thematically.

The group members principally shared their own personal experiences. It often happened that one member's story inspired another member to recount his or her personal experiences. This is what Freema Elbaz-Luwisch (1992, p. 423) calls narrative echoing. A joint story was created in the discussions through dialogicality and reflection on one's own experiences. This joint discussion offered a meaningful environment for self-reflection, allowing the participants to mirror their own conceptions with those of the others.

The target group thus consisted of teachers navigating through their first years in the classroom. The transition to the world of work is a critical stage for teachers. Our starting point was the question of whether mentoring groups could be used as a tool to support new teachers. In this chapter we focus on examining what teachers recounted in the mentoring sessions when discussing their work.

While conducting the research, Tuuli Maunu described her sentiments and insights on her own growth into teachership as follows:

> When undertaking research on the basis of newly graduated teachers' stories about their first teaching years, I'm on an expedition into my own future. The research has consolidated my view that one does not graduate as a teacher. I do not believe I'm qualified when I get my degree certificate. Professional development begins during one's studies – but it continues throughout one's career. I'm pondering my own initial years of teaching. The statistics may look gloomy, but I hope to be on the bright side of them. In any case, I believe I will face challenges and adversities in working life. This research allows me to share my thoughts about teaching. The expedition might also allow me to progress some steps along my own professional development path.
>
> (Maunu, 2008, p. 5)

During their four meetings, the groups managed to discuss teaching broadly. These discussions often concerned human relations: interaction between colleagues, as well as teacher–parent and teacher–pupil interactions; for instance, how to address negative issues with pupils or their parents tactfully. In this respect, the themes discussed by the young teachers were not surprising – teaching has, after all, often been described primarily as based on relationships (e.g. Estola, 2003; Kohonen & Kaikkonen, 1998, p. 135; Laine, 1998, p. 117). Teachers' daily work was manifested in the narratives as multifaceted and intensive. New educational standards are also reflected in the job description for teachers. Teachers' work is not confined to the classroom but includes various other responsibilities as well (Willman & Kumpulainen, 1998, pp. 149, 161). In the following chapters, we will examine a recent graduate's work more closely based on the mentoring discussions. We will refer to the group members using the names that were used in the original research: Elina, Mari, Mikko, Minna, Suvi, Petra, and Tiina (leader).

Joys amid the rush

The group members talked about rushing in each of the sessions – in various contexts, including the free-form coffee meetings. Rushing was experienced as stressful. Planning and preparing materials also takes up a lot of free time. The teacher would like to do things properly, but there is not enough time for everything. Right in the first meeting, one of the group members suggested that rushing should be discussed as a theme of its own in some later session. Rushing seems to be a real problem in teaching. It is seen as a factor that hinders teachers' coping at work (Estola et al., 2007).

According to Hargreaves, the lack of time is a permanent theme about which teachers complain. The amount of time that teachers can employ in their work in addition to actual teaching – such as collaboration with co-workers and self-reflection – is significant for change, progress, and professional development (Hargreaves, 2000, p. 15). Other studies have also yielded similar results (Santavirta et al., 2001). This is how Petra described work stress and how her work followed her home:

> PETRA: I just don't do anything else but work at home, and particularly with this flu I can't go out and infect others; so I may as well just work, like now I'm just preparing some extra material ... Then my husband has occasionally made me feel guilty by saying that I'm married to my job, even though he also works a lot; I've told him that I just have to work. But then if one has a migraine or something else completely preventing one from working, it's strange that – one is still alive the next day. I just have the feeling that I have to work, even if I actually wouldn't have to.

The other teachers in the mentoring group shared Petra's view that the amount of time the teacher used in class preparation was connected to the success of class. In the study by Hargreaves (2000, p. 128), teachers also expressed that the quality of their teaching improved when they put more time into its preparation. The mentoring group teachers' stories clearly demonstrated their desire to employ time for class preparation, but their time resources were limited due to their own coping and the other responsibilities included in the job. Suvi explained how for the first three years she had brought her books home with her and worked there, but had since then changed her work habits. Now she leaves the books at school in order to separate her work from her personal life and to avoid doing what she had done in the first year: eating right after returning home, only to work for the rest of the evening until going to bed.

The junior teachers also reflected on how well teacher education meets the needs of working life. They found that many of the contents studied in subject teacher education at the university were too demanding to be applied to basic education. The workload of teachers increases when they notice that the studied contents are not relevant to their work. The teachers hoped that subject teacher education would contain more didacticism and a practical approach to teaching. Class teacher education, on the contrary, was experienced as very practically oriented, which is one of its strengths.

The teachers also experienced a lot of joy in their everyday work, for example when receiving empathetic attention from their pupils. This had a positive impact on teachers' coping and professional identity. Earlier studies also indicate that teachers get strength from pupils (Syrjäläinen, 2002, p. 110) and experience student feedback as one of the bright spots of their work (Haikonen, 1999, p. 105). The following address by Mari reflects the diverse feelings generated by the work. After some groups or lessons, a teacher may feel like a complete failure; but then there are many days that are brightened by empathetic pupils.

> MARI: One thing was positive: Monday sucked, it was really crappy, but then my own class saved my day on Tuesday – simply put, the pupils were just easy and nice, and I thought that there might be some hope left for the future after all [laughs], and that one might go on teaching, as there still are some occasional nice moments as well.

Work community

The teachers in the mentoring group regarded integration into the work community as highly important. Many of them had also experienced how hard the beginning could be. Rushing is also a problem here: few teachers have time to socialize with their colleagues in the teachers' room. They hardly know their co-workers or just know a few of them. Colleagues do not always provide the support and understanding that a newcomer in the profession might most need. Finding one's place in the work community can thus be difficult.

> SUVI: This week I've had all sorts of unpleasant things, and when I came to work in the morning, one of the teachers asked me if I had slept at all; I thought – there you are, I have not slept at all . . .

Suvi's description gives us the impression that she did not experience her colleague's comment as encouraging, but rather as a mild insult. Several group members shared the opinion that positive feedback could be given and received more often.

The discussions also contained descriptions of young teachers being treated in a bitter and deprecating way by their colleagues. Belittling comments may make a junior teacher feel that he/she is not taken seriously. Young teachers may also feel that the expectations set for them differ from those set for their senior colleagues. Petra described these expectations as follows:

> PETRA: I used to have a teacher colleague who was bitter about my youth . . . my only sin was that I was young, and she found all young people somehow . . . She just always implied that due to my youth I had to manage everything; all her comments were somehow like that. And even now I am expected not to complain about anything and to cope with everything because I am young . . . Young teachers are expected to be somehow so relaxed all the time.

In some cases, belittling is channelled to a young teacher's appearance; for example, their small size, as in the following extract from a conversation:

> MARI: Yes, somehow they don't take you seriously because you are young. I've often been told irritating things, also in my previous job, about being so small.
>
> PETRA: Yes, that's what I also hear quite often: '. . . well you are so small'.

The teachers also discussed the cultural codes that exist within the school community regarding teachers' physicality. The most visible of these codes is related to the manifestation of gender through dressing. At least part of the group members clearly seemed to be aware of the school dress code.

> SUVI: At home you can even wear a bikini or whatever, but not at work.
>
> ELINA: I think teachers can have their own individual styles, but morality sets a certain limit; so clothes may be too daring or tight, and I think they should not be too low-cut either.
>
> SUVI: I think one can be youthful but not sexy and sort of show it all.

Female teachers admitted considering what they wear at work, as teachers also communicate through their manner of dress. A few participants actually mentioned a teacher who attracts attention within the work community for her revealing clothing. Many other studies have also found that female teachers have to reflect on their physicality and the cultural expectations related to it (Mitchell & Weber, 1999, pp. 124–163).

The expectations set for young teachers within work communities were experienced by many of them as very challenging, as many had additional concerns about finding a permanent job. Newly graduated teachers experience that in a substitute teacher's position they dare not express their opinions in the same way as those working in a permanent employment relation. At the end of one session, there was discussion about power struggles in a work community, after two teachers had been speaking about applying for a position. The application period had just begun and would last a couple of weeks. The teachers' stories described the social interaction within the work community as a power struggle. One of the teachers had experienced that loud teachers are noticed and remembered. This is why she thought they would have better odds in the competition for positions.

> MINNA: Sometimes I feel everything here is under a magnifying glass, oh my goodness . . . after all, we are all teachers – and I thought I would be welcomed into some cradle of humanity when choosing this profession, but then life is somehow terribly cruel.

According to earlier research, recently graduated teachers feel a strong desire to demonstrate what they can do and that they can manage in spite of their inexperience. They also feel a need to prove and show their abilities to themselves, in addition to the work community (Eisenschmidt et al., 2008, p. 131). As demonstrated in other studies (Kelchtermans & Ballet, 2002), socialization into a profession actually seems to be about learning a kind of micropolitical literacy. One 'literacy' to be adopted is related to the concern about getting a job. Young teachers, for instance, are learning the ways in which to demonstrate their competence and create confidential relations with the persons deciding on jobs. The learning of this kind of literacy seems to apply to Finland as well.

Teacher–pupil interaction

The group members often described their interactions with pupils. Particularly popular discussion topics were the fair and equal treatment of pupils and encounters with different pupils. The building of relationships entails fundamental questions for initiating teachers: how close to pupils can a teacher be; how can pupils be approached in problem situations; and how can one's authority be preserved? The questions were concretized in Mikko's reflections on how to act in a situation in which he has to deal with an offending pupil:

> MIKKO: Have you experienced or thought about how well you can get along with a pupil if, for example, you discover something negative, like bullying, so that if you must be austere, you actually are austere, and how can you then maintain a teacher's role . . .

Mikko returned to the topic of encountering pupils later. He had noticed that a soft approach was better than an aggressive one in a difficult situation. If the teacher is aggressive, the pupils immediately take up a defensive position. The other group members shared Mikko's view. Mikko also said that in order to get a better idea of his 'own' pupils, he has observed them in other teachers' classes as well. In these lessons he was able to build different interactive relations with them from in his own classes. Mikko's story may have served to encourage the other group members to try something similar. Peer-group mentoring is, indeed, a natural way to learn everyday work practices.

Even though behavioural problems have increased over the past years – in particular, at lower secondary schools (Kiviniemi, 2000, p. 126) – the teachers did not frequently address this topic or their encounters with aggressive pupils. The discussions highlighted only the settling of bullying cases outside teaching situations, to which Mikko's example was also related. However, this does not mean that teachers would face no class disruptions. We do not actually know, for instance, what themes the mentoring group addressed after the data were collected.

One example of teacher–pupil interaction was related to pupils' passivity in class. Suvi's problem was how to activate her students, who were actually so passive that they hardly responded to the teacher at all. Elina had had similar problems with lower secondary level pupils. The girls there were nice and the classes easy to control, but no discussion arose either. Instead, the boys answered actively. The mentoring group leader Tiina had previously talked about her own discussions with pupils, so Suvi turned to her and complained about her inability to stimulate conversation.

> SUVI [speaking to the group leader]: As you say, you often discuss, but if I tried to activate a conversation . . . they would not answer me. And even though these are often groups with good pupils, I still don't manage to discuss with them.

The leader said that the passivity demonstrated by the pupils was not necessarily a consequence of Suvi's activities. This comment seemed to help Suvi: maybe she should more clearly demonstrate that she expects nothing extraordinary or 'unreasonable', as she expressed it.

> TIINA: Pupils may often think that everything is terribly subject-specific. For example, when one says that in a mother tongue class one uses handwriting, they think that in a biology essay they need not answer using handwriting but can use block letters instead. And that one need not write complete sentences and so on; in a way, this may also be related to the difficulty of discussion.
>
> SUVI: Yes it can . . . very well. Or then they can have the preconception that they must know something really unreasonable . . . so, I wonder if it could also be due to that.

Teacher–parent interaction

Studies have indicated that teacher–parent interaction is often one of the most difficult aspects of teachers' work (see Estola et al., 2007). The teachers in the mentoring group had at first been nervous about meeting pupils' parents. They had felt very insecure and anxious about the parents viewing them as inexperienced. Some of them, indeed, had experienced being belittled by some of the parents; though for the most part their nervousness had turned out to be groundless, and the parents had not questioned their professional skills. The following quotation demonstrates a young teacher's insecurity, as well as her experiences of more senior colleagues helping and supporting her to collaborate with parents:

> SUVI: It was in my first year that I felt like crying out for help – asking what I actually was supposed to do. But luckily I then found more and more co-workers who, in a way, helped me. If they hadn't included me, told me about the things that can be handled and so on ... In a way they gave me a chance to think about it first, but then gave a hint about what to do ... This was actually quite a shock for me then.

Pupil assessment poses its own special challenge to collaboration with parents. This is a particularly challenging responsibility for a young teacher, for whom pupil assessment is altogether a new thing. The group members found it essential to take into account the different components of performance in assessment, such as active class participation, behaviour, and exam results. Even though assessment was experienced as difficult by the group members, they regarded the assessment discussions conducted with pupils and their parents as highly rewarding. They were seen as meaningful with regard to both pupils' development and teaching work, and they also facilitated overall evaluation. An intensely discussed question among the teachers was how to present negative matters to parents and pupils in a constructive way, both in assessment discussions and other contexts.

Mentoring as a forum for discussing work

The teachers who participated in this study valued the fact that they had the opportunity to share the challenges faced at work with other teachers experiencing similar situations. They felt that peer mentoring had given them new perspectives and ideas to be applied to their work. One of the teachers reported that peer mentoring had promoted her coping at work. 'Peer mentoring has reduced my own pressures and requirements,' wrote another teacher. The fact that the group leader was a more experienced teacher seemed to bring experiential knowledge to the group, which was obviously needed. We can thus present the hypothesis that a suitable portion of similarity and diversity in group composition will bring additional value to the group.

To a great extent, the newly qualified teachers addressed in their discussions topics that are generally seen as challenges in teaching. To a young teacher, sharing experiences in a confidential group can be of crucial importance. In this research group, trust was manifested in a positive atmosphere and through open sharing. The participants dared to admit that they experienced challenges and imperfections in their professionalism, as well as share their personal joys and sorrows. Peer-group mentoring as a forum for discussing work can thus realize expectations related to work and provide help at a critical stage of professional growth.

Which aspects of your work surprised you the most during your initial years as a teacher?

How did your own work community support you as a newly qualified teacher?

Chapter 4

Mentoring as sustainable school development

Peter Johnson and Suvi Alamaa

The new teachers delivering basic education and general upper secondary education in the Finnish-speaking schools of the Kokkola city have been involved in systematic, comprehensive peer-group mentoring since 2003. Over a period of six school years, a total of 120 teachers – nearly a quarter of the city's entire teaching personnel – have participated in these mentoring activities.

So far, mentoring has been seen as an important form of supporting teachers' individual professional development, and as a significant dialogue arena. This chapter focuses on the effects of mentoring on the development of schools mainly from the perspective of change in school culture and increase in dialogue. Can a relatively pragmatic innovation, i.e. the comprehensive adoption of mentoring, influence the development of school communities and the local school organization even more broadly? We will reflect on this question relying on practical experience and literature on school development.

How did mentoring come ashore in the city of Kokkola?

Teachers' peer-group mentoring was launched in Kokkola in 2003, as the City Education Department participated in the TeLL (Teachership – Lifelong Learning) research project carried out by the Finnish Institute for Educational Research (FIER), which aims at supporting teachership in a changing work environment. The survey, conducted as an initial mapping for the research project, indicated that new-teacher orientation had been realized either poorly or not at all in the schools. Based on the survey, it seemed clear that teachership also needed to be supported through means other than the traditional new-employee orientation carried out by principals. However, the objective of mentoring was not only to improve the orientation but also to promote teachers' professional development as effectively as possible and in as many ways as possible.

Right from the beginning, peer-group mentoring in Kokkola has been based on the city of Kokkola personnel strategy, which describes the city's attitude to its personnel. As an employer, the city values and maintains staff competence, well-being and motivation. It encourages self-development and in-service training for its employees and creates the conditions for these activities. The vision of the personnel strategy is for the employees to be skilful, in good form, motivated, and flexible. The objective of orientation is to contribute to new employees' adaptation to the new workplace, its practices and people, and to understand what kinds of expectations the work involves. The supervisor is responsible for the orientation, in addition to the person who implements the orientation in practice, and the orientees themselves.

The mentoring organized in Kokkola has aimed at providing new teachers with more tools for understanding their own school community's professional relationships, interaction, and operating culture. The Kokkola Education Department has regarded mentoring as a new form of organizing continuing education in a way which promotes teachers' professional development and responds to the developmental needs of teachership. This is how a comprehensive school principal describes the impacts of mentoring on the work community's activities:

> Yes, we've noticed it . . . Of course, even the basic character of the teachers involved in mentoring is very positive. At least they've been cheerfully telling about some group assignments they've done there . . . I don't know if they've already got some ideas. They've quite openly addressed certain topics . . . then they've somehow developed and questioned some things . . . and wondered if things could be done in a certain way. Anyway, they've managed to present it all in a way which has not offended anybody.
>
> (A comprehensive school headteacher, 2005)

The TeLL research project ended in Kokkola in 2005, and the feedback it yielded on mentoring was very positive. Mentoring was experienced as necessary and useful, which is why the activities have continued since then, organized by the Kokkola Education Department. By the 2009 school year, a total of 104 teachers had participated in mentoring in Kokkola. In 2009–2010 sixteen new participants and five mentors started in mentoring groups.

Mentoring as an innovation contributing to a new school culture

The literature and research on school development have demonstrated that development at school is slow and that the school organization has defensive features that it can use to resist change (Johnson, 2006). Thanks to the mentoring practices adopted, it has presumably been possible to further collegiality and dialogical skills among teachers. On the other hand, it is preferable to regard the new practices as an opening in a new direction rather than to expect a rapid change in school culture. Nevertheless, we can see that in the new professional dialogue arenas, brought about by peer-group mentoring (see Salo & Kuittinen, 1998), it has been easier to question the prevailing school and teacher culture.

School culture is manifested through shared values and beliefs, i.e. things that people 'consider as true or right' (Fullan, 2005, p. 57). That is why schools may have different school cultures. This has been apparent in groups consisting of teachers who work in different schools. School culture can also be divided into smaller constituents, such as teacher culture and pupil culture. According to Hargreaves (1994, p. 238), teacher culture can exhibit several forms of interrelations: for instance, individualism, collaboration, obligatory collegiality, and balkanization. The prevailing school culture has a great impact on development at school, but at the same time we must acknowledge the fact that school culture reacts slowly to challenges involving change (Johnson, 2006, pp. 80–84).

Sahlberg (2009) considers that – in addition to hard work and good luck – Finland's success relies on creative ideas and innovations. The roots of innovation are set deep in the values, culture and education of a society. Innovation always calls for creativity, and creativity calls for risk-taking and open-minded inventiveness. Social innovations can also be considered to encompass the operational models of organizations and their management innovations.

The mentoring initiative with new teachers that began in Kokkola in 2003 was a simple and practically oriented innovation. It was organized as peer-group mentoring with one mentor and four to six new teachers in the group. This was actually the only feasible starting point as there was a much higher number of new teachers than available mentors, which is why pair mentoring would not have been a realistic option. In addition, the peer support provided by the group was regarded as important to novice teachers.

The peer-group mentoring process advances during the school year as follows. The person in charge of coordination – presently Kokkola Education Department's training coordinator – assigns the following year's mentors in the spring, so that mentoring can start as quickly as possible when the school year begins in the autumn. The first brochure on mentoring is sent to all new teachers along with their admission letters, and they are invited to the initial mentoring session immediately after schools have started. Principals are informed about mentoring in the autumn, also making sure that all the new teachers have actually received the invitation. In the autumn meeting between the coordinator and the mentors, the principles of mentoring are handled and the preliminary mentoring groups are established. The mentoring group activities start at the beginning of September with a group meeting of mentors and new teachers. In this session the purpose, goals and general practices of mentoring are specified to the participating teachers. In the first meeting, the participants are divided into groups and the activities begin under the guidance of the mentor. The mentoring groups have six sessions that last about one and a half hours during the school year. The participants are also entitled to have one private meeting with their mentor. For each meeting the mentors obtain a compensation that corresponds to one hour of overtime.

The new teachers who attend all of the scheduled mentoring meetings are compensated by one training day included in their working hours. According to the Finnish teachers' collective agreement, teachers are obliged to participate in continuing education on three working days every school year. For those who participate in mentoring, this obligation is consequently reduced to two annual training days. At the end of the school year, the mentors and new teachers give feedback that will be used continuously to develop the activities.

'Peerness' and dialogue in mentoring

As we took our first steps in peer-group mentoring in Kokkola, we first had to decide how to engage suitable mentors in the project, and then on their training for the new task. The TeLL project researchers provided us with information on how mentoring had previously been implemented in Finland, and at the launching stage the first mentors familiarized themselves with the information and experience available. No actual training was organized, but the focus was more on agreeing on common principles, which is why equal dialogue was emphasized at the initial stage.

According to the research outcomes (Jokinen & Välijärvi, 2006), peer-group mentoring provided the novice teachers with the opportunity to share their experiences and problems in a confidential atmosphere. Within the groups the participants could pose 'stupid questions' without being criticized or regarded as incompetent. Neither did the new teachers have to worry about their questions influencing their future in the school community. The mentees experienced that mentoring supported and encouraged them in decision-making. The mentors' questions and comments also helped the mentees analyse and critically evaluate their own teaching and related activities. The peer support received in the mentoring group was also experienced as important. The discussions offered tips for one's own work and opportunities to learn from other new teachers' decisions.

The mentors saw themselves primarily as leaders and listeners in the discussions between the new teachers, and as persons who shared their experiences and problems. The mentors wanted to support the novices' decisions and considered it important that teachers learn how to evaluate their own decisions. The mentors emphasized that they did not want to offer ready-made solution models but rather present alternative ways of acting and solving problems. They underlined that they also learned from the group discussions and the mentees' views (Jokinen & Välijärvi, 2006).

The discussion topics in the mentoring groups were mainly based on the issues addressed by the new teachers. The daily problems encountered by the new teachers were often discussed: difficult pupils, pupils' behavioural problems, interaction with pupils' parents, one's own work community, and collaboration with colleagues. The group discussions often highlighted those school practices of which the new teachers had not been told during their orientation. The topics addressed also seem to be associated with the areas that the new teachers said had been neglected in teacher training. The mentoring sessions seldom directly involved teaching-related pedagogical or didactic solutions or arrangements; for example, how a specific topic is taught to specific pupils. These issues were most commonly addressed among general upper secondary school and lower secondary school subject teachers. In the mentoring group that consisted of special education teachers, it was more common than in the other groups to discuss specific pupil cases and the applied measures; these discussions were often conducted as pair mentoring between a mentor and a mentee (Jokinen & Välijärvi, 2006).

Our point of departure was that mentoring can be used as a tool to transfer expertise and tacit knowledge from a more experienced colleague to a younger one. This involves a reciprocal exchange of ideas, discussion and dialogue, which at its best enables both of the parties to learn. The role of mentor is constructed by each mentor him/herself – no ready-made model for mentoring exists (see Karjalainen et al., 2006). That is why the mentoring pioneers in Kokkola started out with humble and open minds. Their central motivation was the desire to help colleagues who are taking the first steps on their career path, for whom it is a challenge to start in a new position and work community. A principal describes the new teacher's paradoxical situation in an interview as follows:

> A new teacher . . . I think she/he must have been selected and recruited in order to fulfil a certain need, to bring strength to some area in the school. Then the new employee is expressly a resource. But the situation is also challenging, and there will be suspicions and fears regarding the newcomer's integration into the work community. Will she/he enjoy working here, and how will cooperation between co-workers succeed. Will there be conflicts and disagreements . . . which always emerge when new, enthusiastic and energetic teachers arrive. It causes tensions with the long-standing teachers.
> (Comprehensive school headteacher, 2005)

According to Karjalainen et al. (2006), in the traditional approach the mentor as the more experienced person offers his/her knowledge and experience to the novice, which makes the relationship one-sided. In an equal mentoring relationship, mentoring is a collaborative, dynamic and creative relationship between peers, based on openness and risk-taking ability on both sides. Equality requires the crossing of professional roles and consequently opening an opportunity for dialogue, in which the line between expertise and inexperience is blurred. Mentoring at its best could thus be interaction between two or more people, based on reciprocal trust and appreciation of the other person's knowledge, skills and competence (Karjalainen et al., 2006).

The positive experiences and feedback received in Kokkola right from the beginning are likely based precisely on the aforementioned success in collaborative learning and equal interaction. As no long-term mentor training

impact on young people's well-being. A readiness to respond to the needs for change as a community by developing teachers' collaboration skills has been highlighted as one of the central goals in teacher education and teachers' on-the-job learning. The change also involves a need to develop the division of tasks and to enhance cooperation with external experts, for example, within the social care sector.

Teachers work in the crux of change in terms of knowledge, skills and values. They attempt to respond to the challenges within the operating environment by maintaining and developing their professional skills through career-long learning. Teachers have lifelong professional needs that are manifested in the maintenance of their professional skills (Hargreaves, 1994). One of future teachers' most important goals is to awake in their pupils a desire for lifelong learning. Teachers do not succeed in this without committing themselves to continuous professional growth. This is also a foundation for successful school community development. Planning and supporting career-long development is the joint responsibility of teachers, schools, education providers, authorities, and central government.

Along with the change in the operating environment, teachers' work with pupils is also changing. The school can be expected to be an example of a learning, development-oriented community that promotes lifelong learning in its members. Teaching is believed to adopt an increasing number of features involved in the human relations professions. This means that teachers must be ready to encounter an increasing diversity in pupils, as well as their diverse motives, skills and ambitions to learn (Välijärvi, 2000). This change implies the need to strengthen teachers' preparedness to encounter a growing number of new things, institutions and people in their daily work. Competence in special education will occupy an important role in all teachers' work and in all school communities' activities. Even meeting their own colleagues in order to develop the entire school community seems to be a challenge for many teachers. Particularly for newly graduated teachers, encountering the increasingly open and multiform environment often appears problematic and demanding. The disparity between the challenges and the experience of one's own skills sometimes seems unreasonably strong.

As a topical and even internationally popular method, peer-group mentoring is a form of supporting teachers' professional growth in line with the general policies used to develop Finnish schools. These development efforts emphasize knowledge and learning, flexible and diversified teaching, the contribution of schools to curriculum creation, and reciprocal support and trust (Sahlberg, 2009).

Implementing peer-group mentoring in the city of Kokkola

The City of Kokkola Education Department made an administrative decision regarding the launching of mentoring in the spring of 2003. This decision was based on the desire to support new teachers' professional growth, but also on the awareness of the high teacher turnover due in the coming years as a result of retirement. Mentoring was consequently started as an experimental project in the autumn of 2003. Kokkola Education Department carries administrative responsibility for the activity. Mentoring is currently part of the regular activities organized within Kokkola Education Department, and all of the new teachers have the opportunity to participate in it, irrespective of their career phase. In the following text, the term 'new teacher' refers to a new teacher in this broader sense.

Peer-group mentoring has been implemented in Kokkola in groups of two to six teachers. There have usually been four to five yearly mentoring groups, depending on the number of new teachers; and six to seven approximately 1.5-hour meetings have been organized between the mentors and mentees each school year. Kokkola Education Department's experienced teachers took on the role of mentors after brief instructions on mentoring at the initial stage. It was not until 2008–2009 that the mentors began to attend longer mentor training organized by the peer-group mentoring project. The mentoring groups were initially heterogeneous. In recent years, separate groups have been provided for special education teachers and teachers at the different school levels: lower level of comprehensive school, upper level of comprehensive school, and general upper secondary school.

Many new teachers and mentors have considered it important to organize the after-school mentoring meetings in a place separate from their own school. They have also emphasized that the mentor should not come from the same school as the mentees: teachers prefer to discuss these matters with outsiders rather than colleagues from their own schools. It is sometimes otherwise impossible to address matters related to one's own competence or problems within one's own school community (Jokinen & Välijärvi, 2006).

Particularly in the first years, peer-group mentoring was a new phenomenon for the new teachers, and even for the mentors (Jokinen & Välijärvi, 2006; Jokinen et al., 2008). The mentees had received relatively little information on the method, and the mentors had only been provided a one-day briefing on the mentoring process and its central principles. The first meetings and discussions mainly focused on clarifying what mentoring actually is.

The topics addressed in the mentoring groups were principally based on issues highlighted by the new teachers. The groups chiefly discussed the daily problems faced by the teachers, such as problematic pupils, pupils' behavioural disorders, interaction with pupils' parents, the work community, and collaboration with colleagues. The groups also frequently addressed those school practices of which the new teachers had not been informed during their induction. Development as a teacher was examined through the new teachers' own strengths and developmental challenges. The groups that consisted of special education teachers highlighted specific pupil cases and related measures more often than the other groups (Jokinen & Välijärvi, 2006).

Compared to traditional pair mentoring, peer-group mentoring in Kokkola has been easy to organize, which has been regarded as one of its strengths. One, sometimes even two mentors as equal participants take care of a mentoring group of several teachers. The Kokkola mentoring model has highlighted a situated apprentice perspective on mentoring (Heikkinen, Jokinen et al., 2008).

The significance of mentoring from individual and social perspectives

Eighteen teachers participated in the study on which this chapter is based, and about half of them had less than two years of work experience. The data on the teachers' experiences were collected via essays and a group interview. In addition, three principals were interviewed. In their essays and interviews, the teachers described their expectations from mentoring and the significance of mentoring for their professional development, occupational well-being, collaborative learning, and for meeting the challenges that arise at work.

Before the teachers started the peer-group mentoring process, their expectations from the sessions were related to professional knowledge, handling problem situations, and interaction with other teachers. Many of them looked forward to receiving peer support and an opportunity to create networks; some wished to get concrete tools for their work and an introduction to new practices.

The study results indicated that peer-group mentoring fulfilled all of the aforementioned expectations so that, at least at a general level, these themes can be read within the research data. For the teachers who had started the process with an open mind, without strong expectations, their sense of the significance of mentoring was often constructed gradually during the actual mentoring process. Significant mentoring experiences are associated with teachers' different expectations from mentoring, as well as with their professional phases and working life transitions.

Processing challenging situations and sharing good practices

The mentoring discussions were often based on concrete daily school situations. It was important for many of the teachers to process the thoughts and feelings evoked by difficult situations confidentially in the mentoring group. The discussions about problem pupils and challenging situations helped them realize that their colleagues also faced similar things. In addition to being supported, they could share their know-how and competence with others.

> Our group was a place where we could air our thoughts, and each of us came there directly from an everyday situation of that moment. It was so great to have a chance to openly chat about school- and work-related matters, knowing that it would remain confidential between the group members.

I've received new ideas for handling overactive pupils and so on. Discussion with other teachers has reduced stress.

Teachers experienced that peer-group mentoring had offered their work concrete methods and tools, for example relating to interaction with challenging pupils or pupil assessment. All of them acknowledged that discussion and their professional sharing were professionally significant.

Individual empowerment at different career stages

The teachers perceived mentoring as a process that helped them to get started in their work, but also to develop and grow in relation to it. The peer-mentoring group supported novice teachers' work and in many ways lowered the threshold to entering the new workplace. The metaphors 'first-aid kit', 'immaterial support' and 'refreshing bath' were used to describe these mentoring experiences. The new teachers wished to use mentoring as a mirror that proportions their teachership, working, and coping. Their confidence had increased during the mentoring. Stress had also been reduced, which enhanced coping at work. Increased confidence enabled them to develop their work and adopt new points of view. Now the teachers felt that they could dare to question practices and evaluate them critically, but also have mercy on themselves.

For some of the experienced teachers, mentoring was primarily an opportunity to create networks and get to know new colleagues. For them mentoring was a channel consciously used to support their coping and broaden their perspective on the profession. Mentoring was also seen as a tool to support the motivation and coping of teachers who were approaching retirement age. The peer-group mentoring model thus enabled empowerment in teachers at very different career stages. Empowerment is a process in which an individual's resources and responsibility for their own development are strengthened (Heikkilä-Laakso & Heikkilä, 1997, p. 347). According to Siitonen (1999), empowerment and life management are conceptually close to one another.

Confidence in one's own skills and scope for action provides a good starting point for managing and actively handling different situations in the working world. The empowered teachers in this study felt that they belonged to the group and were able to influence work-related matters. They discussed their worries and also saw opportunities for change in their work (see Siitonen, 1999, p. 88).

Different backgrounds of experience as a resource in the peer group

According to Siitonen (1999, p. 138), in an environment that allows empowerment, the participants can observe and evaluate themselves and discuss in an atmosphere of trust and confidentiality. The dialogue of peer-group mentoring supported teachers' empowerment. Professional knowledge was constructed through equal conversation. The group members were at different stages of their teaching career and thus had a lot to give to the others, in addition to learning from them. The interface of different ways of action and thinking in the peer-mentoring group also stimulated self-reflection. The mentees' readiness to share their competences was also enhanced by their increased confidence and courage. The teachers' professional identity was strengthened and they became less judgemental of themselves. Mentoring supported their boldness and courage to be themselves.

> It's encouraged and motivated me to continue, and also helped so that I now notice I can combine work and home, motherhood and teachership, these roles I mean. And combining them was a huge challenge.
>   What it strengthened the most was … that even when my working environment changes, I will remain the same. It has brought me some sort of continuity.
>   Mentoring may have given me more courage to be myself, in other words: carry out my job in my own way, more individually.

External and internal transitions related to life situations; for example, becoming a mother or father, or ageing, also influenced the teachers' professional identity. In the midst of change, one looked for integrity and continuity. Empowerment was associated with experiences of increased openness with regard to change, of combining different roles, and of professional confidence. For some of the participants, mentoring implied increased motivation for self-development. Empowered teachers had discovered their individual resources (Siitonen, 1999, p. 134).

The peer-mentoring group promoting coping at work

Many of the teachers highlighted the positive impact of mentoring on individual teachers' mental well-being at work. The peer group helped them proportion their work according to their individual coping.

> Well, in a way talking is some sort of mental support. I think mentoring can be described as a refreshing shower or bath; it's so nice that even when I've gone there tired, upon leaving I've always been happy.
>   The best thing is that every time we had a chance to talk about the most important thing: our own coping exactly that day, week, between the preceding session and that one. I call this opportunity to talk about our own profession 'a therapy session' even if this term in reality can't be used.

The experience that the tools required for renewing one's own work are insufficient can increase work-related anxiety and exhaustion. Välijärvi (2005a, p. 106) states that in teachers' work, change is experienced rather as a factor that threatens coping and well-being than as a factor that opens up new opportunities.

Even though rapid changes may seem threatening, they can sometimes function as opportunities for positive change (Luukkainen, 2005b, p. 145). At any rate, burnout-type exhaustion is common within the field of education.

The factors that augment stress and strain in teachers include continuous close, emotionally coloured interaction; using one's personality as a tool at work, and the infrequency of positive feedback. The fact that it is difficult to define sufficient or good results in education can be also seen to increase strain (Kalimo & Toppinen, 1997). Coping at work is an entity that is affected by one's ideals, models received from the work community, and the individual life situation as a whole. The greatest challenge for an initiating teacher is learning to recognize his/her own limits. These limits are discovered gradually as one's conception of what is essential becomes stronger, and as the idea of oneself as an employee is crystallized (Förbom, 2003, p. 109).

Mentoring represented holistic mental support for the teachers in the study, in addition to alleviating their work stress. The mentoring-group meetings offered them a good environment to draw breath, in which they were provided with peer support and the opportunity to 'recharge batteries'. Many of them experienced that their employers wanted to invest in occupational well-being and take care of their employees. The teachers also felt that by offering the opportunity for mentoring, the employer welcomed them into the work community.

The significance of mentoring for the work community

The first chapters of this book describe the dialogic approach used in peer-group mentoring that promotes the verbalization of things learned at the workplace and the communal construction of professional knowledge. Professional learning takes place through the interaction of practical work and the reflective discussions conducted in the mentoring groups. This is how the schools' operating cultures also interact in the peer-mentoring groups. It is thus fascinating to reflect on the potential significance of mentoring for school communities. Do mentoring activities also convey something new to the communities, or does mentoring only support the individual participants' development?

The teachers who participated in the same mentoring group usually came from different schools, with a few exceptions. They could not directly share their mentoring group experiences within the work community due to a confidentiality agreement. Almost all of them experienced that mentoring did not directly affect the work community, but that its effects came indirectly through the individuals. Individual development and change always has an impact on the work organization's development as well. It reflects back on the workplace atmosphere and mental well-being, opening up new dimensions and boosting courage for creativity. This also benefits the employer. The participants exemplified this indirect impact with the fact that mentoring had enhanced their courage to present ideas in the work community.

> I believe that the greatest benefit for the work community is my own coping and the fact that I have the courage to bring out different views even in the presence of senior teachers.

The stimuli obtained from other schools, as well as comparison of the ways of action, may have brought new initiatives in terms of developing school practices. For example, the idea of peer-group activities had been applied in a school inspired by mentoring.

> The idea of mentoring has been adapted for our work community so that we nowadays have teams that, in a way, are like small mentoring groups.

Peer-group mentoring offered the opportunity to create networks with other teachers and to exchange ideas, at least at the individual level, and potentially even promoted cooperation between various schools. Nearly all of the participants considered that mentoring had opened doors between schools.

The general experience was that mentoring facilitated headteachers' work to some extent, and it was regarded as an important component of new teachers' induction activities. On the other hand, from the principals' perspective, mentoring may also have seemed like an activity that is disconnected from the rest of the school community.

> I underline this long-term team work, in which more experienced teachers share their knowledge with the others; in other words, transfer tacit knowledge. No one needs to uncritically accept everything, but rather mirror their own thoughts against those of the other.
>
> Mentoring brings out many things we didn't have in teacher training. Things related to school practices . . . Well, it is certainly good for the work community if the teacher can handle things in the correct way.

Individual teachers' empowerment experience indirectly promoted interaction in the school community. Mentoring – in the same way as work counselling – had offered a place and time for handling work-related issues and problems. Teachers felt it would be a tool for making things easier for their own work community. The well-being obtained through mentoring was experienced as a benefit and resource for work communities. Within the schools, mentoring also strengthened togetherness between the teachers who had attended the same mentoring group.

Tribe culture and border crossings

Some of the teachers preferred the idea of peer-mentoring groups that consisted of same-subject teachers. If the job descriptions of the group members significantly differed from each other, some participants felt that the discussions remained thin.

> Fortunately we were divided so that each professional group had a group of its own. This allowed us to create networks and hear the others' experiences, and also get to know other schools. We could establish valuable contacts and share experiences.

For a small village school's only teacher of a particular subject, networking with teachers of the same subject offered an important opportunity for professional dialogue. Identifying with one's own professional group and focusing on aspects related to subject teaching were experienced as meaningful. The mentoring group's homogeneity was in this sense a solution that supported the participants' class teacher or subject teacher identity and professional sense of security. However, diverse backgrounds were sometimes also experienced as a positive opportunity.

> I found it nothing but positive that our mentor was a primary school teacher. We heard examples of things that had happened at his school, and how he had handled things in his class. My own perspective was broadened.
> My gain was that it facilitated my adaptation to my new workplace and offered contacts to colleagues at neighbouring schools, and also familiarized me with the city's education department as a whole. It also made me enjoy my work more and face all the new practices with a calm attitude … Among the absolutely best things in mentoring were also the profound, philosophical conversations we often had.

If teachers' expectations from mentoring only concern concrete aspects related to the organization and implementation of work, they fail to benefit from various elements of professional interaction and knowledge associated with different work experiences. Instead of class divisions and school levels, the experiences of teachers – who view the school world based on the idea of shared educational responsibility – emphasized professional communality and shared teachership. Teacher training is divided into subject and class teacher training, which are implemented in separate faculties. Even the academic cultures of different disciplines differ from each other, and after teachers' basic university education in the various faculties, clique development continues within the educational system (Becher, 1989). According to Vuorikoski, teacher tribes are first determined based on pupils' age and school level. Then subject teachers form the tribe of subject experts, which is further divided into sub-tribes according to the subjects taught (Vuorikoski, 2004). Special education teachers and study counsellors naturally constitute their own tribes within general education.

The phenomenon is connected to the history of our school system and teacher education, and breaking it would be challenging but also inevitable from the viewpoint of, for example, developing comprehensive basic education. On the other hand, the questions and expectations related to new teachers' induction phase must be taken into account in mentoring activities and responded to. Besides, broader educational and professional themes related to teaching should be integrated into the mentoring discussions. It would be good to stop and reflect in advance on the construction and composition of mentoring groups in relation to the objectives of mentoring.

Towards a more social working culture

Peer-group mentoring offers mental support to teachers and promotes their coping at different career stages. It is a good way to prevent stress and burnout. Mentoring can also increase motivation for work and professional development (Holbeche, 1996, pp. 24–27). Peer-group mentoring contributes to breaking the tradition among teachers of acting alone. It offers the participating teachers a time and place for collegial dialogue and reflection. It would be worthwhile to create further intellectual and social places like this for professional interaction within and between school communities. The intensity and professional loneliness of teaching can complicate or threaten teachers' professional development and occupational well-being. Teachers need to counterbalance this by listening to themselves and their co-workers, by verbalizing tacit knowledge and, consequently, by reinforcing their reflective consciousness. At their best, mentoring groups contribute to new professional knowledge and empowered identities.

Peer-group mentoring seems to have played a significant role in enhancing teachers' competences. Teachers have developed a broader perspective with regard to their own work and their work community's activities. Mentoring enables them to share experiences, compare forms of action, and learn new things. The teachers' experiences of being able to share their competence also gave them confidence about their own professional development. An increase in competence also releases energy for developing one's activities and coping at work.

. Peer-group mentoring can be a channel to empowerment, provided that the group's atmosphere is safe and its interaction dialogic and equal. The teachers appreciated the mentor's contribution in guiding the group process. Mentor training was not originally part of classical mentoring, but experience and research has demonstrated that it promotes mentoring activities (Hobson et al., 2009, p. 214). Individual teachers' expectations and relations to professional development also affect their mentoring experiences. Teachers' own orientation to active learning enables empowerment.

The teachers who participated in this study saw mentoring primarily as an individual process that, even at its best, only has an indirect link to the work community's activities and development. The obligation to confidentiality within peer-mentoring groups ensures a confidential atmosphere – but also restricts the transfer of knowledge to the work community. In order to increase the impact of mentoring on work community development, it seems that mentoring should first be introduced to the school world, and that its role as a school-community development tool should gradually be recognized. Communality and critical reflection can be promoted in school culture by providing a larger number of the community members with mentoring experiences, and by systematically using mentoring as a staff development tool. The principals' support for mentoring is crucial, and they should also be offered the opportunity to participate in mentoring.

It is useless to make a confrontation between the individual and social aspects of mentoring. The communal effects depend to a great extent on the new teacher's attitude and personality, as well as on the work community's skills and attitudes towards receiving a new employee. It is also a great opportunity for the work community to learn from the newcomer and his/her experience. Peer-group mentoring highlights various aspects of communality and collaborative learning, whose adoption will also help school communities to enhance their operating culture. These aspects include creating an open and confidential atmosphere, emphasizing peer support, encouraging colleagues, highlighting and furthering inclusion, and giving a voice to tacit knowledge.

Mentoring is a holistic process through which one can develop both as a teacher and as a human being. Teachership is more than a profession or position – it is tightly bound to the teacher's personality, and part of the teacher's ego. Basically, it is a question of identity growth and development – a lifelong journey, the path of human growth.

At what stage of your career as a teacher are you in presently?

How have you helped other teachers professionally?

What do you have to offer professionally to colleagues at different stages of your career?

What kind of professional support have you received or would like to receive from other teachers at this stage of your teacher career?

Chapter 6

Diverse landscapes
of mentoring

Päivi Mäki

Peer-group mentoring has been applied in the city of Oulu to promote the professional development and well-being of teaching staff. The first steps towards utilizing narration and action-based methods in groups were taken in peer groups of immigrant teachers and special education teachers at the beginning of the new millennium (Estola et al., 2007). Mentoring among different staff groups has been systematically developed since 2008, as Oulu joined a national peer-group mentoring project. This development work was aimed at creating good practices based on peer-group activities in order to respond to the needs of different staff groups at different phases of their careers.

Right from the beginning, mentoring in Oulu was shaped according to the staff groups' individual needs. Representatives of the staff groups were invited to the one-year peer mentor training described earlier in this book. Four advisory teachers, an instructor from the Municipal Department of Education, the person coordinating school assistant services, and the development manager participated in the training organized in the municipalities involved in the project. The mentors are experts in different fields, which has allowed us to implement mentoring with different professional groups: the supervising teachers have been responsible for teacher groups, the school assistant coordinator for the school assistant group, and the head of development for new head teachers.

In this chapter I will describe peer-group mentoring activities in Oulu based, in particular, on experiences with new principals and school assistants. Our objective in Oulu is to create a peer-group mentoring model applicable to all staff groups. I will thus examine peer-group mentoring as a part of an action model that education providers can use systematically to advance different staff groups' professional development and well-being. Principals and school assistants are interesting groups, because experiences of mentoring with non-teaching staff are not common within the field of education.

What kind of mentoring?

The concept of mentoring is used loosely in education and teacher education. Mentoring at a general level is interpreted as professional interaction in which all of the participants learn. At the same time, mentoring is increasingly shifting towards collaboration, collegiality, and interaction. Today mentoring is increasingly also used to refer to 'learning partnership', which includes the concepts of professional development and sharing experience, reflection, dialogue and interaction, communication, caring, counselling, guidance, coaching, and different means of mutual empowerment (Tillman, 2003; Heikkinen, Jokinen et al., 2008).

In the peer-mentoring groups in Oulu, we have consciously aimed at creating a community based on learning partnership, one in which the participants gather to share experiences and learn. On the other hand, we have tried to encourage the establishment of a kind of 'community of practice', in particular in the peer-mentoring group of head teachers. Wenger (2006) describes this as a group that shares a common concern or problem, or takes an interest in the same topic. The group may, for example, share the desire to meet regularly to deepen their knowledge and expertise with regard to a specific theme. According to Wenger, the deepening of expertise and competence is based precisely on ongoing interaction.

To create a community of practice also includes the introduction of theoretical and conceptual knowledge into the conversation, which has been described earlier in this publication. The integration of theoretical knowledge into the mentoring discussion calls for methods that, on the one hand, enable the reflection and conceptualization of empirical knowledge and, on the other, the examination of conceptual knowledge in the light of experience. In designing a mentoring programme for new head teachers in Oulu, particular emphasis was put on the realization of the theoretical element, as one of the two main objectives was new employee orientation. In order to generate theoretical and practical interaction, the headteachers' mentoring meetings were organized by themes, and an expert in the particular field was invited to each thematic session to participate in discussion and contribute with new information.

The objectives of mentoring in the school assistant group were to create an idea of work and tasks in this new profession and to strengthen professional identity. The first objective also includes the introduction of conceptual knowledge in the group and sharing it in the group so that group members will be prepared to examine, understand, and develop their own practical work as part of the entire school community.

Peer-group mentoring for school leaders

The high retirement rate of principals and the changes that have taken place in school administration motivated us to launch peer-group mentoring among principals in 2009−2010. We needed a model for sharing good practices to a new generation of head teachers. The large number of new principals opened our eyes to the importance of induction and support in this profession as well. Upon municipality mergers, it is also necessary to ease the challenging transitional stages of principals who come from different operating cultures, providing them with orientation and collegial support. The objectives of the mentoring of head teachers can be crystallized as follows: to support principals at the beginning of their careers, and to function as new employee orientation for new principals as well as for experienced principals who move to Oulu.

Information on the launching and principles of peer-group mentoring was disseminated in the principals' training events. The introduction emphasized that the group activities were based on the ideology of collegial support and communality. The peer-group members collaboratively look for solutions to challenging situations and share good practices. The participants do not come to the group to perform, and no particular preparation is needed for the sessions. Joining is voluntary, but membership requires attendance at every session. One group member's absence affects the operation of the whole group. The introduction also underlined the confidentiality of the group discussions. The peer-mentoring group was described as a meditation pool that offers time and authorization for unhurried conversation as a counterbalance to busy managerial work. During the introductory events, many principals registered for the group because they felt it had been designed exactly for them. In addition, invitations were e-mailed to principals who had one to two years of school leadership experience.

The new principals' peer-mentoring group consisted of eight principals – four females and four males. Four of the participants were primary school principals; one worked at the upper level of comprehensive school and one in a special education school; and the two remaining participants were general upper secondary school principals, one of whom worked with adult students. As from the first session, this composition turned out to be the group's strength. In a group of basic education and upper secondary education principals, issues were analysed from a perspective that comprised the entire school path. Employees working at upper secondary level should remember what daily work in basic education is like, and respectively, the representatives of basic education must understand where young people's educational paths lead after comprehensive school. It is important to see the growth and learning continuum of children and young people of which the principals of different school levels are a part. From the first meeting, the members seemed to bring up countless questions about the work of colleagues at different school levels. They emphasized how important it is to learn about and from others. The discussions highlighted how very different the job description, even the working hours, of principals at general upper secondary school for adults were. However, after the first session they could state: 'The management style is clearly the same, irrespective of school level. Everyone performs the same basic work.'

The headteachers' meetings were based on specific themes in compliance with a jointly created schedule. Special experts in the sub-areas of management and leadership were invited to participate in these discussions. The participation of a finance manager, chief of occupational safety, and human resources manager in a peer discussion relying on the principle of collegiality was a new way of sharing competence. The expert guests joined the group as group members and participated in the dialogue and action-based methods on a footing equal to the principals'. The mentoring group of headteachers met six times over six months. The themes in 2009–2010 were as follows:

- Discussing the headteacher's basic tasks
- From school-tending to school management
- From deleting to delegating – school teamwork supporting leadership
- Sub-areas of management: HR management
- Sub-areas of management: financial management
- Sub-areas of management: safety management.

In compliance with the peer-mentoring principle, the invited experts were in the group in order to both give and to receive. In addition to sharing their expertise, they learned to understand the challenges and needs for support of novice teachers in the different sub-areas of management; moreover, they naturally got to know their new cooperation partners. Since the invited managers themselves were new employees within the Oulu Education Department, their participation had a double purpose: they presented their own expert knowledge of the theme, but also learned from headteachers' work and school management. The issues that had been experienced as difficult in the previous sessions, according to the mentor's notes, were processed in expert groups. For example, as human resources issues were discussed, the headteachers wanted to know about the factors that determine how demanding a position is rated, the costs of long-term substitute positions, and school secretaries' responsibilities. The financial management session started with a warm-up task, in which the finance manager and each principal in his/her turn changed roles and told their expectations and wishes to each other – the headteacher to the finance manager and the finance manager to the headteachers. The challenges for financial management were very easy to map, and several individual issues were solved through joint conversation. The session also produced ideas for financial management training that would definitely meet the participants' needs. One of the members described the group's atmosphere as follows:

> Easily and quickly I got the feeling that we were all in the same boat. I think peer-group mentoring is a lot about reinforcing one's ideas and gaining confidence, but also about being able to admit that one doesn't master everything, and that one doesn't even need to, but that help is available.

In the new headteachers' group, a desire and ability to throw oneself into new activities was highlighted. As the group only included novice headteachers, no old established practices burdened them. The group looked for new mindsets and changed old conceptions rather than transferred existing practices or adapted to established schemata. Three of the group's principals, simultaneously with their schools' teachers, participated in a long-term collaboration development project implemented in the Oulu Education Department. They shared with the peer-mentoring group the good practices obtained from this training, such as organizing a communal teachers' meeting, and many other everyday innovations related to operative management. The group members thus also brought new conceptual knowledge and practical experiences to the group.

Developing school assistants' job descriptions

School assistants work in Finnish schools in order to support pupils who have special needs. They have usually completed a vocational education of about two years. The city of Oulu's Education Department has also offered school assistants the opportunity to reflect on their work and professional identity in a peer-mentoring group. Over 180 school assistants work at the lower and upper levels of comprehensive schools, at combined comprehensive schools, and at special education schools in Oulu. They support pupils' learning, function, holistic growth, and development in all learning environments. School assistants often function as adults close to the pupils, who see and hear the pupils' troubles and pay attention to such things as bullying in class. They have a holistic idea of pupils' needs for learning and growth support, because they see their charges' performance in different subjects as well as outside classes. However, school assistants' tasks and roles in the school community are evolving, and the fact that the teacher and the school assistant are a team should be made more widely understood. School assistants' work is still perceived as providing physical assistance to individual pupils, which initially is what this type of work involves; or the assistants are regarded as some sort of general assistants for teachers and schools (interview with school assistant coordinator Bitja Mikkonen, 18 December 2009).

The themes for the school assistant peer-mentoring group were easy to formulate: clarifying the job description, strengthening professional identity, and occupational well-being. The role of school assistant is new in comparison with the century-old tradition of teaching. The peer-mentoring group members reflected on their role as teachers' partners. The work should be based on teamwork, in which both of the parties have their own, jointly agreed responsibilities based on their profession, in order to achieve their goals. However, this is not always the case in schools, which evokes frustration and a sense of powerlessness in the school assistants. The peer-mentoring group offered the participants the opportunity to get support from the group in order to promote their cause at their own school. The group also strengthened the school assistants' professional identity, as they were able to share with colleagues their stories about challenges at work. The school assistant coordinator, who acted as the group's mentor, could also share her knowledge and expertise with the group, thus contributing to group members' professional identity.

Modern school assistant education pays particular attention to early intervention, observation, and multiprofessional cooperation in the best interests of the child. Unfortunately, many school assistant positions are based on fixed-term contracts, or lessons are split based on acute demands. This causes insecurity with regard to employment and makes long-term multiprofessional cooperation difficult. These topics were commonly addressed in the mentoring group. In particular, action-based methods enabled the school assistants to share these difficulties. On the other hand, the group collaboratively tried to identify the empowering elements of their work. The challenges related to employment relationships cannot be solved quickly, and one still needs to cope at work and find the strength to continue.

The coordinator in charge of school assistant services found it important to continue and develop the peer-mentoring activities with school assistants. It is particularly important to strengthen the professional identity of a new employee group. A professionally competent school assistant is an important link in the multiprofessional collaboration of schools in order to promote communality and develop preventive activities. Teachers should be engaged in the collegial discussion of school assistants, because school assistants' work with one or more teachers is teamwork. The team collaboratively plans, implements, and evaluates learning situations according to individual and group needs. The work is directed by individual and group-specific pedagogical goals and an educational, rehabilitative, and therapeutic knowledge base. The education provider, parents, and society set a wide variety of objectives and expectations for teachers. As teaching group sizes grow and demands increase, taking into account every child's individual needs is a challenging task. Professionally competent school assistants provide valuable support to both children's education and upbringing. In joint peer-mentoring groups, assistants and teachers can learn from each other's work and focus on developing their collaboration. It is also important from the education provider's perspective that the resources allocated to school assistant activities yield services that promote well-being and competence in pupils as well as in the entire school community.

Future outlooks

The mentoring experiments carried out with different employee groups demonstrate that the model responds to a variety of needs. Both in the groups of headteachers and school assistants, the aim has been to integrate multifaceted competence into the discourse by inviting experts to the groups. The school assistant group considered it important to develop the activity by including teachers in their groups, as they work in teams with one or more teachers. The group would allow teachers to see school work through the eyes of the school assistant, which would probably increase the appreciation of school assistants' work and the significance of cooperation. When paving the way for newly graduated teachers to the school community, it has also been considered important that the groups consist of teachers with varying amounts of work experience. The new principals' peer-mentoring groups can also be developed by forming mixed groups consisting of experienced principals as group members and as mentors. In such groups, it is fruitful to create a group atmosphere that strives for new action and thought models, so that the more experienced members are also there to learn and the novice members are encouraged to express openly new ideas in the group.

There is need for a new kind of school culture, in which teacher collaboration, support for professional growth, and the development of the school's working culture are the focus of attention. As financial resources are reduced, schools – and municipalities – can achieve better results only by increasing the flexible and expedient utilization of teachers' expertise (Johnson, 2006; Heikkinen, Jokinen et al., 2008; Nummenmaa & Välijärvi, 2006). A future challenge for Oulu is to apply peer-group mentoring as a tool to increase communality and occupational well-being in individual school communities and, in particular, in the new combined comprehensive schools. This can be accomplished only if the schools or school districts have teachers who have completed peer-mentor training, which allows them to bring the collegial development dialogue conducted in peer groups to the school community level as well. The national peer-mentoring project has managed to develop a well-functioning mentor-training model, which can be put into practice even in economically tight times.

Which staff groups would benefit from peer-group mentoring in your school?

What would be benefits and challenges of multi-professional mentoring groups?

Chapter 7

Peer-group mentoring in the context of transforming local administration

Helena Rajakaltio and Eija Syrjäläinen

The Department of Teacher Education at the University of Tampere undertook a study that aimed at finding out how peer-group mentoring can be developed as a new action model of continuing education, and how it can support development within the field of education in a renewing municipal culture.

At the time of the study, a major municipality reform was launched in the city of Hämeenlinna. The contradictory pressures caused by the shaping of a new municipality culture were also amplified by the large nationwide so-called municipal reform upon the municipality merger. A new organization was created based on the purchaser-producer model that originates in the business world. It was used both as a tool for improving services and for cutting costs. In this client-oriented model, committees act as service purchasers and allocate funding for the services. The municipality's residents are service clients and consumers.

The present development trend within the public sector is part of a global change taking place in the name of the competitive society and new public management, in which public services, e.g. education, are adapted to more efficiently meet the requirements for a competitive edge (Beck, 1997; Harvey, 2005; Pollit, 1990; Strange, 1996). The new governance is characterized by the concept of project society, referring to the fact that activities and their administration are organized through projects (Sulkunen, 2006). This implies that development takes place through project chaos rather than long-span strategies and policies. The project approach is also visible in basic education and its development. Development is linked to different programmed projects, for which funding is allocated. This development trend has also implied that municipalities have changed the way in which they organize development work.

In the city of 'new Hämeenlinna', the transition process implied the integration – or 'harmonization', as it was called in the process – of the municipalities' different historical backgrounds and ways of action. The transition was further complicated by the supranational economic recession, which severely hit the public sector and municipality finances. As a consequence, municipal educational administration fell into financial straits. Municipalities cut their resources, which could be seen, for example, in the temporary dismissals of teachers.

Amidst these strong pressures for change, education departments looked for action models that would promote staff well-being. Peer-group mentoring was found to be one of the methods worth developing. Nevertheless, the situation that cast a shadow over school life gnawed at the trust between teachers and their administration. In such situations, people tend to regard new initiatives with suspicion.

> Teachers don't seem to be very fond of anything that now comes from the educational administration; they may feel that mentoring is a 'simulation of wellbeing'.
>
> (Interview with a member of teaching personnel)

Implementing the peer-mentoring study in Hämeenlinna

However, there was some interest in mentoring activities. At this point, the study was undertaken to examine how peer-group mentoring promotes well-being in school communities. Analysing questions related to daily school life in the mentoring groups outside the work communities inspired the participants to reflect on the relationship between mentoring and the work community. How could mentoring serve well-being and its promotion in a work community? Or does it remain a placebo activity for occupational well-being, carried out somewhere outside the work community? The study also focused on the functioning of peer-group mentoring as a new form of continuing education, and how it can be integrated into the education department's development strategy. In addition, the effects of the municipal reform on peer-group mentoring were deliberated.

Peer-group mentoring was offered in the city of Hämeenlinna as a focus of reflective professional growth in which teachers could develop their professional practices through peer dialogue and joint reflection. The mentoring activities were targeted at new teachers, but also at those returning to work after a break, including all the teachers who were interested in sharing their competence and learning together. The Hämeenlinna peer-mentoring project included two mentor groups. Six mentors participated in mentor training, and all of them also took part in the study.

The research data were collected via questionnaires and a focus group interview from the six mentors who participated in the project (Carey, 1994). One mentor group answered an open questionnaire. Of the teachers who acted as mentors one was a subject teacher, two were special education teachers, and three were class teachers. All six took part in national peer-group mentoring training during the study, in 2008–2009. Four of them acted as leaders of mentoring groups during the training, and the special education teachers led pedagogical café activities. The pedagogical café served as a forum in which the mentors and the teachers collaboratively reflected on issues relating to special needs education and respective support measures.

How was peer-group mentoring implemented in the groups?

These peer-mentoring groups included two mentors working in tandem, which turned out to be a fruitful approach: the mentors supported each other and simultaneously experienced that they had learned a lot by 'shadowing' each other. This approach functioned as shared expertise and facilitated the adoption of the new work method.

> It has been agreed that one of the two mentors is in charge of leading the session; so the one who remains in the background may see things in the group that the leader somehow may not have time to notice.
>
> (Mentor)

The mentor groups consisted of class, subject and special education teachers, who worked with pupils of different ages. This dialogic connection crossing the borders of different teacher groups was experienced as particularly mind-broadening and insight-generating, and it helped the participants to view school issues more holistically. All the parties shared this positive experience.

> And especially the fact that Lisa [name has been changed] and I have such different starting points: she has these preschoolers and I have teenagers, which also stimulates a lot of discussion and interaction between us . . . I've also started to reconsider some things in my work, something I had not thought of before.
>
> (Mentor)

> The conversations made me think about the challenges I face from a broader angle. This was possible because the group members came from different schools, so we didn't get stuck on individual cases. It was easy to talk in the group without worrying that somebody would judge you as a poor teacher.
>
> (Mentee)

Teachers from different sides of the municipality merger participated, which promoted the shaping of the new municipality from 'the bottom', the school level, through teachers' voices. Colleagues in the new municipality shared their experiences of different municipality cultures and their practices within the education sector.

> It was nice that we also had participants from schools other than just Hämeenlinna . . . that in a way it was regionally representative. Brand new things and practices were introduced. So the group had much more to share

than they would have if it had been just between the teachers from the city of Hämeenlinna. That kind of interaction then.

(Mentor)

The groups met seven or eight times during the school year. Teachers' resources, ethics in teaching, assertiveness, time management and work development were among the themes addressed in the discussions. The groups applied action-based and narrative methods, such as stories and drama. The discussed themes were also reflected upon on the basis of short articles related to teaching.

Experiences of peer-group mentoring as a learning space

Mentoring has a strong connection to narrative thinking and methods. Through storytelling, teachers can release their emotional baggage, and at the same time, learn about themselves and others by sharing their experiences (Syrjälä & Heikkinen, 2007). The group constitutes a social reality for the members, in which individuals can collaboratively learn better to understand the phenomenon at hand (Lewin, 1948). Expressly, the questions related to work and professional development are addressed through mentoring. The participants' private affairs are not directly discussed, but as teachers use their personality as a tool, the stories are related to each member's own personal history and identity (Goodson, 2005). Because the group members are equal, the group leader can also share his/her work experiences very personally.

In the case of Hämeenlinna, both the mentors and the mentees emphasized that peer-group mentoring had enhanced their professional development as teachers.

This is a form of professional development and training that is linked … this would be good to link to interaction, group processes, our own coping, and our own way of perceiving that world of work.

(Mentor)

School reforms and changes in teachers' work are complex social processes that teachers interpret based on their personal understanding and experiences. Contradictory pressures arise from the fact that there is usually no space for a shared communication process in the busy and fragmented school world. A timetable divided into classes of 45 minutes still sets the rhythm for teachers' workdays. Finding time for the joint interpretation, adaptation and implementation of changes is like getting blood out of a stone (Rajakaltio, 2008). Andy Hargreaves (2001b) has actually stated that time is a teacher's worst enemy.

We are always so busy in the teachers' room, there is really no time to discuss anything more profoundly; but the atmosphere in the mentoring groups has been peaceful, allowing everybody to be heard, express opinions, worries and joys; and it is just wonderful how the group participates . . . It's not that I as the mentor would do everything but rather so that the group does the whole thing by itself. So, one could imagine that it depends awfully much on the group – what kinds of people happen to be in the group. And isn't it actually the mentor's task then just to make the orchestra play?

(Mentor)

The peer-mentoring group offered the teachers a joint 'rest stop' and a space where they could discuss school-related issues. The group can, indeed, be characterized as a learning space that enables interaction and dialogue. Dialogue is close to the principle of equality, on which the peer-mentoring group's activities are also based. A dialogic approach implies dialogue in which the parties collaboratively look for information, share ideas and experiences, and listen to the others. In the space of dialogue, different communication boundaries are crossed and polyphony is recognized, shared meanings and new understanding are constructed (Arnkil, 2008; Isaacs, 1999; Karjalainen et al., 2006). According to the dialogical concept, learning is a socially constructed process, in which new knowledge is created through interaction. The group members have common interests: sharing knowledge, learning from each other, and gaining shared awareness. Mentoring groups can be described, in compliance with Wenger (1998), as a community of practice based on the social learning theory. People who share a common interest form a group, a community of practice, in which they deepen their expertise. This is based on collegiality, the sharing of practical experiential knowledge, and the generation of new knowledge. The foundation for a community of practice is the contextuality of knowledge, which is a fixed part of the continuously transforming practice of the surrounding community and culture. Learning at work is thus a social rather than an individual process (Lave & Wenger, 1991).

In mentoring, tacit knowledge can be explicated and shared through dialogue. Tacit knowledge is personal, experiential knowledge, difficult to verbalize (Polanyi, 1996).

But of course, as an experience it at least gives you the kind of dialogue about work and problems that are also carried out in the teachers' room; but when there is an aim at logic and guided discussion, it gives you much more and also activates you to observe your own work.

(Mentor)

I had time to stop and reflect on my own work, guided by good leaders and supported by peer teachers. I got new ideas and views for observing my work and activities.

(Mentee)

Of course, the narrative approach can also be criticized. Goodson (2005) claims that teachers' narratives should be embedded into a more extensive frame of reference. According to Goodson, the stories can provide teachers with useful breathing space in the circles of power, but they do not abolish the execution of power. If the stories only remain at the personal level, the approach can even ease the execution of power. Goodson claims that storytelling contains a certain paradoxicality: at the same time as teachers are given a voice, the prevailing working conditions and pressures to change are given permission to continue at school, which is manifested in the teachers' stories as uneasiness and powerlessness. It is thus important for teachers to learn to identify the contextual factors affecting the school world, such as the prevailing socio-political trends and educational policies, as well as the local strategies deduced from them. Awareness of all these factors as they determine school life would reduce the sense of pressure on teachers' work.

Connecting mentoring to the promotion of occupational well-being in the school community

Next we shall examine the connection of peer-group mentoring to occupational well-being within the school community. All the group members came from different work communities, so they had no other links to each other's work communities than one individual teacher.

> Maybe the biggest enrichment was having people from different workplaces, so that we could exchange ideas about the solutions made elsewhere and realize something we had not thought of before; different workplaces do require different solutions, but it is also good to hear what others have so that we don't just swim in our own soup all the time, and things can be solved in various ways.
>
> (Mentor)

The group members found it mind-broadening to hear about other work communities' experiences, ideas and solution models. The group discussions also increased the teachers' sensitivity in observing different work processes at their schools and in realizing the significance of collaborative reflection,

> so that we might be able to rise a little above our own everyday lives and above ourselves also in the work community, and observe its phenomena.
> . . . it has tweaked my thoughts so that the group processes, this is how they actually are, the things related to interaction just are like this. Well, that sort of thinking. And when there obviously is a little crisis going on in your own workplace, you notice that it is some phase going on then.
>
> (Mentor)

Work communities and different work cultures are present in peer-group mentoring through the stories the teachers tell about their work experiences.

The culture of acting alone is still characteristic of schools, and the work as such does not require cooperation with other teachers. The adult contacts in the mentoring group therefore proved to be important. A group member with a long teaching career behind her experienced that the mentor group had given her a new kind of experience of working with adults.

> This is actually the first group where I'm with adults . . . In some vocational course I've been teaching adults. But. You just haven't been in touch with adults. That is certainly one thing you have to learn.
>
> (Mentor)

The teachers who participated in peer-group mentoring emphasized that mentoring had enhanced their professional growth, reflection skills, and the ability to observe their own work and things related to their work community from a distance. In this sense peer-group mentoring promotes the individual members' occupational well-being and readiness for active membership in the work community. However, both the mentees and the mentors highlighted that the mentoring experiences were not shared within their work communities. Often the principals did not even know that a teacher in their school participated in the mentoring project. The experiences gained in a mentor group are not, as such, transferable from the individual level to the community level, as every work community and organization has its own cultural features and power relations, which are shaped through the work community members' interaction. School community development can ultimately take place only from the inside, from the work community itself (Rajakaltio, 1999).

> Now I realize that I think about this rather individually. As development of each teacher's professional identity or self-image and, on the one hand, as tolerance for oneself, and on the other, as appreciation of oneself; and maybe consequently so that we then are actors in our work communities and perhaps able to be sort of active members in the work process. But I somehow find odd the idea that some sort of agent troops would be sent to a work community through mentoring . . . but as work communities have their own rules, that leadership and those goals, they may seem quite narrow within a small circle.
>
> (Mentor)

The role of the principal is significant in all the development processes concerning work communities. Principals have juridical power, and they ultimately decide on schools' joint issues, including resource allocation. They play a leading role in development work as well (Rajakaltio, 2005; Syrjäläinen, 2002). Their attitude to change and activities demonstrates what is valuable to the community. In the case of Hämeenlinna, the principals hardly knew about the mentoring project, or at least the participants said they had not made use of it. The teachers experienced that principals' work had become busier. They had no time to exchange ideas with teachers.

> I guess the principal didn't know anything about it. Thus no attitude from his side.
>
> (Mentee)

Studies focusing on the development of public services' cost-effectiveness and working life quality highlight the central role of management and managerial practices. The municipalities' new financial and administrative culture has resulted in management changes. Different management styles, for their part, shape the way in which work is organized at workplaces (Kalliola & Nakari, 2007; Seeck, 2008). The school-related effects of the municipality merger and organizational restructuring implemented in Hämeenlinna were the strongest influences on the work of principals, who operate directly within the sphere of administrative culture change. This was considered to have increased the principals' work load and administrative duties.

The importance of the principal's role is also highlighted in Pyry Kumpuvaara's (2009, pp. 43–44) Master's thesis which focuses on the first year of novice teachers. New teachers experienced the principal's role as crucial for the way in which they were received in the school's work community. As a rule, their experiences were positive – the teachers usually felt that the principals had supported them. In addition to the principal, the culture in the work community was significant. A well-functioning work community is a resource for the new teacher (Blomberg, 2008, pp. 154–155). According to the novice teachers' observations, the tradition of acting alone is still strong in teachers' work culture, which is manifested, for example, as lack of collegial expertise (Kumpuvaara, 2009). In order to solve the induction phase problems, more attention should be paid to developing the work culture at schools and to increasing their communality (e.g. Lindhart, 2008, pp. 44–45; Syrjäläinen, 2002). Eisenschmidt et al. (2008, p. 146) state that the success of novice teachers pursuing the first steps of their career largely depends on the collegial community at the school. According to them, the principal's role is incontrovertible for creating a receptive and dialogic atmosphere and for developing a professional learning organization.

Peer-group mentoring as part of the municipal continuing education strategy

The city of Hämeenlinna's Education Department has adopted mentoring as a central part of its continuing education strategy in order to promote new forms of continuing education. The objective is to develop a dialogic teacher culture, in which the barriers between different teacher groups can be overcome. At the same time, peer-group mentoring is offered as a discussion forum for different themes, for example special-needs education and subject-specific topics. There are also plans to launch peer-group mentoring for principals.

With regard to developing these mentoring activities further, crucial factors will be how the principals utilize the mentor training and how actively the municipal educational administration supports the development of peer-group mentoring. The participants emphasized that support from the municipality, as well as the principals' roles in the process, would be significant for integrating mentoring into the municipality's long-term continuing education strategy.

> The employer should be closely involved in it. This may not have happened in our case, naturally because of the changes and reforms going on in the municipality, which messed up things; so this is not exactly an issue of who was involved, but anyway, the employer should be strongly committed to the activities and know what it's all about. Now we've had to explain to various people what the point here is. When the employers adopt it, they must also be trained for it, so that they will know what it is and what its benefits are, and why it's worth carrying out.
>
> (Mentor)

Even though peer-group mentoring as a project received both positive and negative feedback from the participants, all of the participants thought that it should be included in the municipality's continuing education offerings. According to the study, peer-group mentoring remained too distant from the work communities. The principals had no time to take an interest in it or utilize the opportunities it would offer, which was partly due to the large municipality merger phase and the changes it involved. Nevertheless, the project participants' experiences that the process supported their professional development provide strong evidence for peer-group mentoring as an eligible form of continuing education, which can be profiled in the municipalities, customized to their individual needs. It is important to find more permanent continuing education solutions in the municipalities, so that they do not need to depend on the constantly changing market for continuing education options. Mentoring activities can blossom into a form of continuing education that contributes to school development in compliance with sustainable development (cf. Hargreaves, 2005).

Learning outcomes from Hämeenlinna

The peer-mentoring project in Hämeenlinna coincided with a major municipal reform, which had an impact on the reception of this new form of continuing education. In fact, in the whirlwind of reforms, mentoring activities remained quite restricted and did not involve many teachers. However, the need for various discussion forums increases precisely in these kinds of transitional situations. The interpretation of the transition, reflecting on it, and the sharing of experiences promote coping at work and occupational well-being (Hargreaves, 2001a and 2001b; Rajakaltio, 1999).

It is highly important for mentoring to be linked to the municipality's developmental context, instead of remaining a pursuit disconnected from the education department's development work. The dialogue should also be opened vertically from the mentor groups, so that messages related to school development find their way from the mentor groups to the ears of officials and decision-makers in charge of municipal educational administration.

The peer-mentoring project's participants experienced that the project did not reach the everyday happenings of the work communities. Mentoring is a development approach that supports individual professional growth, and we find it should be kept apart from work community development methods. In some of the group members' schools, the co-workers were not even aware of the project's implementation during the school year in question. In particular, the role of the principal preoccupied both the mentors and the mentees. The principals were too busy to take an interest in the peer-mentoring project. However, it is precisely the principal's role that is crucial in the midst of a major transition. If the aim is to genuinely integrate peer-group mentoring into the municipal continuing education strategy, special attention should be paid to the principals' work situation and workload, as well as their training and informing. A receptive and dialogic working culture is particularly important when solving problems that occur during the induction phase of new teachers, and when preventing the emergence of problems.

Our study indicated that peer-group mentoring is a very fruitful form of continuing education. This conclusion can be justified merely based on the positive experiences of the mentees and mentors in Hämeenlinna. The mentees felt that their professional competences were enhanced, while the mentors learned to share their expertise through the various ways of working – which strongly contributed to their sense of empowerment. Peer-group mentoring was generally experienced as a shared communication process, as a learning space that is only seldom available to teachers in normal school work. The opportunity for joint reflection prevents teachers' work stress and promotes their coping at work.

In conclusion, we want to return to a set of problems in relation to a background factor in the mentoring initiative. This background factor is associated with the concern about new teachers' first steps in the working world. In the worst cases, this 'culture shock' (Syrjäläinen, 2002, p. 94) has made young teachers swap teaching with other professions. From the perspective of teacher education, peer-group mentoring is not an adequate solution to this problem. Young teachers' transition to working life calls for closer dialogue between teacher education and local actors, municipalities and schools in order better to familiarize teaching students with the daily realities in today's schools. Closer interaction with the municipality's comprehensive schools also serves the development of school research. Over the past few years, an interactive model has been developed in teacher training in Hämeenlinna: in-service teachers, principals and other school actors tell teaching students about the current challenges at school in the light of their own experiences. This opens up a dialogue through which the students have the opportunity to hear real-life, encouraging narratives about the school world from teachers – stories that build a natural bridge between research data and practical experiential knowledge.

In your opinion, could peer mentoring offer teachers a forum in which to consider the implementation of current reforms at a local level?

What do you think of peer mentoring as a form of in-service education?

Could peer mentoring offer a natural approach to the professional development of teachers in your local municipality?

What purposes could it serve?

Chapter 8

A multiprofessional mentoring group at a vocational school

Minna Ahokas

This chapter examines the experiences of peer-group mentoring within upper secondary vocational education. The target group consisted of the teachers who participated in peer-group mentoring at Jyväskylä College in 2008–2009. Jyväskylä College is a multidisciplinary vocational institution, in which young people can complete upper secondary vocational qualifications in twenty-five different fields, which offer thirty-nine different vocational qualifications.

The occupational well-being plan of Jyväskylä College emphasized staff competence development, and peer-group mentoring was adapted as a personnel competence development method. The background conceptions were that it is easier to organize work in a democratic and equal work community, and that open interaction and communication contribute to coping at work.

The material for the study was collected from the peer-mentoring groups of vocational teachers at Jyväskylä College. The mentors came from the same organization and participated in mentor training. The research included two groups: a total of two mentors and twenty-four mentees. The aim of this chapter is to discuss how the upper secondary vocational teachers experienced multiprofessional peer-group mentoring. The study investigated what the mentees' expectations were when they took part in peer-group mentoring, and how they experienced the multiprofessional peer-mentoring group. The study also focused on finding out how dialogic the interaction in the meetings was, and how parity was experienced within them.

The peer-mentoring groups had been composed so that they included both teachers who had worked long in the work community and recently arrived teachers. Thematic interviews were used in the study.

The participating teachers represented different vocational fields. Each vocational field has its own ways of working which reflect on teachers' daily work. The peer-group meetings were arranged once a month, always at the same time, which made schedule planning easier for the participants. The meetings had pre-selected themes, jointly agreed upon with a representative of personnel management, based on the mentors' strengths as well as the vocational college's current development challenges. The themes were related to on-the-job learning, internationality, curriculum reform, special need students, and so on. The theme discussions began with an introduction by an expert. This introduction could be in the form of discussion, articles, or the sharing of experiences associated with the theme. After the introduction the group continued to discuss the topic, led by the mentor. The expert was, as a rule, a Jyväskylä College staff member or other person who had gained in-depth knowledge of the theme through his/her work. The meetings always started with coffee and 'small talk'. The mentor asked the members how they were doing, and everyone had the opportunity to share what they believed to be important at that time. The peer-mentoring sessions were experienced as a breathing space during which the members were allowed to be absent from their own posts and spend a moment with their thoughts and be involved in open dialogue. The multiprofessional approach brought to the discussion different experiences and views with regard to everyday matters. Multi-professionalism enriches a group, but it can also create intra-group tensions and even frustration within it. When teachers from various fields were involved in peer-group discussion, attention was focused on pedagogy instead of teaching contents.

Time for discussion and support for professional growth

The motives for participation in peer-group mentoring were associated with the participants' personalities, work, or work personalities. The personality-related motives included, for instance, processing one's individual challenges, or the need to pause. The motives relating to work or work personality arose from everyday situations, problems or challenges, upon which the participants wanted support, help, or guidance; and sometimes they also needed support for coping at work.

> I am curious when something new is offered; I have selfish but in no way wretched aims: to have a forum in which to discuss ... one would get at least some perspective on how the others experience work in a large organization like ours.
>
> (Female, fifty-three years)

The respondent also referred to the issues brought up by the other mentees, such as the desire to gain more confidence in one's own decisions or solutions. When work becomes busier, there is no natural forum in which to share one's thoughts about working and one's individual challenges or job. The participants had experienced that the need to rush had forced them to prioritize, and no time was left for informal conversation. Coffee or lunch table conversations were not enough. There was no time to share professional challenges. They needed time to discuss peacefully with their colleagues the things they personally felt to be important. The peer-mentoring group provided a forum in which to address the experiences of operating in a large work community. One of the interviewees mentioned that her aim was to obtain more support, a broader view, and enhanced confidence for her work; growth into teachership.

Learning by sharing multiprofessional experiences

A multiprofessional organization does not necessarily provide a natural setting for meeting one's co-workers, reflecting on one's responsibilities in the context of practical performance, or for giving feedback on other people's work. Peer-group mentoring optimally responded to this need. The best offerings of mentoring included the sharing of individual employees' work methods and the creation of new practices. Because the groups consisted of people of different ages, who also had worked in the organization for different periods of time and sometimes did not know each other, it was easy to find different perspectives for discussion through the participants' individual experiences. The mentees found it was more pleasant to talk about certain things with complete strangers than with people they knew. One can discuss more openly and critically with strangers. It was also simple for the participants to register for a peer-mentoring group, as they did not know the other members in advance.

> The time is gone when we worked just based on one viewpoint because, for example, the world of work is full of multiprofessional teams . . .
>
> (Female, forty-nine years)

By comparing different speciality fields' ways of work, shared understanding was enhanced and diverse approaches were addressed. This discussion turned out to be fruitful because the participants represented various areas of expertise. In spite of their differences, the various fields have a lot in common in terms of pedagogy.

Best practices were shared in the meetings. However, in the interviews the participants said that there should have been more reflective discussion regarding their work. The reflection may have remained superficial, if it was limited to talking about one's own successes. It was often more thought-provoking to address failures than successes. Sharing only successes may even have irritated the others and consequently influenced group dynamics. If a group member had performed the same expert tasks for a long time, there was the danger of this member dominating the group with his/her expertise, sometimes unconsciously.

> The sessions started to be dominated too much by just one person – it could be seen on many members' faces – that when a theme was presented, this person was always the one who first took the floor; and I actually wondered if there are people who can't stand a second of silence . . .
>
> (Female, fifty-three years)

Broadening perspectives

Perspectives can be broadened if the peer-mentoring group consists of employees from different work communities and different fields. However, comparing the differences between the fields is not always fruitful – it may transform the conversation into competition. The participants tend to perform comparisons and highlight their own competences unconsciously in the meetings, even though their intentions may not be to emphasize their own or their field's importance. Interest in the way in which a professional group performs specific tasks also broadens the outlook on one's own work. Among the benefits of a multiprofessional peer-mentoring group the interviewees listed the fact that a multiprofessional approach gave a broader perspective on work. It enabled the members to see things from a wider angle. One of the mentees said that his work approach had changed as he had heard that the others also 'wrestled' with similar everyday challenges. The group participants shared the opinion that there was too little collaboration between the units, which is why peer-group mentoring was a good and natural way of finding out what practical inter-unit differences there were. Peer-group mentoring can aim at generating new outlooks on issues, at providing new perspectives, and at piecing together a broader overall view.

> Now I've got clued into things, which has opened my eyes so that I no longer see things from a frog's perspective but perhaps from a bird's perspective.
>
> (Female, thirty years)

The group gained new insights by sharing their everyday experiences. One of the mentees described the group as a place that enabled the birth of insights, something that is impossible in the hectic pace of daily work.

Dialogue, openness and confidentiality in interaction

Interaction in the group took place very spontaneously: through participation in ongoing discussion. It was easy to join the discussions. An indication of the quality of interaction was the fact that discussion was active and the mentees were enthusiastically engaged in it. The groups were dialogic, but after a period of silence, it was more difficult to take the floor. The group members quite quickly built mutual confidence. A few mentees felt that the emphasis in the discussions depended on the participating personalities and their experiences. The more experienced a mentee was, the more space was given to his/her ideas and experiences. Critique was given if a colleague spoke a lot or highlighted his/her success experiences. This did not increase trust or openness within the group – quite the opposite.

The experienced one gets to speak more, which as such is not always good, because that person may have the most formulaic ideas.

(Male, twenty-eight years)

If the group includes too many mentees who have previously known each other, there is a risk that discussion among them becomes too dominant. On the other hand, group discussion may begin more naturally between acquaintances than between complete strangers. One of the mentees presented the view that it is easier to act in the group if the members do not know each other. They are then more equal, lacking any professional roles or professional group roles; in other words, they are just themselves. Many interviewees highlighted that their group had shared a sense of confidentiality right from the beginning, and that it felt very natural.

Confidentiality was the basic assumption; since it is repeated to the students from A to Z that these things are confidential, it never even crossed my mind that the contents would be told somewhere else ... trust is like creating a bowl – if no bowl is created, you can pour nothing into it, then it's just talking.

(Male, fifty-three years)

Activeness and positiveness were often linked together, and the group's interaction was described as positive. This also resulted from the fact that all of the participants had independently decided upon participation, which is why they had positive attitudes and high expectations.

Communality

Initially, the colleagues in the same peer-mentoring group were strangers to one another, so the discussion and activities mainly relied on the mentor. As group formation progressed and the members got to know each other, communality became visible. However, the sense of communality is not born in a minute but requires time.

The sense of communality can be associated with a group as well as with an organization. From an individual's viewpoint, it is important to know the organization and the people in it. The peer-mentoring group had meetings in the various units, so that the group members got to know each other's workplaces physically as well. A sense of communality requires that each individual understands the importance of his/her own role in creating togetherness.

You learn to know the organization as a whole – the better you know it the better you do your job, and this involves the setting of boundaries, student's interest ... you already know that the organization is big, and in big units you work alone; if they are looking for development, this does give chances for that.

(Male, twenty-eight years)

Parity, roles and support

According to the mentees, parity was manifested in the peer-mentoring meetings as equality. The novices and more experienced teachers were at the same level, no one rose above or remained below the others due to background, years in office, or age.

From the perspective of coping at work, the support received from peer-group mentoring was significant. The participants' work-related anxiety, or, for example, anxiety due to pupils' immaturity, was reduced as the group supported and strengthened their views. The group processing of issues experienced as negative put these issues into perspective, while the group provided collegial support and sparring. A person in the same position is often able to help.

> I like to listen and give comments, it's nice to give support but also to bring out my own stuff, especially things that haven't gone so well; I don't know if I personally needed more support, but people should feel they can openly talk about their failures and nobody judges them; we all do make mistakes.
>
> (Female, fifty-three years)

The mentees were very talkative, which is why the mentor's role as chair was emphasized. The mentor's role was associated with the need to have a 'good eye for game' and the ability to give others space. Everyone should be provided with equal opportunities to speak, and the least talkative ones should also be taken into consideration. However, contribution in discussions should be voluntary – the participants must also have the opportunity to just be there and listen.

Challenges and successes

Why is peer-group mentoring important? Newspaper headlines have long declared that our operating environments are changing. In the same way, the current changes in age structure and the increasing importance of networks have become permanent talking points. How is tacit knowledge transformed into organizational knowledge, and how can we create better and more sustainable networks? Peer-group mentoring can be an ideal tool for that purpose. Changes in the conception of knowledge have also brought new challenges for staff development. Knowledge is no more understood as stable, locked facts but as a changing, flexible structure instead. According to Virkkunen (2002), competence has become more communal: the generation and maintenance of competence has expanded from individuals and small work communities to organizations and organization networks. Competence has also become broader in terms of time: the focus has shifted from competence in implementing a prevailing concept to methodological development and the generation of brand-new competence. Knowledge and competence have undergone a qualitative transformation: there has been a shift from the mastery of separate performances and sub-functions to the development of a basic solution shared by them. In traditional mentoring there is a risk of continuing/reproducing practices as such, whereas this risk is less significant in peer-group mentoring. The participants experienced that they received something that contributes to the development of activities. They wanted to hear both about their colleagues' everyday problems and the solutions to them.

The peer-mentoring group meetings were thematically structured, and they were experienced as fruitful. The theme contents were, in one way or another, associated with the work of all the mentees. In terms of staff development, the themes were linked to strategically important issues or focal points. Examples of the thematic areas covered were on-the-job learning, internationality, curriculum reform, and diverse learners. Some of the interviewees thought that it would be good if each member could approach the subsequent meeting's theme by reading or finding preliminary information about it in some other way. This would ensure sufficient initial knowledge, which would enhance the participants' ability to pose questions or comments about the themes. The results of this study thus support the use of theoretical stimuli, which is recommended in the first part of this book.

Many of the peer-group members, irrespective of their discipline, reflected on similar problems and challenges in their work. A peer-mentoring group is a good place to share experiences and good practices. It also allows the participants to see that they are not alone with their problems, that there is always someone with whom things can be shared. The challenges associated with different professions also became apparent in the meetings, and multiprofessional experiences could be compared to one's own context, though within a completely different vocational field.

The peer-mentoring group's atmosphere was open, and trust was established at an early stage. Confidential issues could also be handled within the group. Nevertheless, it is important for the mentor to remember that peer-group mentoring is not therapy. It is not a place in which challenging work community problems or employees' personal problems are solved. The informality of the meetings was a resource, as no one had to prepare or take down the minutes but, instead, the mentees were expected only to concentrate on discussion and the current theme. Humour was also present, and it lightened the atmosphere; however, if used carelessly, it may also turn against itself.

On the basis of this research, we concluded that, for example, the clarification of roles is among the future development challenges in peer-group mentoring. An employee's supervisor cannot act as mentor in the group, as this would cause role conflicts. The mentees found it awkward if some of the group members were in an employer–employee relationship, although one of the participants stated that he had initially chosen the group because his supervisor acted as its mentor.

The mentor's role was regarded as clear. It was described as that of chair, instructor or leader. This role was important also for groups that included one or more dominating persons. Mentors should be able to intervene and interrupt a too-dominating group member. If this is not done, the situation can result in frustration in the other members, who may even quit the group. Delicacy plays a key role here.

The study indicated that a group of sixteen participants is definitely too large, even though all of them were not habitually present. The ideal group size seems to be approximately six to eight mentees. Group composition should preferably be restricted so that no more than two members come from the same unit. This would ensure that no subgroups are formed within the group.

Peer-mentoring group meetings could employ various methods in addition to the discussion approach. Diverse methods could yield new perspectives on the mentees and the processed themes. It is important to take into account that methods do not play the leading role in meetings – they are applied in order to support the processing of themes. The use of new methods requires courage and a desire to experiment from the mentor.

One of the challenges in the mentoring activities was that mentoring and peer-group mentoring were perceived as new employee orientation. However, orientation is a separate activity of its own. Peer-group mentoring can be used to support it, but it is essential to ensure that peer-group mentoring does not replace orientation.

The interviews with the peer-mentoring group members also highlighted work-related rush and insufficiency of time. Colleagues were usually encountered at coffee or lunch breaks, which generated a spontaneous exchange of views on pressing matters, but lack of time prevented the creation of more extensive partner networks or a more profound collaborative processing of issues. In economically tight times, multiprofessional cooperation often remains rare, even though it would be particularly useful in such circumstances. Multiprofessional cooperation would offer a wide variety of opportunities for redesigning work and adopting new tools for collaboration in order to minimize the sense of rush. No work community is profitable and well-rounded without development.

Have you got new ideas for your work from people coming from other fields?

What kind of experiences do you have of multi-professional working?

Chapter 9

Experiences of peer-group mentoring in homogeneous and heterogeneous groups

Maria Lahdenmaa and Hannu L.T. Heikkinen

This chapter focuses on teachers' experiences of peer-group mentoring (PGM) in two groups that were composed in different ways: one group consisted of teachers from the same work community and the other of teachers from different work communities. We do not aim at determining which group composition is better but at describing how the groups' experiences differed from each other. These experiences were examined from various angles, reflecting on how the results could be used to develop mentoring further. The results represented a similarity in both groups' experiences: all the members were satisfied with their own group and its operation. However, we also observed some differences between the groups.

Composition of the peer-mentoring groups

The group that consisted of teachers from the same work community included six subject teachers, of whom one acted as mentor in the group. All the teachers in this group were females. The age distribution was from under thirty to over fifty years. Most of the teachers had several years' work experience, except for one who was newly graduated and in their first year in post. The group had met a total of eight times during the school year, and the meetings had always taken place at the teachers' own school, in a peaceful library room, approximately once a month, after the end of the school day.

The second group, with teachers from different work communities, was composed of seven teachers, of whom two were mentors. There were both subject and class teachers in this group. One group member was male. The age distribution was approximately similar to the other group, from about thirty to fifty-five years. Most of the members in this group had also worked for several years, some considerably longer than the others. The male teacher had only about two years of work experience. The eight group meetings were arranged at a school at which none of the participants worked, in order to ensure the meeting venue's neutrality for everyone. The meetings took place in the afternoon after work, about once a month, during one school year.

Implementation of the study

The groups were interviewed by applying the focus group method. According to Valtonen (2005, pp. 223–224), essential in the focus group method is that the interpretation of group experience is constructed through interaction between the group members and the researcher. This method is an interpretative process, in which individuals form a conception of shared experiences and their meaning with the help of the group (Kamberelis & Dimitriadis, 2005, p. 903). In the focus group method, interaction can be roughly divided into two major categories: well-structured and unstructured, depending on the interviewer's intentions (Fontana & Frey, 2005, pp. 703–704). This study represented the unstructured approach.

The group discussions were conducted in both peer-mentoring groups' last meetings. The data were examined inductively (i.e. by applying a data-based analysis method), deductively (i.e. by analysing experiences in the light of earlier theories), and abductively (i.e. by making intuitive conclusions based on the data). These basic types of reasoning used in qualitative research were combined with SWOT analysis. The data were thus examined by employing methodological triangulation, i.e. multiple methods were used to study the same data (Denzin & Lincoln, 2005, pp. 5–6; Fontana & Frey, 2005, p. 722; Tuomi & Sarajärvi, 2009, pp. 144–145).

SWOT analysis originates from the business world, in which it was created as a tool for developing, for example, company strategies. SWOT is an acronym for the words *strengths, weaknesses, opportunities*, and *threats*. By evaluating these four dimensions, the analysis aims at determining how they can be either utilized or prevented. SWOT strengths and weaknesses have usually been seen as internal factors, and opportunities and threats as external (Hill & Westbrook, 1997, pp. 46–47). The traditional SWOT fourfold table (Table 9.1) was adapted

Table 9.1 'Intra-group factors' fourfold table

Strengths	Opportunities
PRESENT	FUTURE →
Weaknesses	Threats

for this study, because all the factors were regarded as elements emerging from intra-group features. The SWOT table was also adapted by placing a timeline at its centre. This adaptation allowed us to see the strengths and weaknesses as present factors, and the opportunities and threats as future scenarios. The table was named the 'Intra-group factors' fourfold table. The data were also analysed following the principles of data-based content analysis, listed by Tuomi and Sarajärvi (2009, p. 109).

A homogeneous peer-mentoring group (same work community)

The SWOT analysis of the homogeneous peer-mentoring group is presented in Table 9.2. A particular strength of a peer-mentoring group with members from the same work community was the communality that already existed due to the openness and directness of the school's working culture. The mentoring group members appreciated their supportive and encouraging group culture, in which a lot of feedback was given. In the work community, they were used to caring for their co-workers, and now they had dared to rely on each other in a familiar peer-mentoring group. Coming from the same work community, the members also experienced that they could share their problems with each other and help their peers with their problems, as all of them knew the discussion topics very well. From the individual members' viewpoints, their own school's group had been a great opportunity to get to know their own work community and find their own place in it.

In this kind of a homogeneous group, the members already had predefined roles that had been shaped in the work community – which was regarded as one of the group's weaknesses. A further weakness was the fact that even if the group consisted of colleagues from the same work community, part of the work community was excluded from the group. The challenges for the individual

Table 9.2 Fourfold table analysis for a peer-mentoring group of the same work community

Strengths	Opportunities
– Communality	– Work community development
———— PRESENT ————	———— FUTURE ————▶
– Old roles	– Negative attitude of the others
Weaknesses	Threats

members' coping could also be seen as a weakness: for example, the sense of rush one felt on the way to the group meetings, and the burnout risk that even resulted in career change speculations.

One of the group's future opportunities and goals was to contribute to development in the entire work community. The novice teacher's inclusion into the work community, as well as assistance upon her career start, were also seen as opportunities. The experiences had already provided the teachers with a sense of empowerment, so that coping at work could also be seen as an opportunity. Reflecting on problems together with the other members had helped the participants to see their own teachership in a positive light.

It could be seen as a future threat that the group could remain disconnected from the rest of the work community, and a division into two could take place between the peer-mentoring group members and the rest of the work community. This could involve the risk of the group becoming too cliquey. One definite threat to the group was also its potential breakup, which would influence all of the parties involved: the group, the individual and the entire work community.

A heterogeneous peer-mentoring group (different work communities)

The SWOT analysis of the heterogeneous peer-mentoring group is presented in Table 9.3. One of the strengths of the peer-mentoring group that consisted of teachers working at different schools was the absence of predefined roles. The group members had no role expectations regarding each other as they did not know each other beforehand, nor did they hold any predefined ideas of each other's job descriptions. They had been able to start in the group with a clean slate, without any prior roles affecting the group's activities. They experienced being able better to stick to the point and avoid speaking ill of others, for the

Table 9.3 Fourfold table analysis for a peer-mentoring group of different work communities

Strengths	Opportunities
− Absence of roles	− Individual development
———————— PRESENT ————————	———————— FUTURE ————————▶
− Absence of communality	− Negative attitudes of the others
Weaknesses	Threats

conversations had remained on a non-specific level. The reason for the individual members' participation in PGM had been their desire for self-development.

The group's functioning seemed to be impaired by the lack of communality. A considerable part of the meetings had been spent on group formation, and one participant claimed that this process was still incomplete after eight meetings. As a consequence, the low number and short duration of the meetings in relation to the experienced need, as highlighted by the participants, can be regarded as one of the weaknesses of this approach. The members were still looking for their individual roles and places within the group. Moreover, the group's efficiency was reduced by the fact that the members often felt they had to rush to the meetings, which resulted in weaker commitment.

The opportunities of a heterogeneous group included the group's internal development towards integrity, and the clarification of its goals. From the viewpoint of the individual members, the opportunities – and thus group influences – extended to individual professional development and mental coping through reflection and dialogue related to problems.

The future threats in a peer-mentoring group of multiple work communities were related to the absence of communality, which reduced the members' commitment to the group and made the group's purpose disjointed. It was difficult to see how participation in the group would contribute to the members' work community. In the worst case, it could have had a negative effect on the individual's role in the work community. The negative attitudes of employers, experienced by some participants, were also seen as a threat to the heterogeneous group.

Focus on goals when forming the groups

The strengths of both types of peer-mentoring groups were well-justified and characteristic of their group composition. The existing communality of the homogeneous group was highlighted in the members' experiences, and it differed remarkably from what the heterogeneous group experienced as its own strength – rolelessness. The groups' weaknesses were interesting both compared to each other and in relation to the strengths. Even though the group that consisted of teachers from the same school was strengthened and united by the existing communality, the familiar roles simultaneously weakened the group. Respectively, the group of different schools' teachers had no predefined roles, which was its strength, but also made the group less uniform, so that communality only started to be built during the meetings. The strength that the homogeneous group experienced thus resulted in weakness; and conversely, the weakness experienced by the heterogeneous group was the reason for its strength. The homogeneous group was experienced to have the opportunity to develop the work community as a whole, whereas the heterogeneous group could develop its individuals and their coping – a fact that clearly reflects the differences between the groups. The opportunities, and thus also the goals, of the homogeneous group's activities are targeted both at the entire peer-mentoring group and the entire work community outside of the group, as well as its activities. The opportunities of the heterogeneous group's activities, instead, are targeted at each teacher as an individual, separate from his/her work community. Even though the homogeneous group's impacts are also manifested in the individual teachers, its ultimate goal is to support the work community as a whole.

The threats experienced in both of the groups were very close to each other in terms of the groups' potential continuation or breakup and other employees' attitudes towards the group or its members. The groups' threats could also be seen as contrary to each other: in the same work community, the group's compactness was a threat; while in different work communities, the strongest threat to the group was its disconnectedness. Both groups shared the threat that the other employees would adopt a negative attitude towards the group or its members. However, these negative attitudes would differ from each other: the same work community members' negative opinions might affect outsiders as well, whereas in different work communities this impact could be targeted exclusively at each individual teacher who attends the peer-mentoring group.

The members' experiences in both of the groups, as a rule, indicated satisfaction with their own group's operation. They spoke up for their own group's structure and strengths, but were not opposed to the idea of a group being composed in a different way. The weaknesses of one's own group could be turned into group strengths through reasoning. The group members did not actually find the weaknesses problematic but rather acted in spite of them. They seemed to have a very clear idea of their own particular opportunities and goals. By contrast, they were not fully aware of the threats. The group members of the same work community had, to some extent, taken the threats into consideration by keeping the group open for other employees in the work community as well. The teachers in neither of the groups were conscious of the other employees' opinions about the fact that they were involved in the PGM activities.

As an exception to the general satisfaction, the heterogeneous group's experiences also revealed some critique regarding the group's activities. All the group members thought that there had been too few meetings, and that they had been too short. The effects of these limitations were apparent: the first group meetings had mainly involved so-called small talk, and only recently, not long before the last meeting, had the participants begun to discuss the themes more profoundly. Their group formation process seemed still to be going on. The employers' attitudes were also criticized, as it turned out that not all of the participants would be compensated for their participation as promised.

The study highlighted the most essential differences between the two group types. Both of the groups had their own strengths and weaknesses. The experiences demonstrated that both groups would not necessarily be suitable for every teacher or work community. In order to be effective, a group composed of employees from the same work community would require a desire to develop from the entire work community. It would be worth finding out whether a homogeneous mentoring group like this really influences the work community as a whole and, in particular, how it could even better be utilized in holistic work community development. Based on the results, it is impossible to say whether a homogeneous peer-mentoring group has the intended impact on anyone other than the group itself and its individual members.

A peer-mentoring group composed of teachers from different work communities seems to need more time for group formation than a group whose members know each other in advance and are used to one another, and one another's roles and ways of working. Then again, if the intention is to avoid role formation and group formation processes, the group might not have any reason to meet for longer times or more frequently. However, this could also prevent the group from achieving a more profound level in its discussions. On the whole, the activities of the heterogeneous mentoring group seemed to remain on the level of individual development. The group had no actual communal goal, even though mentoring was realized through the group. The results indicated that in developing the activities of heterogeneous peer-mentoring groups, it might be necessary to better consider the demands and effects of group formation. By the other token, as these groups aim at promoting their individual members' professional development and coping – which we can interpret as having been accomplished – taking into account communal factors is perhaps not the primary target of development.

The members of both the heterogeneous and the homogeneous peer-mentoring groups shared a feature that was clearly highlighted in our research: a desire for spontaneous self-development and enhanced coping at work. This had been the motivation for establishing the groups as well as for joining them. The teachers jointly expressed the wish for more peer-mentoring activities. They placed a lot of importance on this opportunity – a permission, place and time – to discuss issues that they otherwise had no time to address; and precisely this had made the experience empowering for the teachers. One of the teachers crystallized the peer-mentoring group's contribution as follows:

> this is nothing awfully big, but its effect the next day or when you go home from here is still in a way great.

In your opinion, would it be appropriate and useful to have discussions about your teaching with other teachers whom you had not previously met?

Chapter 10

Diversity of mentoring

Leena Syrjälä and Eila Estola

The various chapters in this publication convey a picture of mentoring as a multifaceted process that has been implemented in slightly diverse ways at different stages of the mentoring project. In other practical fields, among developmental psychologists, in the business world or in academic spheres, the concepts of mentoring and mentor have varying meanings. Indeed, researchers have reflected on the responsibilities of the mentor, and concluded that no single word – for example teacher, coach or instructor – expresses clearly enough what a mentor actually does (Leskelä, 2005, pp. 21–22). But hardly anyone has asked the mentors themselves.

However, many people have quite a distinct idea of the meaning of the word 'mentor', as described in this book's first part. The word can evoke an image of a person who has acted as an informal mentor at some point in a person's career. This mentor has had certain ways of action that have made him/her a mentor, even though no formal relationship between the mentor and mentee has been defined. These kinds of mental images may, for their part, shape a person's potential mentoring activities. It is recommended for future mentors to reflect on their own and other people's conceptions of mentors and mentoring. Here, therefore, we focus on the diversity of mentoring based on the conceptions of the teachers who participated in the peer-group mentoring training.

At the end of the chapter, we will examine these conceptions in relation to our earlier experiences of teacher groups in which the participants had been offered the opportunity to discuss their work and share related feelings with their peers through narrative and action-based methods in guided situations (Kaunisto et al., 2009). These groups' activities varied from guided, goal-oriented meetings to get-togethers that resembled spontaneous conversation situations (Estola et al., 2007). The guide/mentor's responsibilities also took slightly different forms in these peer-mentoring groups.

The mentor's responsibilities and the forms of mentoring thus seem to vary. In order to develop mentoring and future mentor training programmes, it is useful to examine these diverse conceptions and their interrelations. In the following we will portray the concise narrative material collected in the mentor training, on which our study is based.

The narrative assignment and its analysis

On the first day of the mentor training in September 2008, the participants were asked to define mentoring and reflect on themselves as mentors. In an action-based exercise, arranged in order to stimulate conversation, a large number of postcards were spread out for the participants to view. Each of them could choose a card that described mentoring and the participant as a future mentor. The cards were eagerly picked up, and it seemed to be easy for the participants to find a picture that described their individual situation. Three of the participants chose the same card, which featured a smiling girl standing at a half-open door. The choices evoked a lively discussion, in which the participants exchanged their experiences and views, simultaneously getting to know each other. At the end of the following day, they had to return to their choice by briefly explaining in writing why they had chosen the card in question, write down what they think mentoring means, and depict themselves as mentors. Finally, they were asked to comment on the beginning of the training and on their expectations from its continuation.

A total of twenty-one participants wrote down their reflections. These answers varied from a few lines to half a page. When examining the answers, one must take into account the considerable variation in the teachers' backgrounds. Some of them had already acted as mentors, whereas others had only recently decided to attend the training and were not sure yet whether they would later act as mentors. The training included teachers from different locations, in which mentoring had previously been implemented in slightly varying ways.

It was easy to identify some central themes about which the participants had written when reflecting on mentoring and themselves as mentors. Within these themes, we could distinguish different respondent types. For some of them, mentoring was clearly something completely new, and they had occasional doubts as to whether they would later act as mentors or be capable of doing so. On the other hand, the training included many teachers who had prior experience with mentoring, a fact clearly visible in their answers. The respondents' ideas of mentoring showed considerable variance: some of the experienced ones described mentoring as listening and 'walking by the mentees' side', whereas the novices emphasized the new solutions or practical skills provided by mentoring. Based on this, five respondent types were established and given a fictive name, either according to their mentoring-related backgrounds or dominant views, as follows: Novice Nora, Doubter Debbie, Listener Lisa, Solver Sophie, and Veteran Vicky. Novice Nora was thus taking her first steps on the mentoring path, Doubter Debbie was not yet sure if she would become a mentor and have the qualities required for mentoring. Veteran Vicky's answers, by contrast, manifested a long experience of guidance activities. Listener Lisa described mentoring and the mentor's primary responsibilities as interaction and 'lending an ear' to the mentees. Solver Sophie emphasized in her contemplations mentoring as the search for solutions to practical problems.

In this approach to reading narrative research data, a new story was created based on the participants' contributions, which are presented in this chapter through plotted dialogues. The following dialogues are thus based on authentic texts. One excerpt consists of the answers by participants of the same respondent type; these are nearly direct quotations, in which the participants' original expressions have been preserved as meticulously as possible. In order to make the dialogue more fluent, some introductory words or notes referring to other answers have been integrated into the text (cf. Erkkilä, 2005, pp. 54–55; Richardson, 2000).

The multiple goals of mentoring

The following dialogues, which thus originate from the teachers who participated in the mentor training, are organized according to the themes established upon examining the material. First of all, the respondents addressed the objectives of mentoring, as well as whether these objectives could vary in diverse mentoring groups in the future.

SOLVER SOPHIE: I don't find defining mentoring easy, and I've been thinking that this might be due to the fact that the former groups' goals in the different cities have slightly differed from each other, which is why the groups' activities have also taken different forms. In Kokkola the emphasis was clearly on supporting new teachers' teachership, while the starting point in Jyväskylä were mostly practical questions related to the themes. It would, in any case, be good to clarify what mentoring actually is. How can we assure employers of the importance of mentoring if we can't clearly tell them what it is?

VETERAN VICKY: I also thought about all the things that mentoring could be and whether it could vary from one group to another. That's what we actually are experimenting with here. We should just have the guts to choose our own way of doing it. Actually, the PGM training as a whole is kind of mentoring, in which we utilize the power of peer support for our own development as future mentors.

LISTENER LISA: After all, don't we all share the viewpoint of promoting each group member's occupational well-being? Teachers must be able to do their job 'with their heads on straight', otherwise the consequences will be ugly. The ultimate objective is children and adolescents' well-being. When teachers can share their thoughts in mentoring groups, it will help them better understand children, in addition to teaching.

The teachers' reflections seemed to highlight that the ultimate objective of mentoring is to enhance teachers' – and consequently pupils' – well-being. The participants shared the idea that the objective of mentoring can vary, but it would be necessary collaboratively to clarify what mentoring refers to.

The participants reflected on mentoring as the group's joint activity and collaborative learning. Group interaction was regarded as an essential factor, and its different elements, particularly listening to others, were deliberated upon. The trust built in the group was considered as a prerequisite for all activities.

LISTENER LISA: I see mentoring as acting and learning together, as seizing the moment. It is active listening rather than talking. It is not 'the right solutions' or underestimation. It is taking responsibility for the group; caring, support, interaction. It is also trust and confidence in something better.

NOVICE NORA: Also for me, mentoring means learning within the group. Its strength lies in the group, it is about personalities meeting each other and sharing in a confidential atmosphere. It feels good that I really don't have to be an 'automatic answer machine' that knows all the answers, because the group is the one that does the mentoring!

DOUBTER DEBBIE: I am a little hesitant and still wonder if mentoring should also involve giving ready-made answers and solutions. I hope not, as I don't think I'm capable of doing that, but I still am a bit worried that that's what the mentees expect.

LISTENER LISA: After having reflected on mentoring, I would crystallize its meaning by saying that it is, above all, growth in listening, identification, verbalization, and in influencing each other, by turns, through discussion. Professional growth and well-being form the red thread running through the entire process.

The above dialogues highlight the novice mentors' fear of the group members expecting the mentor to know everything and to be able to provide ready-made solutions to everyday problems. On the other hand, mentoring was clearly viewed, above all, as collaborative learning and growth.

NOVICE NORA: Mentoring means walking by your colleagues' side and supporting them, learning together, encouraging and giving them strength. It's about discovering your own teachership and developing your competences.

LISTENER LISA: I think the best thing is that in the mentoring group we can practise listening and comprehension skills. We can be heard and develop our self-knowledge, clarify our ideas, both professionally and personally. The group, its members, have a great impact on how and in which direction our discussions – in other words, the interaction situations – lead us.

SOLVER SOPHIE: Well, I actually have similar views of mentoring: it is listening, sharing, and respecting the others as they are. Taking everybody into account equally, peacefully. But it is neither new-employee orientation nor work counselling, and even less psychodrama.

Mentor's responsibilities: supporting daily work, asking, and listening

The mentor training participants also reflected on themselves as mentors in their narratives. These kinds of reflections were, indeed, regarded as a very essential element of the training, for if the mentors are conscious of their strengths, they can better utilize them for the group's best interest. At the initial stage, the teachers naturally also had doubts regarding their ultimate willingness or ability to become mentors.

Mentors' responsibilities were clarified in the training through practical examples from teachers' peer groups. The participants' descriptions of themselves as mentors demonstrate that even though this was only the first training session, they had started to build a mentor's identity. Many of the participants reflected on the issues highlighted in the training in relation to their own idea of themselves as mentors, which is visible in the following dialogue, adapted from the texts.

LISTENER LISA: Back in my school days, and even afterwards, I used to be a good listener. People turned to me. Now I'm trying to rediscover in myself that good listener and encourager. I hope I am a good listener. Through listening I can be reminded that shared knowledge is the best knowledge. I must remember to give room for stories.

NOVICE NORA: I'm still a bit shy towards the narrative method. I don't want to be a work counsellor or therapist, or harm anybody with my own actions. A mentor can make good questions and wants to develop him/herself. But at the moment, I actually have no idea of how I would be as a mentor.

SOLVER SOPHIE: Such an apprentice–master model would be ideal. But I understand the lack of resources, to which peer-group mentoring is a partial solution. The mentor is responsible for supporting teachers in their daily work. I don't want to be involved in educating people as humans, neither do I want to psychologize.

VETERAN VICKY: I want to offer my experience to new teachers. I want to solve, together with them, issues related to their daily work – without getting as deeply involved as in my own job.

The importance of listening seemed to be strongly highlighted among mentors' responsibilities, but, at the same time, it is also necessary to be able to ask good questions. Naturally the answers, as a whole, showed variation, as the training had just begun and some of the teachers had no experience with mentoring. On the other hand, some of the respondents were attracted to the master–apprentice model, in which the mentor is clearly more experienced, a master of subject-specific content, and able to solve daily work problems. Many of the participants emphasized that they do not want to be work counsellors or educate others as humans.

Only a few male teachers took part in the mentor training in 2008, and one of them – we call him Eric here – describes in his answer how he had selected a postcard in which a young woman carries beer to a bunch of men. He identified himself as the girl – as a servant – and imagined his potential activities in a peer-mentoring group that consisted exclusively of female teachers.

ERIC: So far only the women have spoken. I chose the 'tough guy card', in which a bunch of men is sitting around the table and the girl is bringing them beer. I thought about my male role already when coming here. When analysing the picture, I put myself in the girl's role as the group's 'servant'. Serving beer symbolizes my tool, my method to make the group talk. After the photo would be taken, I would sit down at the table and participate with the men. In this frame of reference, it is rather interesting to go and lead a group that may consist of women only. However, I don't see myself as a freak, but rather take this as a challenge. When the project is over, I have had a chance to be part of an adult group. So far my more permanent groups have consisted of children.

It was also important for Eric to be actively involved in a group of adults. This is probably one of the strengths of peer-mentoring groups: teachers are offered the opportunity for work-related discussion among adults. However, the gender issue must not be ignored. In our experience, female teachers are more eager to get involved in discussion groups than male teachers. The PGM project's peer-mentoring groups have included some men, which is a sign that men are also gradually getting involved in mentoring activities. This development is pleasing.

How shall we proceed?

The teachers who participated in the mentor training see mentoring as a multifaceted and challenging process. The focus of mentors' responsibilities therefore varies a lot, depending on the groups' goals, composition, and the mentors' experiences. It is, nevertheless, every mentor's inalienable right to be him/herself, which means that the groups can also be 'coloured' according to the mentors' individual qualities. Based on self-knowledge, mentors can determine their group's potential emphases at an early stage. Of course, it is important to remember that the group members must also have the opportunity to be involved in defining the principles, and that mentoring is always a multidimensional process.

Teachers who intend to become mentors should mull over the following questions, for example:

- What are my experiences of group work?
- Do I have previous education that could be useful in mentoring?
- Am I familiar with teachers' daily work?

- How do I evaluate my own human relations skills?
- Am I a good listener, or could I develop this skill further?
- Am I a fact-oriented mentor rather than a mentor who 'walks by the mentees' side'?
- What are my practical qualifications for mentoring – do I have the time and other resources?
- Am I in an acute professional or personal crisis?
- Can I also get support for my mentoring if the need arises?

The PGM training participants expected the training to provide them with opportunities for regeneration as mentors, or encouragement and support for the initial stage of their mentoring career. They also appreciated practical advice for actual mentoring, as manifested by the following dialogue excerpts (adapted from the participants' answers):

VETERAN VICKY: It is nice to join the group even though I have acted as mentor for a couple of years. I feel quite relaxed, but I would like to develop mentoring a bit, and break the mould, as I have been doing it in the same way all the time.

NOVICE NORA: I for my part am only starting my mentoring journey and look for encouragement, tolerance for trial and error, permission to follow my own learning path at my own pace, and a lot of motherly/fatherly support ... Excessive warning and absoluteness easily cause a sense of insecurity, as it's true that there is not just one correct way of doing it.

SOLVER SOPHIE: I still think it would be important to get practical hints in the training about such things as the FAQs from the mentees, and how to motivate discussion in a potential 'tongue-tied' team. I would need to know, in general, what the mentees expect from their mentors.

The question raised by Solver Sophie – regarding the expectations from mentors – is a problem with which all new mentors wrestle. As a matter of fact, similar expectations are targeted at mentors as those which the mentor training participants themselves pose to their educators in the training. The mentor is expected to be an encourager, listener, reformer, and solver of practical problems. Of course, one has to consider that the participants come to the mentor training for various reasons. Based on our experience, these can include:

- a readiness for change and for working on oneself
- a lack of professional enthusiasm, boredom at work
- a transitional period (initial stage of teaching career, new workplace, final stage of career)
- an interest in helping others in their professional learning process.

From these starting points, the expectations of the mentor as well as those of the group take different forms. All things considered, mentors are entitled to be themselves and quietly to develop an approach to guidance and mentoring that best suits them and each individual group. That is why the future mentor can look into the future with a peaceful mind, as Listener Lisa is doing in the following extract:

LISTENER LISA: I am peeking into the future from a half-open door, with an open mind, just like the girl in the postcard. When the project ends, I hope to be an individual, teacher, listener, supporter – who has given herself and others a chance to be heard around and within professionally relevant issues. However, as mentor I see myself so that when the project ends, I will have the opportunity either to open the door a bit more, or to close it. I hope that the expression on the smiling girl's face won't have changed.

Mentoring was outlined in this chapter based on the written reflections of teachers in PGM training who either intend to become mentors or who already have some experience of mentoring. In conclusion, we could present mentoring on a continuum, with one end representing the solution of everyday problems and the other end general issues related to work and professional identity. Irrespective of where mentoring is placed on this continuum, the mentor's fundamental responsibility is to support and promote teachers' occupational well-being. This broad outlook on mentoring actually provides an optimal foundation for developing mentoring in accordance with the participants' needs.

What kind of mentor would you be?

Chapter 11

The group as a context for peer-group mentoring

Saara-Leena Kaunisto, Eila Estola and Raimo Niemistö

What should the mentor know about the group? In this chapter we shall reflect on the challenges and opportunities that the group context opens up for peer-group mentoring at the various stages of group development. A peer group offers various advantages compared to pair mentoring. The group's strength lies in its members and the responsive interaction between them. Some members can give you something that would not be possible to receive from people who do not have similar experiences. It is not merely about receiving support but also about offering it to other people who are in the same situation (Pistrang et al., 2008).

Peer-group mentoring is based on reciprocal sharing of experiences. When this is done with peers – in other words, with people who are in a similar situation – it evokes a sense of togetherness and strengthens the feeling that you are not alone with your problems. You can be heard in the group with your own challenges and work-related emotions. It can also contribute to coping at work and empowerment. Studies indicate that, for instance, with regard to stress management, it is important to meet people in the same situation (Schiff & Bargal, 2000).

A group based on sharing experiences provides a good opportunity for learning. People often join the group because of a need for change or something new in their personal or professional lives. In group interaction they can collaboratively discover an understanding that integrates the theoretical and experiential dimension. On the one hand, learning can involve group discussion and narration; on the other, learning can take place through the sharing of everyday work practices. In fact, the group is considered to be more than the sum of its members.

We will examine here how the stages of group development and their challenging points may reflect on the mentoring process. Group development has been studied since the 1950s. We will adapt Tuckman's (1965) description of group development stages, which are called *forming, storming, norming, performing,* and *adjourning.* An understanding of the group life cycle is useful to mentors preparing to lead a peer-group mentoring. However, one must remember that every group is a unique whole. The duration of a group and intensiveness have an impact on its stages, and, for example, in short-term groups there may not be enough time for all the separate developmental stages, or they may not be identified. Our text 'material' includes a fictive mentor's voice which, through examples, expresses the mentor's thoughts upon the challenges faced by the group. The mentor's fictive voice is the product of our numerous mentoring experiences with different groups.

Mentors' challenges at the various stages of group development

The empowering elements are not automatically achieved in a group. Therefore, the peer-group leader is in charge of helping the group members develop a group that allows room for open dialogue. How can the mentor respond to this challenge at the various stages of group development? Even though every group's objectives and duration are unique, awareness of the group's potential life cycle will help the mentor find suitable methods. The group process progresses from initial disorientation and conflicts to cooperation.

Forming: challenges and questions

> Well, today it starts, our first meeting. I arrange the room. I lift one chair at a time from the corner to the centre of the room, into a circle. Little by little with each chair I settle down in this room and the group, as if my mind would be emptied of everything else. I try to set the right mood for the group. I'm nervous. I wonder how our meeting will be . . . What if the group members don't 'play' with me, or if I don't manage to create a safe group atmosphere?

The first meeting is exciting both for the mentor and the group members. The aim is to create a framework for the group's activities and help the members get to know each other so that joint group dialogue can begin. In the first meeting, the group's objective, basic principles, commitment, and confidentiality are agreed upon. The group members should feel safe enough to be able to share their experiences with each other. Knowledge of the group's composition and 'rules', as well as a clear, recurring meeting schedule, contributes to a sense of security. For instance, the group may always begin and end with a joint round in which the participants can, in a sense, join the group's shared space by recounting their news and feelings. The initial tensions are reduced by getting to know the other members. At the introductory phase, the participants can share their preliminary expectations, wishes and fears, first perhaps in pairs and then collaboratively with the whole group. After having met each member individually, it may be easier to talk with them as a group as well.

Tuckman (1965) states that at the group forming stage the challenge lies precisely in the group's task orientation and getting to know each other. At this stage group structure is characterized through testing and dependence. The participants observe the reactions of the mentor and other members and 'test' what kind of behaviour is acceptable in the group (Tuckman, 1965).The mentor's competence and abilities to lead the group are also observed and evaluated. At the same time, the participants are dependent on their mentor and the other members.Typical of this stage is a sense of insecurity, which can be exhibited by the participants in different ways, such as anxiety or pronounced conventionality. At the activity level, in this phase the group orientates itself to the basic task (Arrow et al., 2004;Wheelan et al., 2003).After a successful group-forming stage, the members constitute a team and experience a sense of togetherness.

> The second PGM meeting. I start the catch-up round.The participants are not in a talkative mood; they aren't particularly willing to share their news. The conversation seems to progress on a really general level. Nobody says anything based on their own experiences.What in the world can I do?

The mentor's role is crucial for creating the group culture. Particularly in the first meetings, the mentor's behaviour contributes to the creation of group culture; in other words, how people act and speak in the group, and what level the dialogue achieves. Dialogue is often promoted by the fact that the participants speak based on their personal experience instead of on a general level. At the initial stage, 'scarce narration' can be a sign of the members not knowing each other sufficiently, which is why they may not feel safe enough in the group.The threshold of discussion can be lowered by providing the members with the opportunity to chat in pairs for some time about their own situations and pressing questions. After this it may be easier to join the group conversation based on one's own experiences.

It can thus be problematic if the discussion remains on a very general level. The mentor can try to direct it more actively to the members' experiences.This can be done by asking questions such as 'How is this story linked to your life?' and 'What did you find moving?' When the narrator hears about the other participants' similar experiences, he/she does not remain alone with the story that he/she has shared, but the story becomes part of the other members' stories. The mentor can promote a culture of sharing, in which no one's story will be criticized, questioned, or invalidated. Group discussion can easily end up being mere provision of advice and interpretations, if it is not loudly and clearly directed to the sharing of one's own experiences. Sometimes this requires a particular structured form; for example, in psychodrama it is done as a phase of 'sharing' (Aitolehti & Silvola, 2007, p. 13).This implies that the participants are guided only to talk about the feelings someone else's narrative has evoked in them, or about what in the narrative has moved them or seemed familiar to them. Defining or interpreting others or placing oneself above the others as an adviser can prevent dialogue (Haarakangas, 2008).

> In the last session, the teachers were hoping to address school memories next. But now they only talk about the joy of work.

It depends on the group's objective and structure if it proceeds according to predefined themes or spontaneously on the basis of themes that are topical in each session. The mentor's role is to see to the group's basic task. Although a particular theme for a meeting would have been agreed upon beforehand, the participants may not necessarily be in the mood for this theme when the meeting arrives. Therefore, when addressing a new theme for the first time, group members can be given some transition or adaptation time with regard to the theme by asking them to think about a question related to it that preoccupies them, or to call to mind a relevant personal experience. In this way they can outline and express their own relationship to the theme. This can be accomplished, for example, by asking the participants to remember, with a partner, a situation related to a specific theme, or to think about what else they would like to know about the theme. As a concept, this approaches the basic starting point of constructivism presented in the first part of this book: it is important to activate learners' preconceptions in the training.

After a successful initial phase, the members and the mentor share an understanding about how to act in the group and what the group's purpose is. From now on, during the following stages of group development, the mentor is in charge of maintaining and enhancing the group's working capacity.

Storming

> The group seems somehow passive. Some of the members arrive late, some are absent. Out of six, only three attended this time. Is this even a group? Is our group starting to fizzle out? How can I make the participants commit to the group? What is this indirect opposition or conflict?

The name of this stage reflects its storming nature: direct or indirect conflict or resistance is typical of it. It can be manifested in the group as passiveness, resistance, criticism or dissatisfaction. In task-oriented groups, the storming is often discreet and indirect. It usually calms down over the course of time. Tuckman (1965) identifies conflict solving as a challenge at the storming stage. It serves the members' independence process. The group's development may stop if the storming stage is completely skipped. If the mentor demonstrates with his/her comments having noticed the group's atmosphere and states this aloud, the group may experience having been heard and continue its basic task. A group that has settled its storming stage will move on to a more mature level in its development (Niemistö, 1998, p. 179).

According to Tuckman (1965), the storming stage is associated with the fact that the group needs to develop shared goals, values, and ways of action, but the members may disagree about them. As a consequence, conflicts arise – basically because the group members try to express their individuality and resist the forming of a uniform group structure. The uniformity built in the forming stage is now experienced as restrictive to individuality. It is as if the group members were fighting in order to preserve their own individuality, instead of being 'swallowed' into the group. Indeed, this stage typically lacks togetherness. The group's tasks are also reacted to on an emotional level. The reactions may be seen, for example, as resistance to the tasks (Tuckman, 1965). The group's goal at this stage is to find harmony between the needs related to group tasks and the emotional needs of the individual group members. A conflict stage is an unavoidable prerequisite for trust and an atmosphere in which the group members can also freely disagree with one another (Wheelan et al., 2003).

> Kate talks about her challenging employment situation: 'It's lovely that the participants now dare to speak from their personal and emotional perspectives, not just on a general level. But what will happen now?' Ann comments on Kate's story by saying that she is worried about Kate's challenging situation. Ann: 'Are we going to talk about such difficult questions here all the time?' Kate: 'Now I feel that I and my issues don't fit in this group.'

As the group members have got to know each other, they gradually also dare to address difficult themes that preoccupy them, or directly comment on others' opinions. Sometimes the comments can evoke conflicting emotions, such as confusion, offence, or anger. These points are challenging both for the mentor and the group: can the mentor handle these emotions, and what about the group? A problem related to the members' interrelations can sometimes even prevent the implementation of the group's basic task. This situation can be opened up from the perspective of the participants, for example by asking them why it makes them anxious/worried, and how it is connected to their experiences. How did the other members feel upon hearing this kind of feedback? The question can also be targeted at the entire group: What thoughts does the situation evoke in the other group members? Have they had similar feelings?

When a group of separate individuals has become a unit with its own peculiar characteristics, we speak about a group entity (Whitaker, 1989). The group can then be either cohesive or incohesive, but it always has its individual character and mentality, which it manifests through its discussion themes, norms, activities, and atmosphere. The group can occasionally become anxious or paralysed when facing a specific task or question, which prevents it from directly expressing its problem. One of the group members can, nevertheless, 'bear' or represent the theme of the entire group. This member may be able to put into words what the others cannot verbalize. The group's problem is often subconscious, and it is experienced only as a vague sensation. Talking about the sensation will then help the member gradually face the problem. The mentor is responsible for grabbing an expression like this, irrespective of whether it is speech, emotion, or an impulsive action. The mentor can bring the issue to the group level by asking the participants if they have similar experiences or how they feel about it.

> Again, Anna is talking all the time. Maria has not said anything yet. What on earth can I do?

The mentor is in charge of ensuring that all of the members have enough space. The mentor can also offer the opportunity for space to members who show no initiative in this respect. The mentor can, for example, start by saying: 'You have not yet commented on the subject. Would you like to say something or share something with us?' When one participant dares to reveal his/her story, it also serves the others by providing them with the opportunity for identification and by lowering the threshold to talking about their own situation.

Instead of words, one can sometimes express things through actions. The action-based methods influenced by Moreno can be useful in making the participants' inner worlds visible, enabling them to share these worlds with others, and giving a form for a specific theme (Blatner, 1996). The activities can also motivate and deepen a theme's examination or reveal something hidden in speech. Such guidance techniques as 'taking a place on a line segment' or creating a statue of the topic may open up a new perspective on an old theme.

Norming and performing

> Great, now the group's atmosphere seems light and open. As mentor, I can peacefully concentrate on observing the team.

After the storming-stage problems have been solved and inner resistance has been overcome, the norming stage is characterized by agreement on a joint purpose. The group has now formed its own culture and norms. These can be manifested, for instance, in what is spoken about and what is not. At this stage, it is important for the group to preserve its communality and harmony. The mentor is responsible for observing how the team implements its purpose and how its discussion develops. In an ideal group culture, discussion should not remain on the level of advice, interpretations, and questions, which do not enable interactive presence (Mönkkönen, 2007, p. 92). Some group discussions resemble 'monological dialogue' (Seikkula, 1995), in which 'the dialogue parties' statements are not actually connected to each other or based on one another, but the participants rather articulate their own views side by side' (Mönkkönen, 2007, p. 88). Each group member seems to be presenting his/her own 'monologue'; in other words, the dialogue consists of monologue after monologue, none of which ever meet each other because the speakers are unable to hear one another.

The norming stage typically gives way to the performing stage. As the members' interrelations and roles have been formed by now, the group can channel its energy into its actual purpose. This stage is called the performing stage, because it is characterized by intensive team productivity and efficiency. In terms of activities, in this phase the group finds solutions to problems and aims at accomplishing its purpose successfully. The understanding of oneself and others may increase, and new solutions to challenging situations may simultaneously be created (Tuckman, 1965; Wheelan et al., 2003).

It is important for the mentor to identify the group development process. Transition from the storming stage to the norming stage is usually not a particularly dramatic event. The group members do not necessarily even recognize it. The mentor may notice that the atmosphere has lightened and the members reach for harmony again, in particular if disagreements or a tense atmosphere has prevailed. The norming stage represents the members' desire to struggle for group integrity and purpose. This is also a relief for the mentor, who no longer needs to 'stay alert', but can encourage the members towards collaboration and self-expression. In a well-functioning group, the mentor can often perform his/her guidance responsibility in a free and relaxed manner, without disturbing the spontaneously functioning team. Inexperienced mentors may feel a pressure to 'earn their salary' through active guidance, but mentoring in a functioning group ideally implies that the mentor give room for the group's creativity. At any rate, the mentor is required to be physically and mentally present and have an interest in the team. The mentor is like a parent with grown-up children.

At this stage, the mentoring group participants might highlight various themes for discussion. If a particular topic seems to evoke an exceptional amount of discussion among them, the mentor must consider whether to stick to the predefined theme or instead focus on what seems to be the 'number-one topic' at that particular moment. The mentor's decision depends on the group's purpose. In task-oriented groups, it may be justified to stick to the basic task but simultaneously observe the group's current interests; or at least the mentor should express awareness of the circumstances in the group. However, sometimes it is justifiable to provide room for a theme that arouses lively debate within the group; if no opportunity for this is provided, it may progressively begin to draw the group's attention away from its basic purpose.

Adjourning

> It's the last time that I arrange chairs for the group. Our joint journey is almost over. This circle of chairs embraces so many emotions, experiences and problems. I feel relieved. I feel a bit sad and good at the same time.

Mentors must pay special attention to the way in which they begin and end their peer-group mentoring. At the last stage of the group process, preparations are made for the group's termination and it is brought to an end. A wide variety of emotions are in the air: sorrow, nostalgia, gratefulness, separation anxiety, maybe also disappointment about uncompleted tasks. On the other hand, according to our experiences, the participants may also feel peaceful and relaxed, and find that it is time for the process to end.

Peer-mentoring groups' meeting schedules are agreed upon in advance, which is why everyone is aware of the adjournment stage. The adjournment process begins before the last meeting. This is often concretized in the mentor's or mentees' comments regarding the sessions soon being over. The team has travelled a journey that has included several phases. It may also have stagnated at some stage (Arrow et al., 2004; Wheelan et al., 2003). If the peer-group mentoring process is short, the group might not manage to go through all of the stages mentioned above. Either way, the group will be terminated. It is common to spend the last session almost exclusively focusing on the themes of adjournment and process evaluation: what has been accomplished and what has remained unaccomplished.

No one can know in advance what the benefits of the group process are. Machines may be relatively predictable, but not people, let alone groups of people. The experiences of group work are frequently positive – and also often surprising. At its best, the group process liberates the members' creativity. The group process gently reveals the group's theme, which is often not the official topic agreed upon beforehand. Sometimes the group's latent theme overrides the official topic both in terms of importance and fruitfulness. When a bunch of people have become a team, and its members begin to trust each other, they gradually develop enough courage to address specifically the topics they find important. These may be delicate, scary, or even shameful themes that are difficult to discuss with anyone. In addition to its most evident content, the central theme consists of latent content and the emotions evoked by the topic. For example, a teacher group may discuss trouble-making pupils, and the topic may give rise to both irritation and anxiety. The latent content, which usually remains subconscious, could in this example be one's own sense of insufficiency and smallness. The comments that criticize a work community or leadership are another example of this. The critique may certainly be justified, but its hidden content may be the fear of exclusion, or envy. The latent content represents basic human experiences. The theme's deeper layers are often anxiety provoking, and facing them requires a long-enough group process in a safe group. It is not necessary to clarify these latent psychodynamic contents in mentoring groups, but the mentor could take their impact into account. The true benefit of less profound group themes also becomes evident only after the group process has been collaboratively concluded.

The group as resource and challenge

What is the significance of the group context, in particular with regard to peer-group mentoring? Awareness of the group development stages helps the mentor to find suitable modes of action for different situations. The mentor's special duty is to ensure that everyone's experiences are given room – and no one's experience is ignored or nullified. The mentor thus contributes to creating a safe setting and rules in cooperation with the group members. Peer-group mentoring actually requires balancing from the mentor: the mentor must interfere, but not too much, so that the peer group can operate under its own steam.

The group as a mentoring context is also challenging. At its worst, a group can become the source of bruising experiences, for example so that one's personality is questioned or one's voice is not heard in the group. Thus mentors cannot avoid awkward and challenging situations. That is why it is important that they have a place in which to process these challenges – either in connection with consultation or work counselling. This will guarantee that no mentor is left alone with their challenging questions.

The need for change can be one of the reasons for joining a peer-mentoring group. Ultimately, transitions begin when the narrators' own stories change due to something happening within them (Elbaz-Luwisch, 2005).

The group possesses a tremendous amount of professional competence and knowledge, which can be developed further by joint group dialogue. The group members' experiences and tacit knowledge are integrated in the group with the team's shared narrative, which again can be an incentive for the participants' understanding to enter a new, more conscious level. In the space opened up by the group, the members can act in the role of listener, expander, or confidence strengthener, and so on, for each other. The group constitutes a shared 'shoulder' on which everyone can lean. The group can also be the torch that ignites hope and casts light into the dimness (cf. the first part of this book).

The group as a peer-group mentoring context can function as a sort of mirror. In the group the narrator can mirror his/her life and its challenges to the reflections opened up by the other members' narratives. In this mirror, one can find interfaces and identification surfaces, but also roughnesses or scratches that make them unique. The narrator is free to choose where on the mirror to focus his/her look and what to ignore. At all events, the group offers the opportunity for renewal as well as for finding new outlooks on teachers' work.

How would you describe yourself as a team member?

What experiences do you have of team leadership?

Chapter 12

Keys to success

Sini Teerikorpi and Hannu L.T. Heikkinen

What determines a peer-mentoring group's success? What if the group doesn't take wing – what could be the reason? We have been studying this by posing questions to the mentors who attended the Tampere region mentor training in 2009–2010. The questions were not directly related to the mentors' personal experiences; instead, we used the role-playing method for data acquisition. As a mid-term assignment, the mentors were asked to write two fictional stories about a mentoring group on the basis of framework stories. The first fictional story was written about a group in which everything works fine and the second about one in which nothing works properly. In this chapter we shall first describe the role-playing method as a qualitative research tool. Then we shall exemplify a successful and unsuccessful group through the stories written by one of the mentors, after which we shall analyse the narrative material using qualitative content analysis methods.

Why use the role-playing method?

The role-playing method is based on the narration of fictional stories. We decided to choose this method because it may be difficult for mentors to talk about their experiences of failure in leading a group. It is easy for a mentor to experience feelings of personal failure if the group does not function well, even though the reasons might well be rooted somewhere else altogether. In the same way, talking about success may be difficult. The role-playing method can thus be applied to create a vivid and versatile image both of successes and failures, without the respondents feeling that they are being labelled as failing or succeeding as mentors.

Even though the narratives collected through the role-playing method are fictional, the narrators draw upon their own experiences. The strength of the method is that it provides interesting interpretations of social reality: fiction can sometimes crystallize the essence of a matter in a very succinct and illustrative fashion.

The participants are first given a framework story, based on which they use their imagination either to develop the narrative further or to describe what has happened before the situation in the story occurred. There are different versions of the framework stories, in which specific details vary, but otherwise the stories are similar. The analysis focuses on the impact of change in one variable (Eskola & Suoranta, 1998, pp. 111–112).

The mentoring students in the Tampere region were assigned two stories to write entitled as follows: 'A nonfunctional work community or mentoring group' and 'A functional work community or mentoring group'. The participants in the training were teachers at different stages of their careers, all of whom had several years of work experience. They totalled twenty-five, and twenty-two of them were running mentoring groups of their own during the assignment. Since not all of them had groups of their own, they were provided with the opportunity to choose freely whether to write about a work community or a mentoring group in their essay. A mentoring group was chosen for the story by thirteen mentors, and because one of the mentors wrote only one story and the others two, the material comprised a total of twenty-five stories.

The following two narratives from a mentor are examples of a successful and an unsuccessful mentoring group.

A narrative about success in a peer-mentoring group

I cut coloured papers into pieces and scattered them on the meeting room table. I clicked the coffee maker on and set a suitable number of cups on the table. Biscuits into the bowl and a sugar bowl beside the milk pitcher. Everything was ready.

I could hear a buzz of conversation behind the door before they knocked. All five group members arrived together, and after serving them coffee, I guided them to the meeting room. The teaspoons jingled in the cups as I gave them the first assignment. Just like to primary school pupils. The group members chose coloured pieces of paper and wrote their names on them. Without a murmur. While drinking their coffee, the participants took turns in justifying their colour choice for the name tag. Kalevi chose grey because he considered himself to be an old hag. Tero's tag was green – just like he was. As a teacher and conservationist. The group was really colourful.

Minna (with a pink name tag) wanted to take the floor right after the introduction round. 'May I tell you immediately what I would like to discuss here?' she asked, as if forcing herself to say something unpleasant. She was met with approving cheers and continued: 'I'm too kind – and even now I'm ashamed of taking the floor regardless of a potential agenda. In addition to suiting my blouse colour, pink symbolizes me because I want to please people so much that it actually nauseates me. It does not suit school.' After this I only needed to hand the floor over to the group members, who asked Minna to give practical examples and recounted their own experiences of the whirlpool of kindness.

It was four o'clock and there were only crumbs left in the biscuit bowl. I had to end the session with a whistle and asked the participants to write down on the scraps of paper (my scissor-hand was aching after all the shredding) the thought that was uppermost on their minds at the end of the session, and whether they had any wishes regarding the next session. I read the notes aloud; many of them included fine spurring maxims for Minna, as well as topic proposals for the next session. Smiling, they gathered their cups from the table and started to prepare for the frosty weather, satisfied with the support they had either given or received.

I loaded the dishwasher and was satisfied. I had made it. And I even thrived and enjoyed this collegial connection we had shared.

A narrative about failure in a peer-mentoring group

The school became empty – in a fast and determined rhythm, immediately after the seventh lesson. Suddenly I was all by myself in the teachers' room, waiting for my mentoring group to come to its first session. I was intolerably conscious about the fact that in the training we had been advised to organize the meeting outside of the school. In a place that would take our thoughts off school, so that we could relax and discuss what was on our minds. We could sit down comfortably and take a breath. Enjoy some coffee bread and smile at our neighbour in an encouraging way. Discuss with a calm velvety voice . . .

Reality soon caught me with the knock on the door, and I could see five complete strangers through the window beside the door. I opened the door and wished everyone welcome, ready to shake hands with them. 'Due to swine flu, I'm not shaking hands', the first lady started our communication. Embarrassed I drew back my hand and pointed at the rack on which the participants could hang their coats. The rack was filled with adults' academic woollen coats and a few pairs of fur-decorated ladies' leather gloves. I was frightened by their strong perfume smell.

I could already feel red spots on my cheeks as I guided these important-looking people to the meeting room. I had dimmed the light to create a cosy atmosphere. An extremely neat female teacher, dressed in a brown jacket suit, considerably more experienced than me, screwed up her eyes and started digging her glasses out of her handbag in order to see better around her, with no success. She seemed disgruntled.

My hands were slightly shaking as I organized the notes I had prepared in advance. I presented the idea of the group and told about my own peer-mentor training. A young man, dressed in a checked jacked, raised his eyebrows. 'Do you mean that you have – not finished – your training yet?' he marvelled, looking at the other four participants. 'We actually do lead these groups side by side with our own training – and practise mentoring here at the same time.' I repeated what I had already said. 'I see,' the man stated in an apathetic, somehow colourless way.

I distributed pieces of paper to the participants, on which I asked them to write down their expectations from the mentoring group. No one had any. They expected me to take care of it all – to hand out articles to be discussed, and to introduce the topic. I had no article. No topic either. I wanted to proceed on the group's terms, direct the freely gushing, enthusiastic conversation. But it just hadn't gone like that at all.

Analysis of the narratives

The preceding stories were one mentor's fictional descriptions of a successful and an unsuccessful group. They share various aspects with the other stories collected for the research. The following analysis is based on all of the twenty-five essays written about a mentoring group. They were analysed using content analysis, identifying meanings in the text, and trying to create a summarized, generalized description of the topic. The material is simplified in content analysis; in other words, any irrelevant information is screened out of the text through research questions. What then follows is grouping concepts that represent similarities and differences and classifying concepts that have the same meaning. The last stage is to distinguish relevant research data and form theoretical concepts in compliance with the selected information (Tuomi & Sarajärvi, 2009, pp. 103–112).

Findings

On the basis of the narratives, the factors that contribute to success or failure in mentoring can be divided into three main categories: physical and administrative factors, social factors, and the methods used during the meetings. These factors are more closely explicated in Table 12.1.

The group's physical setting, such as refreshments and a cosy meeting room, is present in almost all of the stories. In addition to coffee, biscuits or pastries were often served in the stories. A pleasant space can be found anywhere from the school's meeting room to a vicarage. An additional important factor is finding a time that suits everybody – according to one of the stories, it is definitely not Friday evening. The frequent descriptions of physical settings in the stories indicate the salience of a welcoming space for the sessions. The administrative factors encompass organizational – usually municipal – support. This not only refers to the mentor's fee and the space offered for the meetings, but also to a more general interest within the municipality in personnel well-being, including the willingness to listen to the proposals presented at the meetings.

The social factors embrace the attributes of the group and the mentor, as well as intra-group interaction. The positive group attributes presented in the stories include the participants' motivation, activeness, and common goals. Their activeness and attitude seem to have a strong impact on how the mentor feels when guiding the group, and on how the discussions proceed. The mentees' common goal motivates them to commit to the group and to the goal they have set. The group's activities are also promoted by the fact that the members share an interest and are involved in the activities of their own free will. These factors increase motivation and facilitate the creation of a dialogical connection, both of which are important factors for the functioning of a mentoring group.

The participants' narratives portray good mentors as motivated persons who perform the task of their own free choice. Good mentors are well prepared for group meetings and ready unhesitatingly to address even difficult topics. They should also be able to modify their fixed plans if the conversation veers in new, more fruitful directions. This calls for courage, as the group may also be willing to talk about sensitive and delicate topics. The mentor's lack of self-confidence

Table 12.1 Factors contributing to success or failure in mentoring

Main category	Top category	Subcategory	Original expressions
Administrative and physical factors	Physical factors	Refreshments	'I clicked on the coffee maker and set a suitable number of cups on the table. Biscuits into the bowl and a sugar bowl beside the milk pitcher.'
		Space	'Let's find a cosy vicarage for our meetings.'
	Organizational support	Municipal support	'The head of the municipal department of education also attended the first meeting. He said he was interested in the group's activities and promised to promote them.'
		Mentor's fee	'The municipal educational administration was in favour of the matter and, before the training, signed a contract on Mirja's fee at the mentoring stage.'
Social factors	Group	Motivation	'The group was clearly motivated.'
		Activeness	'They expected me to take care of it all.' (neg.)
		Common goals	'The group started …by outlining common goals right in the first meeting.'
		Starting point: one's own interest	'The Green Patio mentoring group was launched as the teachers discovered that they had a lot in common in terms of their work.'
		Overarching factor	'Subject and class teachers from primary and secondary schools, all of whom share an interest in teaching and developing mathematics.'
Social factors	Mentor	Motivation	'Mirja expressed her willingness to participate in mentor training and consequently applied for the training.'
		Starting point: one's own interest	'Vesa had decided to participate in mentor training because the rector had regarded him as suitable for that task.' (neg.)
		Healthy self-esteem	'I could already feel red spots on my cheeks as I guided these important-looking people to the meeting room.' (neg.)
	Interaction	Motivation and encouragement	'I read the notes aloud; many of them included fine spurring maxims for Minna.'
		Support for the mentor	'One of them stops me when I pass by one day; thanks me for the group … says that she has enjoyed the group.'
		Listening to others	'The discussions often get disjointed, as the participants, as well as the teachers, find it difficult to listen to others and wait for their turn.' (neg.)
		Confidential and open atmosphere	'Then Vesa wanted …to openly share his own "wound" with the group. This was experienced to enhance openness and trust in the group.'

(Continued)

Table 12.1 (Continued)

Main category	Top category	Subcategory	Original expressions
Methods	The group's agreement upon action	Rules	'Taru told us about the rules that had been agreed upon in the latest meeting. She had written them down and wanted to make sure that everyone agreed with them.'
		Time management	'Marja regrets being late and simultaneously tries to observe the environment.' (neg.)
		Themes based on the group's wishes	'Taru also says what the others had wished would be addressed in the sessions. Most of them had had basically similar wishes, but some variety could be found.'
		Agreeing on themes	'The group members were unanimous about the topic and wanted to commit to discussing in the mentoring group how to improve the situation.'
	Meeting structure and content	Introductions, Relaxed start, Guided discussion	'Let's start with introduction rounds and continue with some relaxed conversation.'
		Free discussion	'First we'll have coffee and pastries, chatting on something nice.'
		Solution suggestions	'Taru has chosen "coping at work and occupational well-being" as this session's theme. We'll start by writing down our own sentiments … which will be discussed in pairs and finally together.'
		Sharing thoughts and sentiments	'After this I only needed to hand the floor over to the group members, who asked Minna to give practical examples.' 'Then Taru interrupts by saying that we could next suggest how to solve the problems.'
		Bookkeeping	'Each participant took turns keeping minutes. The notes were always revised after the meetings.'

is highlighted in the negative stories. On the other hand, the group members' responsiveness and encouragement, at their best, support mentors in their task, which also contributes to greater self-confidence.

The texts include a remarkable amount of interactive features. One story concisely depicts the meeting's successful result: its members feeling more complete after the meeting than prior to it. This can be achieved when the group members and the mentor share the same expectations and goals for the group's activities, and when they also commit to the group and its goals. The group functions optimally when both the members and the mentor encourage and support each other, and when they genuinely listen to what the others say. The atmosphere should be open and confidential, as well as allowing for the disclosure of emotion. All the participants ideally enjoy being in the group and leave the meetings 'with a smile on their faces'.

The methods (Table 12.1) applied in the group include the group's agreement on action and the structure and content of meetings; in other words, how the group operates and what is done in it. The agreement on action is not necessarily an official agreement but includes issues that make operation more straightforward and equal. First, the agreement requires that all participants arrive at the meetings on time. This allows the group to use all the time available without unpleasant interruptions. Second, the agreement includes the group's rules that are to be approved by each member. It may be necessary to write down the rules for everyone to read. The third item in the agreement on action is the selection of themes to be addressed within the group. The stories indicate that themes arising from the group members' wishes are of primary importance. It is good for the entire group to approve the chosen discussion topics and to commit to reflecting on them.

The methods also encompass meeting structure and content. Several stories mention the beginning of the session, which in a well-functioning group is free-form and relaxed. The meeting can start with an introduction round or game, or at a later stage, with a cup of coffee and a (casual) chat. The stories offer various perspectives on directing the conversation. Sometimes discussion proceeds in a very controlled way and the form varies from writing down one's own sentiments to dialogue and joint group discussion. But sometimes an inspiring topic may inspire the group, and the mentor hardly needs to be involved in the discussion at all. The group's initiative and topic choice are crucial here. The mentor should have a Plan B for directing the conversation, in case the topic does not catch on.

Mere discussion is not always enough – finding solutions to problems would be better. Discussing proposals for improvement and concrete activities are mentioned in many of the narratives. The issues highlighted in the discussions can be written down either by the mentor or the group members. At the end of a meeting, open sharing of the topmost thoughts and sentiments can be liberating. In almost all of the texts, the mentor's and group members' satisfaction at the end of the session was an indicator of a successful meeting.

The keys to success are several physical, administrative, social, and methodological factors, which together can constitute a well-functioning mentoring group. When the door to a comfortable room has been opened and the coffee maker clicked on, the group can concentrate on creating a safe atmosphere and allow itself to be carried away by fascinating discussion. A culture of open discussion and jointly agreed upon practices will guarantee that everyone's joys and sorrows are heard. A confidential group will also allow outpourings of feelings. The group members' initiative and motivation make good prerequisites for a mentoring group in which 'it is easy to thrive and enjoy a collegial connection', in the words of our exemplary story's author. But if collaboration does not run smoothly or if discussion is awkward, the mentor can dig from the bottom of his/her pocket a spare key to unlock the problem. A common goal and jointly discussed themes motivate the members' commitment to the group, thus sealing a viable end result.

Think about some group you have been a member of. Do you think you could tell a story of that group in two different ways so that the listener would not recognize that you were talking about the same group or the same experience at all?

Part III

Towards collegial learning

In this concluding part we summarize the findings of the studies on peer-group mentoring and take a look into the future challenges. Application of the peer-group mentoring concept into the global education world will be examined from the viewpoint of practice theory.

Chapter 13

Lessons learnt from peer-group mentoring experiments

Jessica Aspfors, Sven-Erik Hansén, Päivi Tynjälä,
Hannu L. T. Heikkinen and Hannu Jokinen

In this chapter we first summarize the findings of the empirical case studies on the Finnish peer-group mentoring model after which we examine the challenges of its application. In the first study (chapter 3), Eila Estola, Leena Syrjälä and Tuuli Maunu examined newly qualified teachers' experiences of their first years of work on the basis of the discussions that took place within peer mentoring groups. Their findings showed that new teachers face the same problems that are generally regarded as universal challenges in teachers' work: the tension between being busy and enjoying the work, problems integrating into the work community, and relationships with the students and their parents. New teachers found peer-group mentoring important for their well-being. Teachers rarely have time for in-depth discussions with their colleagues during their everyday work, and therefore group meetings offered them the much welcomed time, space and opportunity with which to share their experiences.

In chapter 4, Peter Johnson and Suvi Alamaa examined peer-group mentoring from the viewpoint of school culture. Peer-group mentoring can be seen as a shift from a traditional, individualistic working culture in schools towards a more collegial culture. Essential for collegial culture is mutual trust, which is also a prerequisite for sustainable school development.

Anu Hiltula, Leena Isosomppi, Hannu Jokinen and Anu Oksakari continued this discussion in chapter 5 by examining the significance of mentoring with respect to both the individual and the entire work community. Their study indicated that at the individual level, mentoring provided teachers with an opportunity to discuss challenging situations in their everyday work and to share good practices. Many teachers also reported experiences of empowerment and strengthened professional identity through mentoring discussions. Teachers felt that their self-confidence had improved and, as such, they now dared to question established practices. Mentoring was also seen as functional in its support for motivation and well-being. At the community level, implications of peer-group mentoring seem to be possible, but they tend to be indirect rather than direct.

In the city of Oulu, peer-group mentoring was used as a model for professional development and well-being not only for teachers but also for school assistants and school principals. In chapter 6, Päivi Mäki described group-mentoring experiences from the viewpoints of these different professional groups. In the school principals' group, mentoring was regarded more as a forum for discovering new ways of thinking and for conceptual change, rather than as an arena for transmitting existing knowledge. For school assistants, in turn, the peer group provided a constructive environment for professional identity development. School assistant is a new position in the Finnish school system, and therefore its role and tasks are still developing in terms of working in partnership with the teacher. In this situation, school assistants found peer-group support very important for their professional development.

The peer-group mentoring model was introduced into the Finnish school system at a time when education providers were undergoing drastic changes in their administration and organization. Many municipalities were merging to form bigger local administration units. This process affected all sectors of regional services, including education. In chapter 7, Helena Rajakaltio and Eija Syrjäläinen examined the implementation of a peer-group mentoring system in this kind of turbulent situation. Their findings showed that big organizational changes tended to weaken teachers' trust in school administration, from which it followed in turn that teachers had their suspicions towards the introduction of peer-group mentoring as well. However, those who participated in group mentoring reported positive experiences. In this particular case, the mentoring groups were heterogeneous, consisting of diverse teacher groups such as primary and secondary school teachers, and both subject and primary school teachers from different schools. Furthermore, two mentors worked in tandem, sharing the responsibility of leading the group, which made the role of mentor a little different from that in other case studies. All the participants emphasized the rich interactions and reflections in the groups, but it also became clear that the mentoring experiences were not shared in the teachers' work communities. Thus, the findings support those yielded by Hiltula and her colleagues, described above, that the benefits of mentoring for the school community and broader organization remain indirect.

In chapter 8 Minna Ahokas examined peer-group mentoring in a multidisciplinary group in a vocational school. Her findings, which support those of other case studies, clearly indicated that teachers experienced peer-group mentoring with reflective, open, and confidential discussions as very useful for their professional development. Moreover, this study points out that a multiprofessional or interdisciplinary group may bring additional value to mentoring activities. It provides teachers with a forum in which they can meet and share experiences with colleagues with whom they otherwise did not have active contacts. This offers opportunities to get new ideas for and new perspectives on professional problems. Teachers also felt that the interdisciplinary group simulated professional teams typical in the working world.

The study by Maria Lahdenmaa and Hannu Heikkinen (chapter 9) explored whether mentoring groups should be composed of teachers from the same school or from different work communities. Their findings showed that both kinds of group functioned well, although some differences were also found. For example, though socially cohesive from the start, the fixed roles of the participants in the groups of teachers from the same school were considered a negative feature. In contrast, in the groups of teachers from different schools, the absence of old roles was seen to be a strength. The potential of using peer-group mentoring as a tool for developing the whole school community was recognized in the same-school group, while this element was absent in the different-school group.

Leena Syrjälä and Eila Estola (chapter 10) examined peer-group mentoring from the mentor's point of view. Their findings showed the diversity of the meanings that mentors give to this activity. The aims the teachers expressed regarding mentoring ranged from collaborative learning to strengthening of the sense of career well-being, and the tasks of the mentors similarly varied from listening to questioning, and from solving everyday problems to supporting professional identity development.

Group activities always involve certain group dynamics which change over the course of time. In chapter 11, Saara-Leena Kaunisto, Eila Estola and Raimo Niemistö examined the challenges mentors encounter in different phases of a group's development. What is required of a group leader in the starting phase is the ability to establish a functioning group culture and working methods, while later, in a more turbulent phase, it is important to ensure that everyone has an opportunity to share. In a fixed-time mentoring group, it is also important to prepare to the ending of group meetings and the evaluation of activities and achievements.

In the last case study (chapter 12), Sini Teerikorpi and Hannu Heikkinen studied the keys to a successful peer-group mentoring process. In the organization of mentoring, many administrative, physical, social, and methodological factors interact and combine to form the prerequisites for functioning activities. Administrative factors, such as organizational support, and physical factors, for example, a cosy environment, set the general scene for mentoring groups; while social factors, including interaction and group dynamics, as well as methodological factors related to the ways of working, define the actual atmosphere in which the group works. Open communication, trust and commitment create a firm ground for functioning group discussions.

The empirical findings presented in the previous chapters provide a comprehensive and multifaceted image of peer-group mentoring opportunities. The case studies reveal clear patterns comprising seven themes (Aspfors & Hansén, 2011). Six themes touch upon specifically changeable perspectives relating to teachers and peer-group mentoring, while the seventh refers to school management and mentoring. These themes can be grouped into four clearly defined categories. The first looks at the need for *support in the transition to professional life*; the second, the *practical formation of implementing* peer-group mentoring; the third, *the working environment and well-being*; the fourth, *the external structures* which provide the ultimate preconditions for mentoring:

1   Peer-group mentoring and transition to professional life
    • the challenges of transition from teacher education to teaching profession
    • PGM as a flexible tool to support newly qualified teachers
2   Peer-group mentoring in practice
    • group formation
    • role of the mentor
3   Peer-group mentoring for professional well-being
    • potential to develop well-being at work
    • working community
4   Peer-group mentoring and the administrative structures of education
    • essential roles of the principal and the municipality.

Peer-group mentoring and the transition to professional life

The challenges of transition from teacher education to teaching profession

As in many other countries, studies conducted in Finland have shown that the introduction of newly qualified teachers is insufficient in many schools and municipalities, if it exists at all. As a result, there is clearly a need to support the teacher's professional development as effectively and comprehensively as possible. Awareness of the fact that many teachers and principals will be retiring in the next few years accentuates this need for supporting and introducing newly qualified teachers (chapters 4 and 6). In order to address the difficulties faced by new teachers during the transition from teacher education to professional life, such as social integration into the working environment and relations with pupils and their parents, measures taken in the form of mentoring per se are unsatisfactory. Mentoring supports the introduction provided for newcomers to a certain profession but is no substitute for it (chapters 8 and 3).

A more advanced level of interaction is required between teacher education, municipalities and schools in order to prepare new teachers for their professional duties. Greater attention needs to be placed on developing a school's working culture and working environment. During teacher education sessions in Hämeenlinna a recent project took place in which teachers, principals and other school staff from surrounding schools shared their experiences with one another. At the same time, a natural link is established between teacher education and schools as well as between knowledge based on research and knowledge gained from practical experience (chapter 7; cf. Bokeno & Vernon, 2000).

One of the key questions in mentoring is how informal teaching can be linked to formal, abstract, systematic studies. Experiences show that the element concerning formal duties in peer-group mentoring – for example reading literature – is minimal. As a result, the use of literature as a tool for supporting learning needs to be developed in the future. For instance, participants could read various papers between meetings for later discussion in subsequent mentor sessions.

Peer-group mentoring as a flexible tool to support newly qualified teachers

Peer-group mentoring has proved to be a flexible alternative in terms of its form and content. The experiences which have been gathered are encouraging and positive. Its strong point is its informal nature of learning, discussion and sharing experiences, which supports both professional development and well-being at work. Sharing experiences and collective thinking about issues relating to teachers' work contribute to shaping complexities at work.

Compared with one-to-one mentoring, one of the strengths of peer-group mentoring is simplicity and flexibility of *organizing* activities. The town of Kokkola is a pioneer in Finland in the context of systematic support of new teachers (chapter 4). Oulu has also experienced good results from supporting teachers, principals and school assistants with the help of flexible solutions. School assistants in Finland constitute a comparatively new professional group who are in need of specific support to define their job description clearly and strengthen their own professional identity. The role and tasks of school assistants need to be strengthened in relation to teachers, especially when these two parties – teacher and school assistant – operate as a team in the classroom.

This flexibility in peer-group mentoring is regarded as a tool for supporting not only newly qualified teachers but also employees facing new tasks at work – for example, immigrant teachers or upper secondary school teachers embarking upon net-based teaching methods (chapter 6). Peer-group mentoring is thus not bound to one exclusive 'right way' to implement activity but permits many work methods. For instance, it may well be an advantage to employ two teachers as mentors for the same group.

Peer-group mentoring is also flexible in terms of its *content*. In mentor groups teachers can generally decide for themselves about content according to their needs. In groups with new teachers topics discussed have included the disruptive behaviour of pupils, interfaces with parents, their own working environment and interaction with colleagues. These discussions relate to specific areas which participants felt had not been looked at in sufficient depth during their teacher education. In mentor sessions specific pedagogical or didactic solutions or dilemmas are not discussed as frequently. Such issues are more commonly addressed by teachers from middle or upper school years. In groups with special teachers certain pupil incidents and related actions are usually the focus of attention (chapters 4 and 7).

As a result, mentor group discussions are based on specific events from a teacher's working day. The teacher finds it rewarding to be able to share experiences with others while discussing appropriate actions and measures, for example for handling demanding pupils. Thus peer-group mentoring is a flexible form of cooperation (chapter 5).

Peer-group mentoring in practice

Group formation

Within the case studies, participants often discuss optimal group formation in terms of appropriateness and group size. Group formations can be arranged in different ways and various types of experience exist about what works best. In the context of the longest experience of peer-group mentoring, groups with teachers from the same category, such as primary school teachers, subject teachers and special teachers, are seen to be most appropriate (chapter 4). One advantage of homogeneous groups is that participants share similar experiences. There may be a risk here, however, that if teachers in this group already know each other very well, familiar roles will place limits on critical discussion. As a result, it may be easier to discuss openly and critically if participants have not previously met. Many new teachers and mentors thus prefer the option of talking with teachers from a different school instead of colleagues from their own school (chapters 4 and 9). Participants find, in doing so, that a foreman may not be an effective mentor for his teachers or other staff since the situation may lead to a conflict of interest (chapter 8).

Some teachers stress the importance of homogenous mentor groups because discussions may risk becoming superficial and shallow if participants have very different interpretations of their work. Identifying with their own professional group – for example, the opportunity for primary school teachers and subject teachers to discuss their respective jobs – is seen as meaningful. One reason for requesting this type of division is because teacher education, to a great extent, groups primary school teachers and subject teachers into different faculties.

A heterogeneous group of representatives from different professional and subject areas, as well as both new and experienced teachers, can also be enriching by offering new insights and broader perspectives (chapter 7). In the context of teaching, participants often share similar problems and issues regardless of teaching category. Attention, in this case, is focused on common interests concerning practical and pedagogical issues (chapter 8).

However, a very heterogeneous group may also cause tensions and frustration. The danger is that someone with more work experience may dominate group sessions. It is therefore the mentor's task to control and divide up discussions fairly. A 'good sense of fair play' is demanded of the mentor. Further, the prevailing gender order may also establish certain demands, since it is generally women who look for mentoring, as mentors and as participants (chapter 10). A feeling of solidarity is not established straight away but requires a longer period of time. In addition, the precondition for solidarity relates to the size of the group. A group of sixteen participants is far too big. By contrast, groups of six to eight participants are regarded as ideal by many mentors. In addition, groups should ideally comprise no more than two persons from the same place of work, thus preventing the creation of sub-groups (chapter 8).

The mentor's role in a peer-mentoring group

Flexible activity provides opportunities but also places heavy demands on the mentor. Every group is different; thus knowledge about group processes facilitates the work of the mentor. Opening and closing sessions, in particular, require special attention. The mentor is heavily influential on the group culture that is established. The mentor's task when opening sessions is to help participants establish solidarity in the group and secure rules and frameworks with the group. The mentor needs to be able to lead discussions, maintain a balance and ensure that all members have enough time to express themselves. Sometimes a discussion can resemble a collective monologue; the intention behind the contribution is not registered, but each individual talks about himself and his own situation. Contributions to discussions are not coherent because participants are not actually listening to each other but simply preparing themselves for their next contribution. As a result, the whole discussion is characterized by each individual's opinion being conveyed one after another. As mentioned above, a highly developed sense of fair play is required of the mentor, i.e. the ability to help group members respond to each other's intentions and establish coherent discussions. Since meetings are agreed upon in the group, all members know when the last session will be held and can thus prepare themselves mentally for when mentor sessions formally end in their group (chapter 11).

The mentor must also be able to handle expectations which groups sometimes have about ready answers even though there are no 'right solutions'. The mentor must, in particular, be able to ask the right questions at the right time (chapter 10). Applying various work methods within the group also requires courage and an interest in experimenting. Operating as a mentor for a group comprising teachers can in itself be seen as a challenge. As a result, the mentor must have experience, a strong belief in him/herself and the tools to operate as a leader of an adult group. Because the role is demanding, the mentor may also require someone from outside the mentor group to share his experiences with (chapters 8 and 11).

Peer-group mentoring for professional well-being

Potential to develop well-being at work

One clear goal shared by all mentoring participants is the enhancement of well-being at work. Learning together, encouragement, confirmation, respect, active listening and trust are key factors in personal and professional development (chapter 10).

Many teachers mention the positive influence of mentoring on the individual teacher's well-being, mental stamina and workload experiences. Mentorship is an effective way of preventing stress and burnout. Burnout and exhaustion are thus very typical phenomena in today's schools. Even if many teachers find their work interesting and purposeful, the difficulties of establishing one's own limits and the intensive and highly sensitive interaction with pupils, colleagues and the environment suggest a very demanding balancing act. Lack of appreciation and limited opportunities for surveying the consequences of one's work, along with one's own personality as a tool at work, may result in the teacher not being able to cope (chapter 5).

Peer-group mentoring is an effective tool for breaking away from the, by tradition, individual nature of a teacher's job, and building a professional identity based on collective effort. To counter-balance the intensity and exposure of a teacher's job, opportunities are needed to be heard by and with other colleagues in order to put passive knowledge into active words, thereby strengthening reflective awareness. In order to handle stress effectively, it is important to share experiences with others in the same situation (chapter 5).

Working community

One theme regularly discussed is the importance of peer-group mentoring for the working community. A group from the same school will have good preconditions for developing the community. In cases where most participants come from different schools, the chances of sharing experiences in their own community are limited due to confidentiality. Almost all teachers feel that mentoring does not have any direct effect on the working community. Development and change experienced by the individual member of staff may well have an indirect effect on the organization of work, climate of work and mental well-being (chapter 5).

School research shows that development is slow and that the organization puts up defensive barriers towards change. Schools reveal very different types of school culture, in terms of traditions, attitudes and approaches, which leave their mark on the school and determine what may or may not be carried out. Mentor group discussions also expose that various school cultures exist between different schools in the same (local) area. From the perspective of change considered it depends on the type of prevailing school culture. The school organization usually comprises only two hierarchical levels: the teachers and the school management or principals. Teachers are consequently active in the same organization plan, maintaining an attitude of equal importance. However, different teacher groups evaluate and assess one another, consciously or subconsciously, during the school day. While in theory there is de facto equality, in practice various cultures and groupings of teacher are brought to light when conflicts of interest arise – for example, in a process of change (chapter 4).

Peer-group mentoring may be regarded as a way of expressing the need for a strengthened community within the school and greater interaction between the various staff groups. A new school culture is required which focuses on developing cooperation between teachers and professional growth. The transition to cohesive compulsory education (years 0–9) presupposes a school culture involving both primary and secondary levels of education. A mentor group containing representatives from different levels can, as a result, (successfully) conduct discussions on one another's work and create an all-encompassing environment. Mentoring has contributed to development – albeit very gradual – from an individualistic to a collegial school culture. Expanding the school culture in a collegial direction can be further enhanced by other efforts towards development. Reducing the barriers existing between various groups will gradually broaden teaching horizons (chapter 4).

Peer-group mentoring and administrative structures of education

Essential roles of the principal and the municipality

Experiences show that conditions of work vary depending on municipality and that some municipalities do not provide the appropriate support for peer-group mentoring. Depending on which municipality they are employed in, some teachers will be better off than others. The fundamental approach of a municipality or a principal towards mentoring will very often be of great significance as a result. The role and support of the principal, along with an effective working environment, are key factors when receiving new teachers into a school. The workload and stress levels may, however, limit a principal's involvement in peer-group mentoring; for this reason, the principal's work situation, education and knowledge may require close scrutiny (chapters 5 and 7).

For mentoring activities to develop successfully, they must form an integral part of the municipality's school development and not be treated as a separate entity. Mentoring needs therefore to be incorporated into a long-term municipal in-service education strategy. Communication should also be effected vertically so that matters concerning the school's development are passed on from the mentor group to those responsible for education in the local municipality (chapter 7). Mentoring must be recognized in order to have any chance of gaining influence in terms of school development (chapter 5). The case studies reveal that schools represented by some participants did not even know about mentoring as a form of activity (chapter 7).

At times when economic resources are more limited, schools and municipalities may improve their performances by making use of the teachers' expertise in a more flexible and goal-orientated fashion (chapter 6). Peer-group mentoring is

Table 13.1 Summary of findings from the case studies

	Individual	*Community/Organizational*
Prerequisites of functional mentoring activities	• social factors: open atmosphere, mutual trust • methodological factors: rules, agreements	• administrative factors: organizational support • physical factors: time and place convenient
Benefits/implications of peer-group mentoring	• time and space for reflecting and sharing experiences • empowerment and increased self-confidence • professional identity development • conceptual change • increased motivation and well-being	• mainly indirect effects: empowered teachers act as agents of change • more direct effects when teachers come from the same school and when the groups are multidisciplinary

an activity model designed for supporting staff development and well-being at work in an economically beneficial way.

Related to the practical conditions and benefits of peer-group mentoring, the findings of the case studies can be further analysed from four perspectives. On the one hand, we may ask what the prerequisites of successful peer-group mentoring practices are. On the other hand, we may ask what the benefits or implications of PGM may be. Both can be studied on an individual and a social level. The empirical findings for these questions are summarized in Table 13.1.

Challenges in applying peer-group mentoring

Peer-group mentoring has proved to be a flexible and simple social innovation that can be applied in different educational institutions and fields. The experiences are encouraging for both general upper secondary and vocational education. The strength of peer-group mentoring is that informal types of learning – peer dialogue and experience sharing – support both professional development and coping at work (Bokeno & Vernon, 2000; Gardiner, 2010). At its best, the group is an empowering experience of learning together. By sharing experiences and collectively discussing issues related to education, the participants can better discern the complexities of teaching.

Peer-group mentoring seems to be particularly suitable for the Finnish educational system, which is based on teachers' relatively high educational level and professional autonomy. Compared to several other countries, in which schools and teachers are 'controlled from above', Finnish schools are conducted in an independent and self-directed manner. However, more pressure is currently being placed on increasing control in Finland as well. The heightened need for control stems from the rise of neoliberal politics and the new public management approach it has promoted (*New Public Management*; Harvey, 2005).

The new approach to public management is in fundamental conflict with the objective that teachers should be educated to become strong and independent experts in their profession. True professionals do not work under control and standards; rather, they rely on their high-quality expertise and professional ethics. Peer-group mentoring, in which teaching professionals independently further their own expertise, is based on a strong faith in teachers' professional autonomy. Therefore, the Finnish mentoring solution, with its confidence in teachers' reciprocal learning in groups, is very different from some other models of mentoring.

The negative flipside of autonomy is the strong tradition of acting alone which has prevailed in Finnish schools. This challenge has also been highlighted as a popular discussion topic in the mentoring groups. But the genuine meaning of autonomy is not synonymous with individualism – in fact, quite the opposite is true: it is based on a strong communality between professionals. Teachers acting professionally cannot do whatever they want, as their activities are determined by firm professional ethics: whatever teachers do, their ultimate motive is the best interest of the growing and learning child or adolescent. The goal of autonomous teachers' activities is to support these learning individuals' opportunities to lead a good life.

Peer-group mentoring can contribute to breaking the tradition of acting alone and building a more communal professional identity. The communality and reflectivity of school culture are reinforced when collective personnel development models, such as peer-group mentoring, are systematically applied in schools. Peer-group mentoring emphasizes several features of collaborative and cooperative learning (cf. Chaliès et al., 2008), the adoption of which helps school communities advance their operating culture. To achieve this, we must create an open and confidential atmosphere; emphasize peer support and encourage co-workers; underline and promote inclusion; and identify and process the tacit knowledge concealed within the community. Particularly encouraging experiences are yielded from groups that include representatives of different subjects, professions or tasks. Multiprofessional interaction should, indeed, be furthered in various ways, and one effective tool for this purpose is PGM.

The objective of mentoring is to discover tacit knowledge to be processed through words. *Schools should better utilize the fresh perspectives of junior employees.* A new employee in a work community sees with new eyes things that the older ones might take for granted. It is not always easy to receive these observations, and a newcomer's outlook might sometimes be rejected outright. PGM offers a forum for constructive discussion, in which these blind spots of school culture may also be collaboratively scrutinized.

Even though PGM is a promising work method, it is not problem-free. While it has provided good experiences as a tool that promotes communality and autonomy, its challenges and requirements have also been highlighted. The challenges are particularly related to group process management, to finding a balance between formal and informal learning, and to working hours and terms of employment.

The group process is always full of surprises. The mentor needs experience, wisdom, healthy self-esteem, and readiness to act as group leader when necessary, even though he/she in many respects is equal to the other group members. For example, a typical challenge for the group leader is a situation in which a participant starts to dominate the group's activities with his/her speech, overshadowing the others. *The mentor needs support and training in order to be able to act in the correct way within the group process.*

Our experiences of peer-group mentoring show that mentor training is a very important element of the model. In addition to competence related to the group process, mentor training should address the ethics of guidance, themes related to interaction and collective meaning-making process, as well as work community dynamics and well-being. Moreover, mentors should know different practical methods that they can apply as group leaders. Self-regulative competence being one of the major cornerstones of autonomous professionalism, the training should also address themes related to reflectivity and metacognitive skills. These themes are handled in mentor training, whose core content has proved to be expedient. On the other hand, it is important that the content of mentor training remains sufficiently open, so that variations and local conditions can be considered. *One challenge in mentor training is how to better dovetail degree-granting teacher education with mentoring and mentor training.*

One of the key questions in mentoring is how informal learning is linked to formal, conceptual and systematic studying. On the one hand, discussion in groups is very liberating in its informality, thus promoting coping at work. But on the other hand, learning can reach a more profound level if the experiences can be conceptualized, put into words and summarizing theories. Ideally, a balance between formal and informal learning is established in a mentoring group.

The experiences have so far evidenced that the proportion of formal knowledge – for example, reading the literature – is relatively low in the groups. *The utilization of professional literature to support learning in the groups is a future challenge.* It would be possible to apply the Scandinavian tradition of study circles more efficiently in PGM, with its long traditions in adult education. The study circle method involves the group members reading different texts between the meetings and then discussing them. Another method in the utilization of conceptual knowledge is the use of introducers. A brief introduction by an outside expert is usually enough in terms of understanding the phenomenon and opening the key concepts. However, literature or introducers must be brought to PGM in a way which does not extinguish the free, informal conversation, which is the group's core strength.

Our experiences also highlight that the present terms of employment within the field of teaching do not optimally support peer-group mentoring. A common question in teachers' groups is how participation in a mentoring group is seen with respect to a teacher's working time. Traditionally, both mentors and mentees use their working time for mentoring. It is natural that the staff employed within the teaching profession also expect this general principle to apply to themselves. The issue of working hours is strongly highlighted through both positive and negative examples. In the vocational institution, this was not a problem due to the use of a total working time system. In the same way, school assistants' working hours have been clearly fixed as daily working hours, which easily encompass mentoring. By contrast, teachers' working hours are usually determined on the basis of the number of lessons. *Adapting the total working time system for teachers as well would foster the utilization of peer-group mentoring as a social learning innovation.* It would also solve some problems experienced more generally in continuing education.

The transition to working life is a great challenge not only for every teacher and school, but also for the school system and society. However, it would be fruitless to try to solve it as a separate issue. The support provided to teachers in their induction phase is a part of the continuum of teachers' professional development, which begins with teacher education and continues throughout their entire career. Developing teacher education and training to constitute a lifelong process requires the input of several parties: cooperation is needed between teachers, schools, education providers, labour associations, researchers, teacher education institutions and central administration.

Chapter 14

Future perspectives
Peer-group mentoring and international practices for teacher development

Stephen Kemmis and Hannu L. T. Heikkinen

Practices of teacher development

The research and development work to support new teachers in Finland has resulted in a novel peer-group mentoring model (PGM). One of the special features of this model is the inclusion of more experienced teachers alongside new teachers within these groups. The Finns have launched a comprehensive national programme to support new teachers which utilizes the PGM model (Heikkinen et al., 2010). In this chapter, the practices affiliated with this model are studied from an international perspective within the theoretical framework of practice theory.

The need to support new teachers is a global challenge. In Finland, the attrition rate of teachers is still small and, from an international perspective, we might say that attrition is not a serious problem there. Internationally, however, the increasing number of new teachers resigning from teaching has become a concern for educationalists. Despite greater efforts to support early career teachers, problems in the induction phase have increased in some countries. Any procedures and policies to meet this challenge are therefore of great interest (Cochran-Smith & Power, 2010; Hong, 2010; Kutilek & Earnest, 2001; Marvel et al., 2007; Nasser-Abu Alhija & Fresko, 2010; Scheopner, 2010; Tynjälä & Heikkinen, 2011; Välijärvi et al., 2011).

Internationally, the solutions to support new teachers have many similarities, but there are also differences, in part due to the dissimilarities between societies and national educational cultures. In many cases, support for new teachers is almost synonymous with mentoring. In Finland, mentoring is also a key concept of the PGM model. Nonetheless, the PGM model seems not only to be about mentoring in traditional terms but also to present a new *hybrid of practices*. PGM still includes some features of classical mentoring (e.g. Field & Field, 1994) but it also resembles practices such as *study circles* (Rönnerman et al., 2008), *reflecting teams* (Friedman, 1995), *memory work* (Haug, 1987), *peer networking* (Rhodes et al., 2004) and *coaching* (Brockbank & McGill, 2006).

The practices of PGM are so far removed from what is often called mentoring that we may ask whether this is mentoring at all, or something else. Mentoring practices are usually based on an interaction between more experienced and less experienced persons. Mentoring in the traditional sense mostly refers to bilateral guidance, in which a more experienced employee advises a less experienced one. The term mentor is used to refer to this experienced and often socially esteemed person who guides the younger one:

> Mentoring is a process for the informal transmission of knowledge, social capital, and the psychosocial support perceived by the recipient as relevant to work, career, or professional development; mentoring entails informal communication, usually face-to-face and during a sustained period of time, between a person who is perceived to have greater relevant knowledge, wisdom, or experience (the mentor) and a person who is perceived to have less (the protégé).
>
> (Bozeman & Feeney, 2007)

Mentoring usually includes activities and actions such as providing feedback, being a role model and a counsellor, and sometimes even an evaluator who is responsible for assessing the performance of the new teacher. In PGM, the basic arrangement is fundamentally different. The practices are more about dialogue and collaboration than counselling, assessing, providing feedback or transferring (tacit or explicit) knowledge from more experienced teachers to newcomers. Is it appropriate to use the concept of mentoring in this context? Yes, it is, we think. There are features in PGM practices similar to practices in classical mentoring. One of the key elements is that the newcomers in a working society are taken care of by more experienced colleagues.

Still, we may also ask: what is the 'correct' meaning of mentoring? If we put the question like this, we refer to a correspondence theory of truth which implies that the words must have a correspondence with entities that exist regardless of language (Heikkinen et al., 2001). In other words, we should clearly distinguish practices of mentoring which differ characteristically from any other practices. Alternatively, instead of focusing on the correspondence between sentences (the semantic-linguistic realm) and things out in the world (spatial-physical-material realm) we might take a Wittgensteinian view on language. In the latter phase of his career, in *Philosophical Investigations* (1953), Ludwig Wittgenstein located meaning not in words or ideas and their correspondences with entities (objects, states of affairs or events in the world), but in *language games*, that is, the ways in which people use language to orient themselves in the world in the same way. In turn, Wittgenstein located these language games in shared forms of life which make the language games interpretable to those participating in them. Meaning and knowledge are to be found in the 'doing' and the temporally and historically located 'happening' of practices in which particular words are used. In this view, characteristic of social constructivism, concepts are nothing more than temporal agreements in social interaction. On this Wittgensteinian view, there are no 'right' or 'wrong' meanings of 'mentoring'; instead, there are various understandings and conceptualizations of mentoring grounded in different kinds of language games that orient speakers in different kinds of social practices of mentoring (Kemmis, Edwards-Groves et al., 2011; Schatzki, 2002). There will continue to be confusions about what 'mentoring' means because people use the term to describe different kinds of practices, and while they do, the confusion will not be dispelled by agreeing to a definition – a form of words. What would be needed to overcome the confusion, says Wittgenstein, is not an agreement in words but in forms of life – an agreement in the ways mentoring is practised.

The PGM model reflects certain characteristics of international discussion, in effect the *language games of teacher induction*. In the international discourse of induction, the practices to support new teachers have been reduced to the concept of mentoring. Thus, the word 'mentoring' has also been adopted into the Finnish language in quite a straightforward way. Nevertheless, mentoring has become an international mantra in teacher induction, and there seem to be various understandings of (1) the relevant concepts; (2) the activities and actions involved; and (3) the relationships between the people and organizations involved with new teachers. The PGM model is a living example of this. To understand the particularities of the PGM model in an international context, we will take a closer look at teacher development from the perspective of *practice theory*. We will first discuss the notion of *practice architectures* and then *ecologies of practices* (see also Kemmis, Heikkinen et al., 2011; Aspfors et al., 2011).

Practice architectures of teacher development

Mentoring has sometimes been described as 'a practice which is ill-defined, poorly conceptualized and weakly theorized' (Colley, 2003). Our attempt in this chapter is to understand lifelong teacher development as *practices* which are made possible through the particular *practice architectures* that support them. We will study the relationships between the (1) language; (2) activities and 'set-ups'; and (3) social relations in mentoring, teacher education and continuing professional development. These practices may also be understood as *subpractices* of more comprehensive *metapractices* of education and politics (Heikkinen, 2011; Kemmis & Grootenboer, 2008; Kemmis & Smith, 2008; Kemmis, Edwards-Groves et al., 2011).

According to the theory of practice architecture, practices are organized bundles of 'sayings', 'doings' and 'relatings' that 'hang together' (Schatzki, 2002) in the project of a practice – the 'project' of the practice being the overall purpose that gives it some coherence (even if it also contains contradictions). This is a strong claim: that all practices are composed in three dimensions, not in just one or two. The three dimensions are (1) the *semantic* dimension (in which it is possible to say things and be understood); (2) the dimension of *physical space-time* (in which it is possible to carry out relevant activities); and (3) the *social-political* dimension (in which it is possible to relate appropriately to others in the practice).

A practice does not come into existence by producing sayings, doings and relatings out of thin air. It draws upon existing possibilities in each of these dimensions: it is composed from existing *cultural-discursive arrangements* like the languages and specialist discourses that describe and justify the sayings that occur in particular practices; existing *material-economic arrangements* that make possible the doings – the activities – that compose the practice; and existing *social-political arrangements* that make possible the relatings that compose the practice. Peer-group mentoring has a specialist discourse that names and justifies what it is and does; it involves particular distinctive activities, like facilitation and participation in discussions; and it involves distinctive roles aimed at building solidarities among participants rather than the hierarchies of other forms of mentoring that suggest reliance upon the authority of experts. While peer-group mentoring can *now* draw upon *existing* discursive material and social arrangements, these arrangements did not always exist. Like other new or emerging practices, peer-group mentoring came into existence by *transforming* the arrangements characteristic of older practices of mentoring of a novice by a master, arriving at a 'new settlement' in a new specialist discourse, bundled together with new kinds of activities for peers and facilitators, and new, more egalitarian, social relationships between the people involved. When these were bundled together in the new practice, they formed a new complex that makes peer-group mentoring distinct from older, more hierarchical, forms of mentoring.

According to the theory of practice architectures, practices are also *distributed* among and across people – different people may have different parts of the knowledge and 'sayings' and language that constitute the practice as a whole, be involved in different activities in the complex of related activities that constitute it, and play different parts or roles among the complex of parts or roles that together constitute the practice. In the practice of mentoring, for example, some people will have more specialist knowledge of the discourse of mentoring theory even though others successfully participate in the practice without that specialist knowledge; some people will be involved in different activities from others in the process, for example facilitating discussions rather than joining them on the same basis as other participants; and some people will play different roles in the mentoring process – such as the different roles of mentor or facilitator or mentee. The practice, then, is not just held together in the sayings, doings and relatings of a single person, but is both distributed and held together in discursive, material and social interactions among people who are connected to one another in and by the practice.

This last point is also important. Practices are not only *distributed*, they are also *orchestrated*. People do not just join the activities of a practice blindly; with greater or less awareness of the whole, they join into the overarching *project* that the practice accomplishes – they become part of the collective project of the practice. In doing so, they are *stirred in* (Kemmis, Edwards-Groves et al., 2011) to the sayings, doings and relatings characteristic of the practice. That is, they learn 'how to go on' (Wittgenstein, 1953) in their part of the practice, and they come to understand how they are oriented in the practice as a whole, even if they see it mostly from their particular location in the practice without necessarily understanding the whole complex of relationships that are held together in it (in the way that the student in a school classroom doesn't necessarily understand how the teacher's role in the practice of teaching is enabled and constrained by the principal, by the national curriculum or by international PISA testing).

In terms of the theory of practice architectures, then, knowledge of the induction phase in teachers' professional development is distributed among participants and in specific discourses in (1) *semantic space*. Second, activities, such as mentoring, are distributed among participants and in activity systems or networks in (2) *physical space-time*. Third, participants of teacher induction and participation in it are distributed in particular kinds of relationships to one another, and to other objects, in (3) *social space*. Practices of mentoring, in their various forms and at various levels, *hang together* (1) in language and discourses about how to support teachers in their work; (2) in practical arrangements, actions and activity systems intended to provide this support; and (3) in relationships – usually intended to relationships of care and support – among individuals, groups, institutions and others involved (Kemmis & Grootenboer, 2008; Schatzki, 2002). Orders and arrangements in these three kinds of spaces hang together in a more or less coherent *project* (the overarching purpose) of supporting teachers. Nevertheless, this overaching project is realized in various different ways of supporting newly qualified teachers. We can explore these differences in terms of the different ideas (language and discourse) they employ to describe and justify mentoring, the different kinds of activities involved, and the different kinds of relationships they establish between participants in the practice.

Drawing on what has been introduced above, practice is defined in the following way:

> A practice is a coherent and complex form of socially established cooperative human activity in which characteristic arrangements of activities (doings) are comprehensible in terms of characteristic arrangements of relevant ideas in discourses (sayings), and when the people and objects involved are distributed in characteristic arrangements of relationships (relatings), and when this complex of sayings, doings and relatings 'hangs together' in a distinctive project.
>
> (Kemmis, Edwards-Groves et al., 2011)

From this standpoint, teacher induction is a special kind of social project, a practice constituted of characteristic arrangements in the sense that it is conceptualized in a given way, composed of particular activities and actions, and distributed through characteristic social arrangements between the people involved. The practice develops and is held in place both in terms of the *agency and actions of individuals*, and in terms of the *cultural-discursive, material-economic and social-political enabling preconditions* that make practices of induction possible.

Practices are always situated in time and space, and unfold in site ontologies (Schatzki, 2005). They are not merely set in, but always already shaped by, the particular historically given conditions that exist in particular localities or sites at particular moments. Specifically, practices of teacher development are always constituted in and through the particular cultural–discursive, material–economic and social–political conditions that exist in the site. This embeddedness is illustrated in Fig. 14.1.

Schatzki (2002) describes practices as 'the site of the social'. As a practice, or family of practices, then, teacher development is a *social site* – it is where people coexist for the particular purpose of assisting teachers to develop other practices – their practices of teaching and professional learning, for example. The material site, in space and time, inhabited by practices of teacher development, is also home to other practices. That is, other practices overlap with practices of teacher development in physical space and time. Practices of teacher development not only overlap, but also have resonances with, educational practices found in initial and continuing teacher education, in the administrative and collegial practices of schools, in the administrative and professional development practices of municipalities, in the industrial and advocacy practices of teacher unions, and in the practices of other related educational and political institutions, professions and social networks. Elements of these different kinds

Individual and collective *practice* constitues, and is constitued in, action via	Characteristic	Dimension/medium	Practice architectures constitute, and are constituted in, action via	The world we share:
	Characteristic **'sayings'** (and *thinking*)	The *cultural-discursive* dimension (*semantic space*) realized in the medium of *language*	Characteristic **cultural-discursive** arrangements	
The individual: **Education and the good for each person** Education for living well	Characteristic **'doings'** (and **'set-ups'** of objects)	The *material-economic* dimension (*physical space*) realized in the medium of activity and work	Characteristic **material-economic** arrangements	The world we share: **Education and the good for humankind** Education for a world worth living in
	Characteristic **'relatings'**	The *social-political* dimension (*social space*) realized in the medium of *power*	Characteristic **social-political** arrangements	
	which are bundled together in characteristic ways in distinctive *projects*.		which are bundled together in characteristic ways in *practice traditions*.	

Figure 14.1 Practice architectures (Kemmis, Edwards-Groves et al., 2011)

of practices jostle together in ways that enable and constrain and thus give distinctive shapes to particular practices of teacher induction and mentoring as they occur in particular locations. Those other practices come together in different ways to shape the overarching project of support for teachers differently in each place where it occurs – though with family resemblances that make these shapes comprehensible as (a project of) teacher development. In one kind of induction practice, for example, the emphasis may be on supporting a new teacher to adapt to the administrative procedures of the workplace; in another, the emphasis may be on continuing the professional education of the teacher in a transitional phase understood to exist between the initial teacher education phase and mid-career continuing professional development.

The semantic space of teacher development

In order to comprehend a practice as a practice of teacher development, it must exist in a semantic space populated by ideas (sayings or potential sayings) that appear in some discourse – that is, in some discursive arrangement that makes ideas about teacher development meaningful. In *(1) semantic space*, we can find various expressions which people use to discuss what is going on in schools as new teachers enter the profession. Some speak about *new teachers* and others refer to *young teachers*, which is not necessarily the same thing. In the Nordic languages, there are expressions such as *nya lärare* (Swedish), *nyutdannet lærere* (Norwegian), *algajate õpetajate* (Estonian) and *uudet opettajat* (Finnish) which refer to new teachers. These concepts carry specific connotations within these different languages and they are not always directly synonymous with each other. There are also concepts such as *novice* or *novice teacher* which carry heavy connotations relating to the practices of preparing members of religious orders in the Catholic Church, and apprenticeship practices in the guilds of the Middle Ages, referring to less experienced young people following more experienced and older role models. Lately, the concept *newly qualified teachers* or the abbreviation *NQTs* has become more popular, especially in the UK, and has rapidly spread to other countries, even to non-English-speaking areas. In Australia, the expression *early career teachers* is commonly used.

The semantic space of *mentoring* is a contested space. For example, there has been lively and intense discussion on the similarities and differences between the concepts of *coaching* and *mentoring* (e.g. Brockbank & McGill, 2006). In many countries, the concept of *induction* has taken the primary role in conceptualization. In Danish, Swedish, Norwegian, Swedish, Estonian and Finnish this word has been adopted with slight linguistic finetuning. In the Estonian national context, teacher educators talk about *kutseaasta*, which refers to the induction year (Poom-Valickis, 2008). The support for new teachers is usually conceptualized as *mentoring*, with national variations such as *mentorlus* in Estonian. Mentoring has also been conceptualized as *veiledning* in Norwegian, which literally means 'leading someone the (right) way'. A very similar expression is the Swedish *handledning* which means that someone takes the newcomer by the hand to lead him/her the (right) way.

In Finnish, the concept *mentorointi* also comes directly from English. This conceptualization has gradually turned more into expressions such as *ryhmämentorointi* ('group mentoring') and *vertaisryhmämentorointi* ('peer-group mentoring'), along with a growing emphasis on equal interaction between peers in the international discussion of mentoring (Gardiner, 2010; Le Cornu, 2005; Rhodes et al., 2004). In Finland, a special national tradition, close to mentoring, is the practice tradition called *työnohjaus*. This concept is difficult to translate without additional overlays of meaning being added to the original Finnish expression. Sometimes *työnohjaus* has been translated as 'clinical supervision', sometimes as 'work counselling', sometimes simply 'supervision'. There are many similar elements in *työnohjaus* and peer-group mentoring: both aim at professional development and well-being through professional discussion in groups. *Työnohjaus* and PGM are, however, based on different theoretical and conceptual frameworks, and there are also differences in the practical arrangements and actions involved, and the kinds of social relations expected among the participants. For example, the facilitator of the *työnohjaus* group is an expert in supervision but not typically an expert in the professional field concerned, whereas a PGM mentor is another teacher who shares educational expertise with the other participants of the group.

These examples illustrate how practices of mentoring have been differently conceptualized, with different overtones of meaning – sometimes in contrasting ways (for example, conceptualizing mentoring as based on a hierarchical relationship between mentor and mentee versus conceptualizing it as a process of peer support among newly qualified teachers). We could continue with more examples in languages throughout the world. The spectrum of expressions used in this field is vivid and versatile. The international language games of teacher induction and mentoring are blended and intermingled with national language games in many ways.

Brockbank and McGill (2006, p. 1) believe that the terminology in the mentoring research literature is confused and confusing. For us, such 'confusion' is an excellent example of what takes place in the *semantic space* of practice. That practices are conceptualized in various ways within as well as between countries makes it possible to *discuss* what is done and what should be done so that the participants of the discourse can understand each other. Through all these *sayings* (Kemmis & Grootenboer, 2008), people aspire to clarify their ideas and better communicate with one another. However, it should not be supposed that particular words mean the same thing for all participants in a discourse. Each participant in the discussion has individual perceptions and experiences and understands the world on the basis of their own concepts, assumptions and ideas. Therefore, it is impossible to think that the concepts could actually carry the same meanings for all the participants of the practice. Discussion, nevertheless, helps to maintain practice in a reasonable and productive way, and, as Wittgenstein

(1953) showed, participation in language games allows participants to orient themselves to the world in common ways.

The physical time-space of teacher development

Practices of teacher development also take place in the dimension of *(2) physical time-space*, in the *activities and actions* that occur to support a new teacher entering a school, for example, and the material 'set-ups' or arrangements of physical objects to be found at the sites where teachers actually experience induction. Practices of induction are formed through certain ways of *doing* things in teacher education institutions and schools in the course of *time*. The dimension of the physical time-space of practice can also be understood in terms of *time-space geography* which traces its roots back to the Swedish geographer Torsten Hägerstrand (1975). In his theory, he built a model which demonstrates the interconnectedness of the temporal factor and the spatial factor in human activities and actions. *The time-space path*, devised by Hägerstrand, shows the movement of an individual in the spatial-temporal environment with the constraints placed on the individual by these two factors. Hägerstrand's theory on time-space geography is a sophisticated way to describe a person's behaviour in a given physical setting. In the theory of practice architectures, the time-space dimension is studied at various levels of generality. We may study the activities and actions of a teacher in a given school context but we may also study the practices of teaching within the physical time-space dimension at a very high level of generality.

According to Schatzki an activity is a 'temporalspatial event' (2010, p. 171). He writes:

> The event of activity has a structure quite unlike that of other events. It is a temporal event in the sense of the temporality of the activity. More specifically, it has three temporal dimensions, namely, coming toward that for the sake of which one acts (the future), coming or departing from that to or in the light of which one reacts (the past) and acting itself (the present). I summarily abridged this structure as teleologically acting motivatedly. Activity is a temporal event.
>
> (Schatzki, 2010, p. 170)

Unlike Hägerstrand, Schatzki sharply distinguishes *the time-space of human activity* from the abstract matrix of space and time (2010, pp. 1–20). The time-space of human activity is the time and space that unfolds as a particular activity unfolds through time in particular places. He says: 'The timespace of human activity consists in acting toward ends departing from what motivates at arrays of places and paths anchored at entities' (2010, pp. 38–40) and 'The timespace of human activity is acting toward an end from what motivates at place-path regions anchored at objects' (2010, p. 41). When we observe activities in teacher development, therefore, we look for the particular *ends* that guide the activities (like helping teachers), *the things that motivate* them (like the difficulties teachers face in developing their practice), and the *paths* and *places* those activities go through (like the path from a discussion group to a lesson where an idea is tried out and to another discussion – a path that passes through places and times for collective and individual reflection).

In the dimension of physical space-time, we refer to specific arrangements of objects and activities to support teachers early in their career, including the final stage of pre-service education and the initial phase of an in-service career. In some countries and traditions, new teachers are not supported at all; in others they are well supported. We may call the former a 'sink or swim' mindset; in other words, new teachers are just thrown into school and gradually it becomes apparent whether they will survive or not. Even more, it appears that in some places and traditions where the 'sink or swim' view is found, new teachers sometimes have excessive burdens placed on them in their first years of teaching (Bjerkholt, 2011, p. 9; Howe, 2006, pp. 289–291).

In other contexts, mentoring and support are organized more or less formally. There are remarkable variations between activities and actions between and within nations. Methods used to promote professional development include mentoring, orientation, workshops, distribution of written materials, classroom observation, internship, reduced work load and time given for reflection and collaboration with colleagues. The most common component of induction programmes is to assign a suitable mentor to a new teacher (Alhija & Fresko, 2010; Howe, 2006; Ingersoll & Smith, 2004; Wong, 2004). Howe's (2006, p. 287) review of teacher induction programmes in Australia, Britain, Canada, France, Germany, Japan, New Zealand and the United States concluded that the most effective teacher induction programmes include opportunities for new and experienced teachers to learn together in a supportive environment that promotes time for collaboration and reflection (Aspfors et al., 2012).

The activities and arrangements in the PGM model fit well with Howe's description of best practices of induction. In PGM, the key element is the peer-group meeting, where new and more experienced teachers meet in a supportive setting. The peer group allocates time for sharing actual and challenging issues experienced by group members so as to enable reflection and to empower the participants of the peer-mentoring group.

The social space of teacher development

Practices of induction and mentoring also take place in a social setting, in the dimension of *(3) social space*. Practices are always social by nature. Practices *are* practices because they involve characteristic relationships between people *and* between people and objects. Social space is relationally constituted – that is, in relations between persons. In different kinds of mentoring, new teachers and more experienced teachers relate to each other in different ways. These patterns of relationships are not only constituted *formally* within the educational system with its apparatus of curricula, grades and diplomas, but also *non-formally* in the everyday life of schools outside formally established learning, and *informally*, as part of the non-intentional and sometimes incidental learning that occurs in the personal meaning-making processes of everyday life. The learning and professional development of teachers might best be seen as a continuing process combining formal, non-formal and informal learning throughout their careers, supported by a variety of educational practice architectures that constitute the sayings, doings and relatings of teachers' practices in different ways in different settings.

In the social space of teacher induction, the relationship between a mentor and a mentee is of great interest. In chapter 1 of this book, Heikkinen, Jokinen and Tynjälä suggest that mentor and mentee may be regarded as equals at the *existential level*, whereas there are differences between them at the *epistemic level* in terms of knowledge and expertise. At the *juridical level*, in terms of duties, rights and responsibilities, we also find some differences between the mentor and the mentee. The mentor is the one responsible for the activities in a way that supports the professional development of the mentee in line with the aims which have been negotiated together with the employer (usually but not always, in Europe, the municipality). On the other hand, the PGM mentor is also paid for the running of the peer-mentoring group, unlike the other participants. Thus, there are some aspects at the juridical level which mean that PGM mentors are not equal to the others in the group. It is important to detect these three levels in the social space at the micro level of a peer-mentoring group clearly enough. The fact that the PGM mentor has more responsibilities and duties at the juridical level does not predict that there are any differences at the existential level.

At the macro level, we may also detect social *metapractices* (practices that shape the form and conduct of other practices) which affect the practices of teacher development. Social space is not only constructed of the person-to-person (lifeworld) social relations between individuals but also about the (system) relationships between educational and political organizations and institutions. Among the metapractices shaping the conduct and conditions of teacher development are:

- metapractices of *initial and continuing teacher education* that form and shape the practices of teacher development and how these, in turn, are shaped by and shape
- metapractices of *politics and administration* that determine the resources, infrastructure and policies that influence the conditions for educational practices, including those of teacher development, and how all of these are shaped by and shape
- metapractices of *educational research and evaluation* that shape and are shaped by the practice of education and the other metapractices by suggesting how

these other metapractices can be understood, and by monitoring the conduct and consequences of the other metapractices, as well as

- metapractices of *student and teacher learning in schools* that shape the form and conduct of teacher development practices as they actually occur, and, in turn, are shaped by the effects of teacher development on the ways teachers teach and create conditions for learning for students and for teacher colleagues.

Peer-group mentoring is an essentially Finnish way of organizing support for new teachers – a new practice that is evolving in the educational system which has sometimes been ranked the best in the world (Foroohar, 2010; Sahlberg, 2011; Simola, 2005). The PGM model has been developed within a specific social setting, one in which Finnish educationalists, teacher unions, politicians and educational administrators relate to each other in a particular way. The practices of induction are formed within local, national and international metapractices. Educational practices are bound to societal practices in general. To some extent, educational practices are constituted by the jurisdiction of the state via its administrative and leadership apparatus and practices. All this, to a greater or lesser extent, determines the content and conduct of educational practices in schools. But there are also professional practices which are not so directly derived from administration and jurisdiction. The more autonomous the profession, the more practices are built up by professionals on the basis of the expert knowledge of the profession.

Nevertheless, the metapractices of politics and education are mutually interdependent, influencing and being influenced by one another. In different parts of the world, and within individual states, the complex of metapractices that constitute contemporary schooling vary locally, but they still have 'family resemblances' (Wittgenstein, 1953) while varying in their content and conduct across states, regions and schools.

In particular, one current political metapractice requires closer attention. In recent times, internationally (and especially in OECD countries) there have been reforms in public administration described as new public management (NPM). NPM is a management philosophy used with the intention of modernizing the public sector to imitate practices said to be characteristic of the private sector. NPM is based on the classic Taylorian division of labour, in which the planning and control of work are separate from its performance. According to this theory, work performances must be itemized so that they can be unambiguously measured and controlled. Applied in the field of educational policy and administration, NPM has fostered initiatives that have led to the standardization of teaching. Another of the main hypotheses of new public management is that a greater market orientation in the public sector will lead to greater cost efficiency. According to Pasi Sahlberg (2010), this neoliberal movement has been adopted as the official agenda or accepted as educational orthodoxy in many countries, including the USA, the UK and Germany. Thus, educational practices, including those related to teacher development, have been affected by political metapractices rooted in neoliberal beliefs. This has led to a growing interest among policy makers and government officials in the standardization and control of educational practices, including those of teacher development.

At the macro level, we view the Nordic models of teacher development in the context of a (post-) welfare state, drawing from Nordic traditions of democracy, being challenged by the neoliberalist trends which have influenced many education reforms throughout the world. Generally speaking, Finnish education systems have remained quite unreceptive to the neoliberal wave (Sahlberg, 2010). The PGM model reflects the Finnish way of educational reform which has a high level of teacher autonomy. Finns seem to build on a culture of responsibility and trust that values teachers as professionals (Sahlberg, 2010, p. 11). Contrary to many of the mentoring programmes worldwide, no elements of assessment, standardization or control are involved. Instead, working in a peer-mentoring group offers opportunities for both new and experienced teachers to learn together in a supportive environment that promotes time for collaboration and reflection. Thus PGM is in line with the general pedagogical trends in Finland which emphasize the social construction of knowledge (Heikkinen, Jokinen et al., 2008). As Jouni Välijärvi and Hannu Heikkinen describe in chapter 2 in this book, the high professional autonomy of teachers, based on trust, seems to have a highly significant role in the excellent results in student achievement in an international comparison.

Ecologies of practices for teacher development

In the previous section, we used the metaphor of 'practice architecture' as our starting point. This is a typical metaphor for a scientific theory: it uses vocabulary which is rooted in the conceptual sphere of construction and architecture. We often see theories as buildings: we establish a *foundation* for a theory, and we speak about a *framework*. A good theory is *supported* with *strong* arguments, *buttressed* with facts, etc. George Lakoff and Mark Johnson have suggested that metaphors are not just about the style and form of text and communication, but that metaphors are fundamentally important cognitively. Metaphors serve to facilitate understanding through expressions that relate to another, more familiar conceptual domain, typically a more concrete one. Human thought is rooted in using metaphors. In *Metaphors We Live By* (1980), Lakoff and Johnson say that metaphors are pervasive in everyday life, not just in language, but also in thought and action. They explain how a metaphor is simply understanding and experiencing one kind of thing in terms of another. Lakoff and Johnson give several examples of the use of daily metaphors; our conceptual system is fundamentally rooted in metaphors.

Any metaphor has its strengths and weaknesses. A problem of the basic metaphor typical for science, construction and architecture is that it creates an image of something static and stationary, like a building that was planned long ago and remains a stable and fixed form. Practices, however, are not static but in constant motion: practices are something mobile and changeable; they are in progress; they change and develop endlessly over the course of time. We think we have good reason to say that practices can be understood very much like *living things* (Kemmis et al., 2012; Kemmis et al., 2009). Moreover, practices are interdependent with other practices to which they are connected. These attributes are taken into account in the theory of *ecologies of practice*.

This theoretical apparatus is not an alternative to the metaphor of *practice architectures* but complementary to it. The metaphor of practice architectures suggests how a practice is supported by language and discursive arrangements, temporal and physical arrangements, social-political arrangements and an overarching project that constitute it. By enabling and constraining practices, practice architectures prefigure the social world for those who inhabit the practice.

The framework of *ecologies of practice* (Kemmis et al., 2012; Kemmis et al., 2009) draws our attention to the interdependence among particular clusters of practices, and the ways particular practices interact and influence one another, so that one practice produces outcomes or products that are taken up in others. This is invoked in the notion of *Zusammenhang* or 'hanging together' (Schatzki, 1996; Wittgenstein, 1953) by which human beings and human lives coexist in 'the social' and 'sociality'. The theory of ecologies of practice explores whether and (if so) how practices are ecologically connected with one another (Kemmis et al., 2012; Kemmis et al., 2009).

Kemmis and Mutton say:

> By ecologies of practice we mean distinctive interconnected webs of human social activities (characteristic arrangements of sayings, doings and relatings) that are mutually necessary to order and sustain a practice as a practice of a particular kind and complexity (for example, a progressive educational practice).
>
> (Kemmis & Mutton, 2011, p. 15)

We are accustomed to thinking about relationships between practices in terms of the relationships between the *practitioners* who relate to one another in practice, but we are less familiar with thinking about relationships between *practices themselves*. The focus in ecologies of practice is on how practices relate to one another, not so much with how participants of the practice relate to one another. Practices exist in ecological relationships with one another and in whole ecosystems of interrelated practices.

Kemmis et al. (2012) and Kemmis et al. (2009) have shown how it makes sense to say that practices live in ecological relationships with one another using principles derived from Fritjof Capra's principles of ecology (Capra, 2004 and

2005; see also Center of Ecoliteracy, 2011). Capra describes this notion of living systems in the following way:

> First, *every living organism*, from the smallest bacterium to all the varieties of plants and animals, including humans, is a living system. Second, *the parts of living systems* are themselves living systems. A leaf is a living system. A muscle is a living system. Every cell in our bodies is a living system. Third, *communities of organisms*, including both ecosystems and human social systems such as families, schools and other human communities, are living systems.
>
> (Capra, 2005, p. 19)

Capra lists eight principles of ecology which can be applied to any practices, including educational practices. Here, we follow Capra's specification, but we add a ninth principle of ecology, that is *ecological niches*. Throughout these nine principles, we intend to show how (1) practices, by analogy with species, and (2) ecologies of practices, by analogy with ecosystems, meet the criteria implied by these nine principles of ecology. Our aim is to show how practices related to teacher development behave in accordance with these principles (Table 14.1).

To explore these principles in the context of teacher development and especially in the Finnish peer-group mentoring model, we introduce the following examples of the principles of ecology:

Networks

> Different practices derive their essential properties and their existence from their relationships with other practices.

The practices of teacher induction are developed in networks of other educational and political practices (Hedegaard, 2008). A practice like teacher induction derives its essential properties and its existence from its relation with other practices, for example the social practices of a society or state which the practice of education informs and influences, and which, in turn, inform and influence the conduct and content of education. These networks are not always well defined and explicit but more often tacit and implicit in nature. The networks in schools, teacher education and continuous professional development are more often informal and based on self-organization. Some of the networks are explicit and take a formalized form.

The Finnish PGM model has been developed within a number of networks which are both formal and informal. In this book there are descriptions of various kinds of networks in the empirical articles. Actually, a peer-mentoring group itself is a small network, and the mentors who guide the peer-mentoring groups form networks with each other more or less formally or informally. Nationally, the network of Finnish teacher educators Osaava Verme has

Table 14.1 Ecological principles

Ecological principles	If practices are living things and ecologies of practices are living systems, then ...
Networks	Practices derive their essential properties and their existence from their relationships with other practices.
Nested systems	Different levels and networks of practice are nested within one another.
Niches	In ecology, a niche is the relational position or function of an organism in an ecosystem of plants and animals. The ecological niche describes how an organism or population responds to the distribution of resources and competitors and how it in turn alters those same factors. Likewise, there are 'niches for practices' within other practices.
Interdependence	Practices are dependent on one another in ecology of practices as are ecologies of practices.
Diversity	An ecology of practices includes many different practices with overlapping ecological functions that can partially replace one another.
Cycles	Some (particular) kinds of matter (or in education – practice architectures, activities, orders or arrangements) cycle through practices or ecologies of practices – for example, as in a food chain.
Flows	Energy flows through an ecology of practices and the practices within it, being transformed from one kind of energy to another (in the way that solar energy is converted into chemical energy by photosynthesis) and eventually being dissipated.
Development	Practices and ecologies of practices develop through stages.
Dynamic balance	An ecology of practices regulates itself through processes of self-organization, and (up to breaking point) maintains its continuity in relation to internal and outside pressures.

Source: Cf. Capra, 2004 and 2005; Center of Ecoliteracy, 2011; Kemmis et al., 2012; Kemmis et al., 2009.

contributed to the PGM model. This network has been clearly formalized, but there are also plenty of other more informal networks which have influenced PGM, such as networks of narrative research, action research and 'slow science', some of which have been built up and reshaped over years, and others of which are rapidly emerging in social media. Internationally, contributions to the PGM model have been made in particular by Australian, Nordic and Estonian advocates of teacher education and educational action research. An example of a formally established network that has contributed to PGM is the NQT-COME network which is focused on teacher induction. Another well-established network with a significant impact on PGM is the international Pedagogy, Education and Praxis (PEP) group, constituted mostly of Australian and European researchers, which has contributed to the practice theory. In all these networks, practices derive their properties and their existence from their relationships with other practices. PGM mentoring is one of the practices which exists in relation to other ways of supporting new teachers, ways of developing these practices, conceptualizing them, and doing research on the various practices of induction.

Nested systems

Different levels and networks of practice are nested within one another.

The complex of practices that constitute the PGM mentoring model appear to be 'nested' in other practices and in this way to be ecologically related. This book offers examples of nested systems, especially in Peter Johnson and Suvi Alamaa's chapter (chapter 4) which introduces the interesting idea of sustainable development for educational practices. Their chapter indicates how mentoring is tightly nested in the school practices and educational administration in the city of Kokkola. The practices of teacher induction are constituted in a complex of metapractices of education, initial and continuing teacher education, educational policy and administration, and educational research and evaluation. Together, these metapractices may be said to form an ecology within which the different metapractices are *nested*. Each of these metapractices shapes and influences the others that are 'external' to it, and each metapractice, in turn, shapes and influences other practices that are internal or subsidiary to it. Teacher induction, for example, is nested in the practices of teacher education and the continuing professional development of teachers, which in turn are nested in the practices of education. A simplified illustration of this nestedness is visualized in Fig. 14.2.

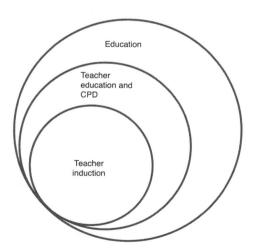

Figure 14.2 The nestedness of practices of teacher development

These practices are nested in the sense that they enable and constrain one another. They are also nested in another sense, namely, as similar kinds of activity across different levels of metapractices like collaborative learning in groups in Finnish pre-service teacher education, in peer-group mentoring, and in the education of PGM mentors, all of which are expected to demonstrate collaborative forms of work. There are other forms of nesting, too, from large scales of activity to lower levels of activity, and from overarching long-term projects to the short-term projects of particular professional learning or student classroom learning practices.

Niches

> In ecology, the concept of niche refers to the distribution of resources and competitors necessary for the survival of an organism. Practices also exist in niches that are composed of bundles of cultural-discursive, material-economic and social-political arrangements, distinctive of that particular practice, that are necessary for the practice to be enacted and even to exist.

The concept of 'niche' is close to the idea of 'nestedness', but emphasizes instead the particular substantive content of an environment that provides an organism – or a practice – with the conditions it needs to survive. According to Smith (1999), drawing upon the ideas of Gibson (1986), an ecological niche is

> that into which an animal *fits* . . . The niche is that in relation to which the animal is habituated in its behavior (Gibson, 1986, p. 129). It embraces not only things of different sorts, but also shapes, textures, boundaries (surfaces, edges), all of which are organized in such a way as to enjoy affordance-character for the animal in question in the sense that they are relevant to its survival. The given features motivate the organism; they are such as to intrude upon its life, to stimulate the organism in a range of different ways.
> (Smith, 1999, p. 126)

Its 'niche' similarly motivates and stimulates a practice, providing it with motivations (points of departure), purposes (ends), and the characteristic places and paths in and through which it is enacted (cf. Schatzki, 2010, on the time-space of human activity). The niche supplies the discursive means for the distinctive sayings, the material means for the distinctive doings, and the social-political means for the distinctive relatings that are enacted when the practice is conducted. Without its niche, the practice cannot be enacted and it cannot survive. On the other hand, a suitable niche can exist and then be colonized by a practice (as when a school that has been closed re-opens, and classroom teaching once again comes to exist there). This relationship is complex, however, because many aspects of the niches of practices do not occur in the absence of human agency but as a result of it – as languages and discourses are made and developed by linguistic communities, for example. In this sense, practices appear to build the niches that support them. Put more precisely: both niche and practice develop and evolve in interaction with one another.

The concept is used not only in ecology but also in business and economy. A niche market is the subset of the market on which a specific product focuses; therefore the market niche defines the specific product features aimed at satisfying specific market needs. In both contexts, the entity (an organism or a product) finds its ideal living space in relation to other entities in given conditions and circumstances.

We may claim that in Finland there seems to be a niche for peer-group mentoring. The model has found its relational position in the ecologies of practices of teacher education, continuing professional development and other educational practices. We may also claim that the classical one-to-one mentoring has not found a niche in Finland. This traditional model of mentoring was actually launched in the capital and surrounding area of Finland at the beginning of the 2000s, but it faded away within a number of years and practically no remnants of it seem to be left. Instead, the PGM model is being disseminated in the area of the capital. Why this niche exists is a question that still needs to be more closely examined. Nevertheless, something in the Finnish niche of teacher induction has made it possible for PGM mentoring rather than the classical model to prevail. However, some new attempts have lately been made to implant an American model of mentoring into Finland. History will show how imported practices survive within the local ecosystem of educational practices. The new species might also modify a niche more suitable for it; practices for teacher induction and the niche which exists within educational metapractices develop in interaction with one another.

Interdependence

> Different practices (understood as different species of practices, manifested in particular individual instances of that practice) are dependent on one another in ecologies of practices (understood as ecosystems) and can be sustained only in interaction with these other practices. In turn, whole ecologies of practices are dependent upon their relationships with other ecologies (as a coastal rainforest may be dependent on an alpine ecology above it), and sustainable only by their connections with these other ecologies.

All educational practices, like teacher induction, are dependent upon one another and dependent upon their relationships with the processes and practices of the wider society in which they exist. Some of these practices are even *symbiotic*. In Europe, specific national educational practices may also be more or less interdependent with practices in other countries, as well as with other metapractices (like educational leadership and administration) nationally and transnationally. At the international level, a clear indication of the interdependence of the practices of teacher induction is that the European Union and the OECD have released a number of political outlines for teacher education and also for teacher induction (European Commission, 2001, 2006, 2007, 2010; OECD, 2000, 2005).

In this book, examples of interdependence between the practices at the national level can be found. In the introduction of this book, the career-long continuum of teacher professional development is based on the interdependence between initial teacher education, the induction phase and in-service education. The PGM model is also interdependent with other educational and political practices such as the collective labour agreements of teachers.

Diversity

> An ecology of practices includes many different practices with partially overlapping ecological functions that can partially replace one another.

In teacher induction, many practices seem to co-exist and overlap with one another – like group facilitation and group participation; individual and collective self-reflection; group meetings and meetings of members outside scheduled whole-group meetings; and peer mentoring and mentoring by experts. At particular moments in the overall practice of mentoring, one of these pairs of activities may substitute for or replace the other.

In Finland, the PGM model seems to be an emerging approach, but there are other practices, such as *työnohjaus* ('clinical supervision'), which come very close to PGM. At the national level, there are also other more informal and spontaneous ways to support new teachers creating diversity. In many schools, there are special local practices through which new teachers are supported. These arrangements diversify according to the size of the school and municipality as well as, for example, the geographical and population structures. In the capital area, for example, the practical arrangements are very different from those in northern Finland. In Lapland, a new teacher has to travel long distances to find another new teacher, whereas in Helsinki and other places new teachers can find many peers in a small geographical area.

At the international level, we may find a lot of diversity in the practices of teacher education and induction. In many countries, the practices of induction are more or less based on classical mentoring. Sometimes the term 'tutoring' is even used synonymously with mentoring. In the school context, tutoring often refers to older students, i.e. tutors, acting as advisers, guides and 'databanks' for younger students or pupils. Tutoring activities have been actively developed in various educational institutions; for example, most universities provide yearly tutor training for students to be able to support new students. Tutoring is sometimes also provided by teachers: at the initial stage, student groups are guided by one of the school's teachers. Here the main difference between tutoring and mentoring is the context: tutoring is mainly used in an educational context while mentoring mainly occurs in working life. In other words, tutoring is associated with formal education, while mentoring is a form of non-formal training and guidance implemented in the workplace. As the forms of non-formal and formal education overlap, it is natural that the interpretations of mentoring and tutoring also overlap to some extent.

Sometimes, however, the term tutor is used in the context of working life, for example in the UK where the term 'induction tutor' has been introduced. The induction tutor is a more experienced teacher who has day-to-day responsibility for monitoring, supporting and assessing a newly qualified teacher. Induction tutors are expected to provide guidance and support, and make judgements on the performance of the new teacher through formative assessment activities that include observations and meetings to review progress at least every half term. The induction tutor is expected to provide formative assessment and often to be involved in the formal, summative assessment at the end of induction (Training and Development Agency for Schools, 2011).

Coaching has been adopted into working life as a staff training method. Its meaning is fairly broad and vague, and its relations to the concepts of mentoring and on-the-job-instruction are interpreted in a variety of ways. It is common for training enterprises to offer coaching and mentoring simultaneously. Educational services are marketed under the concept of coaching, often in the context of such names as *change coaching*, *solution-based coaching* and *life coaching*. The educational market even uses the concept of *brain-based coaching*, which is said to rely on the latest scientific brain research. The courses are fairly expensive and intended as training for business staff. When exploring the offerings of commercial educational enterprises, we cannot avoid getting the impression that expensive educational product brands are deliberately built on mental images associated with scientific research. A closer look at them often demonstrates that the scientific warrant for their claims is thin.

The concept of coaching has also been linked to mentoring outside business staff training. In the context of teacher education, the term 'coaching' is often used synonymously with 'mentoring'. Mentoring in these contexts is associated with supervision and control, whereas coaching provokes the mental image of support provided to students in a way that respects their autonomy, in order for them to achieve the goals they have set for themselves. This interpretation, however, has not been broadly used within the international teacher education debate.

In international comparisons, we also find very special kinds of system such as the German two-step model into the profession, *Vorbereitungsdienst*. This includes mentoring, a reduced teaching load, formal theoretical seminars, and informal learning through gradual introduction to teaching with explicit feedback (Lohmar & Eckhardt, 2010). In the UK, the induction year includes measures such as a 10 per cent reduction in teaching load, meetings with a named induction tutor, an individualized programme of support and monitoring, half-termly observations of teaching and an assessment meeting each term (Williams, 2003; Jones, 2006). We may say that these systems are examples of the diversity of practices of induction; they have overlapping ecological functions that, in principle, might partially replace one another.

The diversity between practices may be identified in the three dimensions described earlier. We may find variation in (1) the conceptualization of induction in *semantic space* as well as (2) a variety of practical arrangements and actions (in *physical space-time*) and (3) social relations (in *social* space). A good example of this diversity is the Norwegian practice of *veiledning* related to that of 'mentoring'. The Norwegians seem not to have a national consensus about the meaning of the concept of *veiledning* (Olsen, 2011, p. 16). There are also some advocates of 'mentoring' in Norway, and this conceptualization seems to be associated with a specific group of educationalists who highlight certain differences in how things are done within the practice of 'mentoring'. Thus, the diversity is not only about the concepts but also about actions and arrangements, and about a collective identity of researchers and teacher educators. The collective identity of advocates of 'mentoring' is being achieved through a sense of 'otherness' from the people associated with *veiledning*. The diversity between these practices also shows us the interconnections between the three spaces of practice: the 'hanging together' of semantic space, social space and physical space-time. How things are done in different places is related to how those actions and arrangements are conceptualized, and to how the agents and actors are socially interrelated as individuals and social groups.

Cycles

It is possible to observe some kind of matter cycling through practices.

From this perspective we observe some kind of matter cycling through practices as in a food chain. Although the concept of 'chain' seems linear, it is in fact a cycle in which the predators at the top of the food chain die and are eaten by creatures further down. Specific practices cycle through history in the form of practice traditions that vary across time and space. For example, a child becomes a student who practises learning from a teacher who practises teaching, and goes on to become a teacher teaching students in the rising generations that follow. In turn, a new teacher enters the practice traditions of the school and the national educational culture. Some of these practice traditions seem to carry features of the initiation rites of ancient tribes: the newcomer has to meet with pain and public humiliation so as to achieve the status of adult and full member of the tribe. In military service, for example, there is a long tradition of humiliation of newcomers, and we may easily find sad examples of those practices being reproduced by new generations within the school tradition. The long practice tradition of mentoring, by contrast, emphasizes support and care for the newcomer.

In this cyclical process of circulating practice traditions, specific kinds of ideas (knowledge of education or mentoring, etc.), particular kinds of activities (assessment, lecturing, giving feedback, group work, etc.), and particular kinds of relationship (the relationships between new teachers, experienced teachers, school principals, etc.) are reproduced over time and over generations. These practice traditions are not, however, reproduced without variation of difference; they are also constantly being transformed in the light of changing historical, social and local conditions. Thus, ideas that first emerged centuries or millennia ago still circulate today with changed nuances or more elaborate meanings – or even come to mean something very different from what they once meant. And the same holds true for different kinds of activity and different kinds of relationship between people in different roles. For example, the relationships between more experienced teachers and new teachers and students are being reproduced and transformed in cyclical way. When new practices emerge, they are composed of elements or features of previous practices which are being circulated in new composition.

Circulation of practices is evident in the various national practices of supporting new teachers. They circulate practices related to each other and to the local traditions. The national Norwegian practice of *veiledning* in support of new teachers is an example of this. It circulates fruitfully many of the practices common to many of the pre-service teacher education programmes in the Western world, such as professional autonomy, reflection and professional identity work. In the Finnish PGM model, we also find the cyclical processes of international and national practices used in pre-service teacher education. In initial teacher education in Finland today, reflection in peer groups is supported in quite similar ways to those of PGM. There are also some practices of reflection in PGM which are familiar from the tradition of action research – practices that are adopted in Finnish pre-service teacher education as well as in PGM. These reflective practices are recycled in the peer-mentoring groups, and these educational ideas are also circulated in the education of mentors. Thus, the circulation of practices takes place in many ways and at many levels, and the 'food chains' may be longer or shorter, as they are in ecology.

Flows

> Energy flows through ecologies of practices and the practices within them, being transformed from one kind of energy to another (in the way that solar energy is converted into chemical energy by photosynthesis) and eventually being dissipated.

In ecology, physical energy is transformed from one form to another as it flows through biological systems. In relation to the human and social world, we might think analogously about the different kinds of energy transferred and expended as people conduct practices. Like other biological organisms, of course, the participants in a practice need and expend *physical energy*. That is, physical energy flows through practices as it does through the 'doing' of the people involved in a practice. We want to suggest, however, that there are also different forms of energy that flow through practices: what we might call *semantic energy*, which flows through practitioners' 'sayings' in practice, and *social energy* that flows through practitioners' 'relatings' in practice. In each of these additional dimensions, then, we suggest that there is a flow of energy analogous to the flow of physical energy through the biological entities participating (Kemmis et al., 2012; Kemmis et al., 2009).

Adapting Kemmis et al. (2012) and Kemmis et al. (2009), we may say that three forms of energy flow in and through the practices of teacher induction:

1 *Meaning* in the semantic dimension, transmitted in the medium of language, which flows through the sayings characteristic of a practice. For example, the conceptualization of mentoring and teacher induction that flows from the national and international discourse of educational researchers to the national semantic space of teacher education and school practices;
2 *Physical energy* in the dimension of material space-time, transmitted in the medium of activity and work; as, for example, when money and other material resources flow from Finnish and European taxpayers into the public funds to be expended in practices like research on teacher induction, PGM, and other forms of support for new teachers;
3 *Social connectedness* (which includes *social differentiation* and *distinction* as well as *solidarity*) in the dimension of social space, transmitted in the medium of power, which flows through the relatings characteristic of practices, such as relationships between researchers, teacher educators, teaching unions, and educational policy makers and administrators in municipalities.

Development

Practices develop through stages, and ecologies of practices also develop through stages.

It is evident that practices of teacher induction have evolved from the practices of mentoring over a long time. The origin of the concept of mentoring is based on Homer's (eighth-to-sixth-century BCE) epic poem *The Odyssey* about Odysseus, King of Ithaca. In this ancient tale, Odysseus asked his friend Mentor to watch over his son Telemachus while he fought in the Trojan War. The first recorded modern usage of the term has been traced to another book, *Les Aventures de Telemaque*, written by Francois Fénelon in 1699 in France. This is regarded as the source for the modern use of the word 'mentor' in the sense of trusted friend, counsellor or teacher, usually a more experienced person. In traditional one-to-one mentoring, newcomers are paired with more experienced people, who advise them and serve as role models. Today, mentors often provide expertise to less experienced individuals to help them advance in their careers, enhance their education, and build networks. In education, this kind of mentoring seems still to be the most common internationally. Newer forms of mentoring practice such as PGM have emerged in more recent years, however – so the practice of mentoring seems to be developing.

Likewise, mentoring as a part of the induction arrangements for new teachers is developing within wider ecologies of practices. In places where teacher education is regarded as the formation of each individual teacher, and where induction is seen as the responsibility of an employer to each individual employee, then more individualist forms of mentoring are likely to be found: an individualist perspective pervades the whole ecology of practices. In other places, however, more communitarian or collectivist kinds of practices relate to one another in more collectivist ecologies of practices. Thus, for example, when collective self-reflection is a key element in pre-service teacher education on the one hand, and in school development (e.g. through action research projects) on the other, a more collectivist form of mentoring like PGM is likely to thrive because a collectivist ethic pervades this ecology of practices.

The practices of PGM have clearly developed through stages. The development of the PGM model in Finland started from the classical one-to-one model. In the city of Kokkola there were not enough mentors for all the mentees in 2005, and the educational administrators of the city decided to put more mentees together in a group guided by one mentor. This arrangement was found beneficial, and the group-mentoring model was implemented more consciously as the support systems for new teachers were developed through action research in the cities of Hämeenlinna, Jyväskylä, Oulu and Tampere. Later on, the education of mentors was further systematized and formalized, and the PGM model was implemented nationwide by all teacher education institutions. Thus, there have been many developmental stages in the social space of teacher induction in Finland. In the semantic space, we may also distinguish clear stages. Initially, the method was simply called group mentoring. Over time and with international collaboration, a conceptual-theoretical energy flow in the semantic dimension and the medium of language, and a growing emphasis on reflective discussion among peers, the method was conceptualized as peer-group mentoring, the final step being the acronym PGM.

Dynamic balance

Ecologies of practices regulate themselves through processes of self-organization, and maintain (up to breaking point) their continuity in relation to internal and outside pressures.

Living systems are not static. They are in a dynamic balance rather than the kind of balance reached when opposing forces are equal, things are in stasis, and action stops. Living systems are characterized by constant change, as are practices in the day-to-day life of a school or classroom. Teacher education and the continuing professional development of teachers may be understood as a form of biological ecosystem that also illustrates this kind of dynamic balance. But keeping things in balance is possible only within limits. As Capra (2004) indicates, living systems continually bring themselves back into balance when they encounter crisis points, resistance, critical incidents, confusion, instability, lack of flexibility and disturbance.

In the case of the practices of teacher induction, we may say that many national practices of education have reached a crisis point or a critical stage as the number of teacher retirements and resignations has increased. To address a crisis in the teaching workforce, governments have been finding new balances within and between different ways of conceptualizing the process of beginning teaching, the material–economic resources allocated to teacher education and induction, and ways of connecting the students and teachers involved in pre-service teacher education, teachers in schools, new teachers coming to schools, and the people who assist them in making their transition into school work and school as a workplace. As they do so, they are developing a variety of individual practices that make up this ecology of practices, thus assisting the development of the ecology as a whole.

The need to maintain a dynamic balance can also be detected in smaller practices, such as PGM. For example, the regional needs in the capital area of Finland have to be balanced with those of other regions, some of them sparsely populated rural areas with long distances between schools and fewer municipal resources. Thus, the national resources which may be allocated to support new teachers must be balanced within this complicated field of practices.

Conclusions: Peer-group mentoring as an emerging practice

The professional development of teachers is a multifaceted issue. It can be understood as a specific kind of *practice* which is constituted through doing things and conceptualizing things related to professional development in a certain way, all of this taking place in a complicated social setting. In order to understand the practices of teacher induction and professional development, relationships between language, the activities and actions, and social relations must be taken into account. Thus, within the theory of practice architecture, practices of teacher development must be studied in *cultural-discursive, material-economic* and *social-political dimensions*.

In this book, the focus has been on the Finnish model of teacher development and teacher induction – PGM model. This book is based on theoretical and philosophical background as well as empirical evidence on the model. The

PGM model has been studied both in an international setting and in the context of its specific national characteristics. On the one hand, this model may be considered a typically Finnish practice: it is based on the comparatively high level of autonomy of Finnish teachers and the high academic level of pre-service teacher education. On the other hand, the practices of PGM reflect international currents in teacher education: aspirations to reflective practices in teacher education with a view to building bridges between educational theory and practice. Peer-group mentoring also links to ideas of autonomy and emancipation that have been emphasized in the long tradition of educational action research, which, according to Wilfred Carr and Stephen Kemmis (1984, p. 221), aims at providing a means by which 'teachers can organize themselves as communities of enquirers, organizing their own enlightenment'. Peer-group mentoring is a living example of 'communities of enquirers'. At least it gives some space for teachers to create communities for enlightenment. However, it remains to be seen how this space will be used and how it will develop; how the emerging 'niche' for PGM will be constituted in the future in the ecologies of practices of education in Finland and elsewhere, and how it will, in turn, have an effect on the ecologies of practices of teacher development internationally.

References

Aitolehti, S. & Silvola, K. (2007). Mitä psykodraama on? In S. Aitolehti & K. Silvola (eds), *Suhteiden näyttämöt: Näkökulmia psykodraamaan* (pp. 11–22). Jyväskylä: Gummerus.

Alhija, F. & Fresko, B. (2010). Socialization of new teachers: Does induction matter? *Teaching and Teacher Education*, 26, 1592–1597.

Almiala, M. (2008). *Mieli paloi muualle – opettajan työuran muutos ja ammatillisen identiteetin rakentuminen.* Joensuu: University of Joensuu.

Angelique, H., Kyle, K. & Taylor, E. (2002). Mentors and muses: New strategies for academic success. *Innovative Higher Education*, 26(3), 195–209.

Arnkil, R. (2008). Remembering the future: Future dialogue and the future of dialogising. In J. Lehtonen & S. Kalliola (eds), *Dialogue in Working Life Research and Development in Finland* (pp. 131–143). Frankfurt Am Main: Peter Lang.

Arrow, H., Poole, M., Henry, K., Wheelan, S. & Moreland, R. (2004). Time, change, and development: The temporal perspective on groups. *Small Group Research*, 35(1), 73–105.

Aspfors, J. & Hansén, S.-E. (2011). Gruppmentorskapets många ansikter – en metanalys av möjligheter och utmaningar. In J. Aspfors & S.-E. Hansén (eds), *Gruppmentorskap för nya lärare* (pp. 108–124). Stockholm: Södeströms.

Aspfors, J., Hansén, S.-E. & Heikkinen, H. (2011). Nya lärares erfarenheter av gruppmentorskap i ljuset av praktikens arkitektur. In J. Aspfors & S.-E. Hansén (eds), *Gruppmentorskap för nya lärare* (pp. 79–93). Stockholm: Södeströms.

Aspfors, J., Fransson, G. & Heikkinen, H.L.T. (2012). Mentoring as dialogue, collaboration and/or assessment? In P. Tynjälä, M.-L. Stenström & M. Saarnivaara (eds), *Transitions and Transformations in Learning and Education*. Dordrecht: Springer. In press.

Ax, J. & Ponte, P. (2008). *Critiquing Practice*. Rotterdam: Sense.

Becher, T. (1989). *Academic Tribes and Territories: Intellectual Enquiry and the Cultures of Disciplines.* Stony Stratford: Society for Research into Higher Education.

Beck, U. (1997). *The Reinvention of Politics*. Cambridge: Polity Press.

Bereiter, C. (2002). *Education and Mind in the Knowledge Age*. Mahwah, NJ: Erlbaum.

Bereiter, C. & Scardamalia, M. (1993). *Surpassing Ourselves: An Inquiry into the Nature and Implications of Expertise*. Chicago, IL: Open Court.

Berg, G. (2003). *Att förstå skolan*. Lund: Studentlitteratur.

Bickmore, D.L. & Bickmore, S.T. (2010). A multifaceted approach to teacher induction. *Teaching and Teacher Education*, 26(4), 1004–1014.

Bjerkholt, E. (2011). Veiledning av de nye lærere i barnehage, grunnskole og videregående upplæring. In E. Høihilder & K.-R. Olsen (eds), *Veiledning av de nye lærere i skole og barnehage* (pp. 8–13). Oslo: PEDLEX.

Blatner, A. (1996). *Acting-in: Practical applications of psychodramatic methods.* New York: Springer.

Blomberg, S. (2008). *Noviisiopettajana peruskoulussa – aloittelevien opettajien autenttisia kokemuksia ensimmäisestä lukuvuodesta* (Tutkimuksia No. 291). Helsinki: Helsingin yliopisto, Soveltavan kasvatustieteen laitos.

Bokeno, R. & Vernon, W. (2000). Dialogic mentoring. *Management Communication Quarterly,* 14(2), 237–270.

Boreen, J. & Niday, D. (2000). Breaking through the isolation: Mentoring beginning teachers. *Journal of Adolescent & Adult Literacy,* 44(2), 152–163.

Bourdieu, P. (1986). The forms of capital. In J. Richardson (ed.), *Handbook of Theory and Research for the Sociology of Education* (pp. 241–258). New York: Greenwood.

Bozeman, B. & Feeney, M.K. (2007). Toward a useful theory of mentoring: A conceptual analysis and critique. *Administration & Society,* 39(6), 719–739.

Brockbank, A. & McGill, I. (2006). *Facilitating Reflective Learning through Mentoring & Coaching.* London: Kogan Page.

Burke, L.A. & Miller, M.K. (1999). Taking the mystery out of intuitive decision making. *Academy of Management Executive,* 13(4), 91–99.

Capra. F. (2004). *The Hidden Connections: A Science for Sustainable Living.* New York: Anchor.

—— (2005). Speaking nature's language: Principles for sustainibility. In M. K. Stone & Z. Barlow (eds), *Ecological Literacy: Educating our Children for a Sustainable World* (pp. 18–29). San Francisco: Sierra Club Books.

Carey, M.A. (1994). The group effect in focus groups: Planning, implementing, and interpreting focus group research. In J. M. Morse (ed.), *Critical Issues in Qualitative Research Methods* (pp. 225–241). London: Sage.

Carr, W. & Kemmis, S. (1984). *Becoming Critical: Education, Knowledge and Action Reseaerch.* London: Falmer.

Center of Ecoliteracy. (2011). *Ecological Principles.* Retrieved from http://www.ecoliteracy.org/nature-our-teacher/ecological-principles.

Chaliès, S., Bertone, S., Flavier, E. & Durand, M. (2008). Effects of collaborative mentoring on the articulation of training and classroom situations: A case study in the French school system. *Teaching and Teacher Education,* 24(3), 550–563.

Cochran-Smith, M. & Power, C. (2010). New directions for teacher preparation. *Educational Leadership,* 30(3), 6–13.

Colley, H. (2003). *Mentoring for Social Inclusion: A Critical Approach to Nurturing Mentoring Relationships.* London: RoutledgeFalmer.

Cross, S. (1998). Roots and wings: Mentoring. *Innovations in Education and Training International,* 35(3), 224–30.

Denzin, N.K. & Lincoln, Y.S. (2005). The introduction: The discipline and practice of qualitative research. In N.K. Denzin & Y.S. Lincoln (eds), *Handbook of Qualitative Research* (pp. 1–32). Thousand Oaks: Sage Publications.

Eisenschmidt, E., Heikkinen, H.L.T & Klages, W. (2008). Strong, competent and vulnerable. Experiences of the first year as a teacher. In G. Fransson & C. Gustafsson (eds), *Newly Qualified Teachers in Northern Europe. Comparative Perspectives on Promoting Professional Development* (Research publication No. 4, pp. 125–147). Gävle: University of Gävle, Teacher Education.

Elbaz-Luwisch, F. (1992). Hope, attentiveness, and caring for difference: The moral voice in teaching. *Teaching and Teacher Education,* 8(5/6), 421–432.

—— (2005). *Teachers' Voices: Storytelling and Possibility.* Greenwich, CT: Information Age Publishing.

Eraut, M. (2004). Transfer of knowledge between education and workplace settings. In H. Rainbird, A. Fuller & A. Munro (eds), *Workplace Learning in Context* (pp. 201–221). London: Routledge.

Erkkilä, R. (2005). *Moniääninen paikka – Opettajien kertomuksia elämästä ja koulutyöstä Lapissa* (Acta Universitatis Ouluensis No. E 79). Oulu: Oulun yliopisto.

Eskola, J. & Suoranta, J. (1998). *Johdatus laadulliseen tutkimukseen*. Tampere: Vastapaino.

Estola, E. (2003). *In the Language of the Mother – Re-storying the Relational Moral in Teachers' Stories* (Acta Universitatis Ouluensis No. E 62). Oulu: Oulun yliopisto.

Estola, E., Kaunisto, S.-L., Keski-Filppula, U., Syrjälä, L. & Uitto, M. (2007). *Lupa puhua Kertomisen voima arjessa ja työssä*. Jyväskylä: PS-kustannus.

European Commission. (2001). *Making a European Area of Lifelong Learning a Reality*. Brussels: Commission of the European Communities. Retrieved from http://www.bologna-berlin2003.de/pdf/MitteilungEng.pdf.

—— (2006). *Operational Guide for Clusters and Peer Learning Activities (PLAs) in the Context of the Education and Training 2010 Work Programme*. Brussels: European Commission.

—— (2007). *Improving the Quality of Teacher Education*. Communication from the Commission to the Council and the European Parliament. Brussels: Author. Retrieved from http://ec.europa.eu/education/com392_en.pdf.

—— (2010). *Developing Coherent and System-Wide Induction Programmes for Beginning Teachers: A handbook for Policymakers*. European Commission Staff Working Document SEC (2010) 538 final. Brussels: Commission of the European Communities. Retrieved from http://www.kslll.net/Documents/Teachers%20and%20Trainers%202010%20Policy%20handbook.pdf.

Field, B. & Field, T. (1994). *Teachers as Mentors: A Practical Guide*. London: Falmer.

Fontana, A. & Frey, J.H. (2005). The interview: From neutral stance to political involvement. In N.K. Denzin & Y.S. Lincoln (eds), *Handbook of Qualitative Research* (pp. 695–727). Thousand Oaks: Sage Publications.

Förbom, M. (2003). *Mentori – aloittelevan opettajan käsikirja*. Helsinki: Tammi.

Foroohar, R. (2010). The best countries in the world. *Newsweek, 156*(8/9), 30–38.

Fransson, G. & Gustafson, C. (eds). (2008). *Newly Qualified Teachers in Northern Europe. Comparative Perspectives on Promoting Professional Development* (Research Publications No 4). Gävle: University of Gävle, Teacher Education.

Friedman, S. (ed.). (1995). *The Reflecting Team in Action: Collaborative Practice in Family Therapy*. New York: Guilford Press.

Fullan, M. (2001). *The New Meaning of Educational Change*. New York: Teachers College Press.

—— (2005). *Leadership and sustainability: System thinkers in action*. Thousand Oaks, CA: Corwin Press.

Gadamer, H.-G. (1975). *Wahrheit und Methode*. Mohr: Tübingen.

Gardiner, W. (2010). Mentoring two student teachers: Mentors' perceptions on peer placements. *Teaching Education, 21*(3), 233–246.

Gibson, J.J. (1986). *The ecological Approach to Visual Perception*. Hillsdale, NJ: Lawrence Erlbaum Associates.

Glass, N. & Walter, R. (2000). An experience of peer mentoring with student nurses: Enhancement of personal and professional growth. *Journal of Nursing Education, 39*(4), 155–160.

Goodson, I.F. (2005). *Vad är professionell kunskap? Förändrade värderingar av lärares yrkesroll*. Lund: Studentlitteratur.

Haarakangas, K. (2008). *Parantava puhe*. Helsinki: Magentum.

Hadot, P. (1995). *Philosophy as a Way of Life*. Oxford: Blackwell.

Hägerstrand, T. (1975). Space, time and human conditions. In A. Karlqvist, L. Lundqvist & F. Snickars (eds), *Dynamic Allocation of Urban Space* (pp. 3–14). Lexington: Lexington Books.

Haikonen, M. (1999). *Konflikteista aiheutuva stressi ja siitä selviytyminen opettajan työssä* (Tutkimusraportteja No. 1). Helsinki: Helsingin yliopisto.

Hargreaves, A. (1994). *Changing Teachers, Changing Times. Teachers' Work and Culture in the Postmodern Age*. London: Castell.

—— (1998). Pushing the boundaries of educational change. In A. Hargreaves, A. Lieberman, M. Fullan & D. Hopkins (eds), *International Handbook of Educational Change* (pp. 281–294). Dordrecht: Kluwer Academic Publishers.

—— (2000). *Changing Teachers, Changing Times: Teachers' Work and Culture in the Postmodern Age* (5th edn). New York: Teachers College Press.

—— (2001a). Emotional geographies of teaching. *Teachers College Record, 103*(6), 1056–1080.

—— (2001b). The emotional geographies of teachers' relations with colleagues. *International Journal of Educational Research, 35*(5), 503–525.

—— (2005). Sustainable leadership. In B. Davies (ed.), *The Essentials of School Leadership*. London: Sage.

Hargreaves, A. & Fink, D. (2006). *Sustainable Leadership*. San Francisco: Jossey-Bass Publishers.

Harvey, D. (2005). *A Brief History of Neoliberalism*. Oxford: Oxford University Press.

Harris, M. & Chisholm, C. (2011). Beyond the workplace: Learning in the lifeplace. In M. Malloch, L. Cairns, K. Evans & B. N. O'Connor (eds), *The SAGE Handbook of Workplace Learning*. London: Sage.

Haug, F. (1987). *Female Sexualization: A Collective Work of Memory*. London: Verso.

Hedegaard, E. (2008). Development of networking and networks. In G. Fransson & C. Gustafsson (eds), *Newly Qualified Teachers in Northern Europe. Comparative Perspectives on Promoting Professional Development* (Research Publications No. 4, pp. 148–166). Gävle: University of Gävle, Teacher Education.

Heikkilä-Laakso, K. & Heikkilä, J. (1997). *Innovatiivisuutta etsimässä. Irtiotto keskinkertaisuudesta* (Julkaisusarja No. B 57). Turku: Turun yliopisto, Opettajankoulutuslaitos.

Heikkinen, H.L.T. (2001). *Toimintatutkimus, tarinat ja opettajaksi tulemisen taito. Narratiivisen identiteettityön kehittäminen opettajankoulutuksessa toimintatutkimuksen avulla* [Action research, narratives and the art of becoming a teacher. Developing narrative identity work in teacher education through action research; in Finnish] (Jyväskylä Studies in Education, Psychology and Social Research No. 175). Jyväskylä: Jyväskylän yliopisto.

—— (2003). *Becoming a Teacher – Struggling for Recognition*. A paper presented at the European Congress on Educational Research, Hamburg, Germany. Retrieved from http://www.leeds.ac.uk/educol/documents/00003446.htm.

—— (2011). *Understanding Induction of New Teachers as Practice Architectures*. A paper presented at the NERA, Jyväskylä, Finland. Retrieved from http://ktl.jyu.fi/ktl/nqtne/presentations.

Heikkinen, H.L.T. & Huttunen, R. (2008). Hiljainen tieto, mentorointi ja vertaistuki [Tacit knowledge, mentoring and peer support; in Finnish]. In A. Toom, J. Onnismaa & A. Kajanto (eds), *Hiljainen tieto, tietämistä, toimimista, taitavuutta* [Tacit knowledge. Knowing, acting, knowing how; in Finnish] (Aikuiskasvatuksen vuosikirja No. 47, pp. 203–220). Helsinki: Kansanvalistusseura/Aikuiskasvatuksen tutkimusseura.

Heikkinen, H.L.T., Huttunen, R. & Kakkori, L. (2001). This is my truth tell me yours. Some aspects of action research quality in the light of truth theories. *Educational Action Research, 9*(1), 9–24.

Heikkinen, H.L.T., Jokinen, H. & Tynjälä, P. (2008). Reconceptualising mentoring as a dialogue. In G. Fransson & C. Gustafsson (eds), *Newly Qualified Teachers in Northern Europe. Comparative Perspectives on Promoting Professional Development* (Research Publications No. 4, pp. 107–124). Gävle: University of Gävle, Teacher Education.

—— (2010). *Verme. Vertaisryhmämentorointi työssä oppimisen tukena* [Supporting learning at work through Peer Group Mentoring; in Finnish]. Helsinki: Tammi.

Heikkinen, H., Tynjälä, P. & Kiviniemi, U. (2011). Integrative pedagogy in practicum. In M. Mattsson, T.V. Eilertsen & D. Rorrison (eds), *A Practicum Turn in Teacher Education*. Rotterdam: Sense Publishers.

Hill, T. & Westbrook, R. (1997). SWOT analysis: It's time for a product recall. *Long Range Planning, 30*(1), 46–52.

Hiltula, A. & Oksakari, A. (2010). *Mentorointi – Matka opettajana kasvamiseen. Ryhmämentoroinnin merkitys opettajien ja rehtoreiden kokemana* (Master's thesis). Jyväskylä: Jyväskylän yliopisto, Kokkolan yliopistokeskus Chydenius, Opettajankoulutuslaitos.

Hobson, A., Ashby, P., Malderez, A. & Tomlinson, P.D. (2009). Mentoring beginning teachers: What we know and what we don't. *Teaching and Teacher Education, 25*(1), 207–216.

Holbeche, L. (1996). Peer mentoring: The challenges and opportunities. *Career Development International, 1*(7), 24–27.

Hong, J.Y. (2010). Pre-service and beginning teachers' professional identity and its relation to dropping out of the profession. *Teaching and Teacher Education, 26*, 1530–1543.

Honneth, A. (1995). *The Struggle for Recognition. The Moral Grammar of Social Conflicts*. Cambridge: Polity.

Howe, E.R. (2006). Exemplary teacher induction: An international review. *Educational Philosophy and Theory, 38*(3), 287–297.

Huber, C. (2010). Professional Learning 2.0. *Educational Leadership, 31*(3), 41–46.

Huttunen, R. (2003). *Kommunikatiivinen opettaminen – Indoktrinaation kriittinen teoria.* Jyväskylä: Sophi.

Ingersoll, R. (2003). *Is There Really a Teacher Shortage? A Research Report.* Seattle, WA: University of Washington, Center for the Study of Teaching and Policy.

Ingersoll, R. & Smith, T. (2004). Do teacher induction and mentoring matter? *National Association of Secondary School Principals Bulletin, 88*(638), 28–40.

Isaacs, I. (1999). *Dialogue and the Art of Thinking Together*. Garden City, NY: Doubleday.

Jakku-Sihvonen, R. & Niemi, H. (2005). *Thirty Years Research-Based Teacher Education – a Finnish Case.* Paper presented at the symposium A Nordic Dimension in Education and Research – Myth or Reality? of the Nordic Educational Research Association (NERA). Oslo, Norway.

Johnson, P. (2006). *Rakenteissa kiinni? Perusopetuksen yhtenäistämisprosessi kunnan kouluorganisaation muutoshaasteena* (Doctoral dissertation). Kokkola: Jyväskylän yliopisto, Chydenius-instituutti.

Johnson, P. (2007). Peruskoulun kehittämisen mahdollisuudet. In P. Johnson (ed.), *Suuntana yhtenäinen perusopetus.* Jyväskylä: PS-kustannus.

Johnson, P. & Salo, P. (2008). Koulun kestävän kehityksen edellytyksistä. In P. Johnson & K. Tanttu (eds), *Kestäviä ratkaisuja kouluun.* Jyväskylä: PS-kustannus.

Jokinen, H. & Sarja, A. (2006). Mentorointi uusien opettajien tueksi. In A.-R. Nummenmaa & J. Välijärvi (eds), *Opettajan työ ja oppiminen* (pp. 183–198). Jyväskylä: Jyväskylän yliopisto, Koulutuksen tutkimuslaitos.

Jokinen, H. & Välijärvi, J. (2006). Making mentoring a tool for supporting teachers' professional development. In R. Jakku-Sihvonen & H. Niemi (eds), *Research-Based Teacher*

Education in Finland: Reflections by Finnish Teacher Educators (Research in Educational Sciences No. 25, pp. 89–101). Turku: Finnish Educational Research Association.

Jokinen, H., Heikkinen, H.L.T. & Välijärvi, J. (2006). *Mentoring in Supporting Newly Qualified Teachers' Professional Development: Individualism or Organisation Development.* Paper presented in ATEE 2005 Conference web publication (pp. 219–222). Retrieved from http://www. atee2005.nl/publ/papers.htm.

Jokinen, H., Morberg, Å., Poom-Valickis, K. & Rohtma, V. (2008). Mentoring of newly qualified teachers in Estonia, Finland and Sweden. In G. Fransson & C. Gustafsson (eds), *Newly qualified teachers in Northern Europe. Comparative perspectives on promoting professional development* (Research Publications No. 4, pp. 76–106). Gävle: University of Gävle, Teacher Education.

Jones, M. (2006). The balancing act of mentoring: Mediating between newcomers and communities of practice. In C. Cullingford (ed.), *Mentoring in Education: An International Perspective* (pp. 57–86). Aldershot: Ashgate.

Kalimo, R. & Toppinen, S. (1997). *Työuupumus Suomen työikäisellä väestöllä.* Helsinki: Työterveyslaitos.

Kalliola, S. & Nakari, R. (2007). Renewing occupational cultures – bridging boundaries in learning spaces. *International Journal of Education Research, 46*(3/4), 190–203.

Kamberelis, G. & Dimitriadis, G. (2005). Strategic articulations of pedagogy, politics, and inquiry. In N.K. Denzin & Y.S. Lincoln (eds), *Handbook of Qualitative Research* (pp. 887–907). Thousand Oaks: Sage Publications.

Kansanen, P. (1999a). Research-based teacher education. In J. Hytönen, C. Razdevšek-Pu ko & G. Smith (eds), *Teacher Education for Changing School* (pp. 135–141). Ljubljana: University of Ljubljana, Faculty of Education.

—— (1999b). Teaching and teaching-studying-learning interaction. *Scandinavian Journal of Educational Research, 43*(1), 81–89.

Karjalainen, M., Heikkinen, H.L.T., Huttunen, R. & Saarnivaara, M. (2006). Dialogi ja vertaisuus mentoroinnissa. *Aikuiskasvatus, 26*(2), 96–103.

Kaunisto, S.-L., Uitto, M., Estola, E. & Syrjälä, L. (2009). Ohjattu vertaisryhmä haavoittuvuudesta kertomisen paikkana. *Kasvatus, 40*(5), 454–464.

Kelchtermans, G. & Ballet, K. (2002). The micropolitics of teacher education. A narrative-biographical study on teacher socialization. *Teaching and Teacher Education, 18*(1), 105–120.

Kemmis, S. (2008). Preface. In S. Kemmis & T. Smith (eds), *Enabling Practice. Challenges for Education* (pp. xi–xiii). Rotterdam: Sense.

Kemmis, S. & Grootenboer, P. (2008). Situating praxis in practice: Practice architectures and the cultural, social and material conditions for practice. In S. Kemmis & T.J. Smith (eds), *Enabling Practice. Challenges for Education* (pp. 37–62). Rotterdam: Sense.

Kemmis, S. & Mutton, R. (2011). Education for sustainability (EfS): Practice and practice architectures. *Environmental Education Research.* Manuscript submitted for publication. doi: 10.1080/13504622.2011.596929.

Kemmis, S. & Smith, T. (eds). (2008). *Enabling Practice. Challenges for Education.* Rotterdam: Sense.

Kemmis, S., Edwards-Groves, C., Wilkinson, J. & Hardy, I. (2012). Ecologies of practices. In P. Hager, A. Lee & A. Reich (eds), *Learning and Practice.* Dordrecht: Springer. In press.

Kemmis, S., Heikkinen, H.L.T., Aspfors, J. & Hansen, S.-E. (2011). Gruppmentorskapets arkitektur och ekologi. In J. Aspfors & S.-E. Hansén (eds), *Gruppmentorskap för nya lärare* (pp. 54–78). Stockholm: Södeströms.

Kemmis, S., Wilkinson, J., Hardy, I. & Edwards-Groves, C. (2009). *Leading and Learning: Developing Ecologies of Educational Practice.* Paper presented at a Symposium Ecologies of

Practice at the Annual Meeting of the Australian Association for Research in Education, Canberra, Australia.

Kemmis, S., Edwards-Groves, C., Hardy, I., Wilkinson, J. & Lloyd, A. (2011). *On Being 'Stirred' to Practice*. Unpublished manuscript.

Kim, K., Hagedorn, M., Williamson, J. & Chapman, C. (2004). *Participation in Adult Education and Lifelong Learning: 2000–01.* Washington, DC: US Department of Education.

Kiviniemi, K. (2000). *Opettajan työtodellisuus haasteena opettajankoulutukselle. Opettajien ja opettajankouluttajien käsityksiä opettajan työstä, opettajuuden muuttumisesta sekä opettajankoulutuksen kehittämishaasteista* (Opettajien perus- ja täydennyskoulutuksen ennakointihankkeen (OPERPO) selvitys No. 14). Helsinki: Opetushallitus.

Kohonen, V. & Kaikkonen, P. (1998). Uudistuva opettajuus muutosten ja vaatimusten ristipaineissa. In H. Niemi (ed.), *Opettaja modernin murroksessa* (pp. 130–143). Jyväskylä: Atena.

Kumpuvaara, P. (2009). *'Mun äiti sano, että sä olet tosi nuori.' Noviisiopettajien kokemuksia ensimmäisestä työvuodesta* (Master's thesis). Tampere: Tampereen yliopisto, Opettajankoulutuslaitos, Hämeenlinnan yksikkö.

Kutilek, L. & Earnest, G. (2001). Supporting professional growth through mentoring and coaching. *Journal of Extension, 39,* 334–346.

Laine, T. (1998). Opettajakin on ihminen. In H. Niemi (ed.), *Opettaja modernin murroksessa.* Jyväskylä: Atena, 110–119.

Lakoff, G. & Johnson M. (1980). *Metaphors We Live By.* Chicago: University of Chicago Press.

Lapinoja, K. (2006). *Opettajan kadonnutta autonomiaa etsimässä* (Doctoral dissertation). Kokkola: Jyväskylän yliopisto, Chydenius-instituutti.

Lave, J. & Wenger, E. (1991). *Situated Learning: Legitimate Peripheral Participation.* Cambridge: Cambridge University Press.

Le Cornu, R. (2005). Peer mentoring: Engaging pre-service teachers in mentoring one another. *Mentoring and Tutoring, 13*(3), 355–366.

Le Maistre, C. & Paré, A. (2006). A typology of knowledge demonstrated by beginning professionals. In P. Tynjälä, J. Välimaa & G. Boulton-Lewis (eds), *Higher Education and Work: Collaborations, Confrontations and Challenges* (pp. 103–113). Amsterdam: Elsevier.

Leskelä, J. (2005). *Mentorointi aikuisopiskelijan ammatillisen kehittymisen tukena* (Doctoral dissertation) (Acta Universitatis Tamperensis No. 1090). Tampere: Tampereen yliopisto.

Lewin, K. (1948*). Resolving Social Conflicts. Selected Papers on Group Dynamics.* New York: Harper.

Lindhart, L. (2008). *Hvor laerer en laerer at vaere laerer? Unge Paedagoger,* (3), 41–45.

Linnakylä, P. (2004). Finland. In H. Döbert, E. Klieme & W. Stroka (eds), *Conditions of School Performance in Seven Countries: A Quest for Understanding the International Variation of PISA Results* (pp. 150–218). Munster: Waxmann.

Lohmar, B. & Eckhardt, T. (eds). (2010). *The education system in the Federal Republic of Germany 2008. A description of the responsibilities, structures and developments in education policy for the exchange of information in Europe.* Bonn: Secretariat of the Standing Conference of the Ministers of Education and Cultural Affairs of the Länder in the Federal Republic of Germany. Retrieved from http://www.kmk.org/dokumentation/das-bildungswesen-in-der-bundesrepublik-deutschland/dossier-englisch/publikation-zum-download.html.

Luukkainen, O. (2005a). *Opettajan matkakirja tulevaan.* [Teacher's travel guide for the future; in Finnish] Juva: PS-kustannus.

—— (2005b). Yhteiskuntasuuntautunut ja tulevaisuushakuinen opettaja (pp. 143–164). In O. Luukkainen & R. Valli (eds), *Kaksitoista teesiä opettajalle.* Jyväskylä: PS-kustannus.

Marsick, V.J. & Watkins, K.E. (1990). *Informal and Incidental Learning in the Workplace*. London: Routledge.

Marvel, J., Lyter, D.M., Peltola, P., Stirizek, G.A. & Morton, B.A. (2007). *Teacher Attrition and Mobility: Results from the 2004–2005 Teacher Follow-Up Survey*. Washington, DC: Government Printing Office.

Maunu, T. (2008). *Opettajat kertovat ensimmäisistä työvuosistaan vertaismentorointiryhmässä* (Master's thesis). Oulu: Oulun yliopisto, Kasvatustieteiden ja opettajankoulutuksen yksikkö.

Merriam, S., Caffarella, R. & Baumgartner, L. (2007). *Learning in Adulthood: A Comprehensive Guide* (3rd edn) New York: Wiley.

Mitchell, C. & Weber, S. (1999). *Reinventing Ourselves as Teachers: Beyond Nostalgia*. London: The Falmer Press.

Mönkkönen, K. (2007). *Vuorovaikutus. Dialoginen asiakastyö*. Helsinki: Edita.

Murray, M. (2001). *Beyond the Myths and Magic of Mentoring: How to Facilitate an Effective Mentoring Process*. San Francisco: Jossey-Bass.

Musanti, S. (2004). Balancing mentoring and collaboration. *Curriculum and Teaching Dialogue*, 6(1), 13–23.

Nasser-Abu Alhija, F. & Fresko, B. (2010). Socialization of new teachers: Does induction matter? *Teaching and Teacher Education*, 26, 1592–1597.

Niemi, H. (2000). *Teacher Education in Finland: Current Trends and Future Scenarios*. Proceedings of the Conference on Teacher Education Policies in the European Union and Quality of Lifelong Learning, European Network on Teacher Education Policies, Loulé (Algarve), Portugal.

—— (2002). Active learning – a cultural change needed in teacher education and school. *Teaching and Teacher Education*, 18, 763–780.

Niemistö, R. (1998). *Ryhmän luovuus ja kehitysehdot*. Helsinki: Helsingin yliopiston Lahden tutkimus- ja koulutuskeskus.

Nummenmaa, A. R. & Välijärvi, J. (eds). (2006). *Opettajan työ ja oppiminen*. Jyväskylä: Jyväskylän yliopisto, Koulutuksen tutkimuslaitos.

OECD (2000). *From Initial Education to Working Life*. Paris: OECD.

—— (2005). *Teachers Matter: Attracting, Developing and Retaining Effective Teachers*. Paris: OECD.

Olsen, K.-N. (2011). Aktører og roller. In E. Høihilder & K.-R. Olsen (eds), *Veiledning av de nye lærere i skole og barnehage* (pp. 14–18). Oslo: PEDLEX.

Opetusministeriö. (2007). *Opettajankoulutus 2020* [Initial teacher education 2020; in Finnish] (Opetusministeriön työryhmämuistioita ja selvityksiä No. 44). Helsinki: Author.

Palmer, K. (2007). Why teachers quit? *Teacher Magazine*, 18(6), 45.

Pesonen, J. (2011). *Opettajat oppijoina* [Teachers as learners; in Finnish] (Physical Education and Health No. 165). Jyväskylä: University of Jyväskylä. Studies in Sport.

Pistrang, N., Barker, C. & Humphreys, K. (2008). Mutual help groups for mental health problems: A review of effectiveness studies. *American Journal Community Psychology*, 42, 110–121.

Polanyi, M. (1996). *The Tacit Dimension*. Garden City, NY: Doubleday.

Pollit, C. (1990). *Managerialism and the Public Services. The Anglo-American Experience*. Oxford: Basil Blackwell.

Poom-Valickis, K. (2008). *Algajate õpetajate profesionaaline areng kutseaastal* (Dissertations on social sciences No. 33). Tallinn: Tallinn University. Retrieved from http://www.tlulib.ee/files/arts/95/poom.c688c1dfeb2de2aae41da137c3523b81.pdf.

Rajakaltio, H. (1999). Breaking with tradition: Towards collaboration in the education sector. In S. Kalliola & R. Nakari (eds), *Resources for Renewal. A Participatory Approach to the Modernisation of Municipal Organisations in Finland* (pp. 59–79). Amsterdam: John Benjamin.

—— (2005). Sosiaalisen pääoman kehkeytymisen ehdot kouluyhteisössä. In E. Poikela (ed.), *Oppiminen ja sosiaalinen pääoma* (pp. 127–151). Tampere: Tampere University Press.

—— (2008). Finnish school – the PISA star and dialogical paradox. In J. Lehtonen & S. Kalliola (eds), *Dialogue in Working Life Research and Development in Finland* (pp. 195–210). Frankfurt am Main: Peter Lang.

Rhodes, C., Stokes, M. & Hampton, G. (2004). *Practical Guide to Mentoring, Coaching, and Peer-Networking: Teacher Professional Development in Schools and Colleges*. London: Routledge Falmer.

Richardson, L. (2000). Writing. A method of inquiry. In K.D. Norman & Y.S. Lincoln (eds), *Handbook of Qualitative Research* (pp. 923–948). Thousand Oaks: Sage Publications.

Roberts, A. (2000). Mentoring revisited: A phenomenological reading of the literature. *Mentoring & Tutoring, 8*(2), 145–169.

Roehrig, A., Bohn, C., Turner, J. & Pressley, M. (2008). Mentoring beginning primary teachers for exemplary teaching practices. *Teaching and Teacher Education, 24*, 648–702.

Rönnerman, K., Furu, E. & Salo, P. (2008). *Nurturing Praxis: Action Research in Partnerships between School and University in a Nordic Light*. Rotterdam: Sense.

Roth, G., Assor, A., Kanat-Maymon, Y. & Kaplan, H. (2007). Autonomous motivation for teaching: How self-determined teaching may lead into self-determined learning. *Journal of Educational Psychology, 99*(4), 761–774.

Sahlberg, P. (2009). Ideat, innovaatiot ja investoinnit suomalaisen koulun kehittämisessä. In M. Suortamo, H. Laaksola & J. Välijärvi (eds), *Opettajan vuosi 2009–2010. Terve työympäristö* (pp. 13–56). Jyväskylä: PS-kustannus.

—— (2010). Educational change in Finland. In A. Hargreaves, A. Lieberman, M. Fullan & D. Hopkins (eds), *Second International Handbook of Educational Change* (pp. 323–348). New York: Springer.

—— (2011). Lessons from Finland. *American Educator, 35*(2). Retrieved from http://www.aft.org/pdfs/americaneducator/summer2011/ae_summer11.pdf.

Salo, P. (2002). *Skolan som mikropolitisk organisation: En studie i det som skolan är* (Doctoral dissertation). Åbo: Åbo Akademi.

Salo, P. & Kuittinen, M. (1998). Oppiiko koulu organisaationa? *Kasvatus, 29*(2), 214–223.

Santavirta, N., Aittola, E., Niskanen, P., Pasanen, I., Tuominen, K. & Solovieva, S. (2001). *Nyt riittää. Raportti peruskoulun ja lukion opettajien työympäristöstä, työtyytyväisyydestä ja työssä jaksamisesta* (Helsingin yliopiston kasvatustieteen laitoksen tutkimuksia No. 173). Helsinki: Helsingin yliopisto.

Sarason, S. B. (1971). *The Culture of School and the Problem of Change*. Boston: Allyn & Bacon.

Schatzki, T. (1996). *Social Practices: A Wittgensteinian Approach to Human Activity and the Social*. Cambridge: Cambridge University Press.

—— (2002). *The Site of the Social: A Philosophical Account of the Constitution of Social Life and Change*. University Park: Pennsylvania State University Press.

—— (2005). Peripheral vision: The sites of organizations. *Organization Studies, 26*(3), 465–484.

—— (2010). *The Timespace of Human Activity: On Performance, Society, and History as Indeterminate Teleological Events*. Lanham, MD: Lexington.

Scheopner, A.J. (2010). Irreconcilable differences: Teacher attrition in public and catholic schools. *Educational Research Review, 5*(3), 261–277.

Schiff, M. & Bargal, D. (2000). Helping characteristics of self-help and support groups. Their contribution to participants' subjective well-being. *Small Group Research, 31*, 275–304.

Schmidt, M. (2008). Mentoring and being mentored: The story of a novice music teacher's success. *Teaching and Teacher Education, 24*, 635–648.

Seeck, H. (2008). *Johtamisopit Suomessa*. Helsinki: Gaudeamus.

Seikkula, J. (1995). From monologue to dialogue in consultation with larger system. *The Journal of Systemic Consultation and Management, 6*, 21–42.

Siitonen, J. (1999). *Voimaantumisteorian perusteiden hahmottelua* (Acta Universitatis Ouluensis No. E 37). Oulu: Oulun yliopisto.

Siivonen, P. (2010). *From a 'student' to a lifelong 'consumer' of education? Constructions of educatibility in adult students' narrative life histories*. Jyväskylä: FERA.

Simola, H. (2005). The Finnish miracle of PISA: Historical and sociological remarks on teaching and teacher education. *Comparative Education, 41*(4), 455–470.

Sinclair, M. & Ashkanasy, N.M. (2002). Intuitive decision making amongst leaders: More than just shooting from the hip. *Mt Eliza Business Review, 5*(2), 32–40.

Smith, B. (1999). Truth and the visual field. In J. Petitot, F.J. Varela, B. Pachoud & J.-M. Roy (eds), *Naturalizing Phenomenology. Issues in Contemporary Phenomenology and Cognitive Science* (pp. 317–329). Stanford: Stanford University Press. Retrieved from: http://ontology. buffalo.edu/smith/articles/tvf.html.

Strange, S. (1996). *The Retreat of State. The Diffusion of Power in the World Economy*. Cambridge: Cambridge University Press.

Sulkunen, P. (2006). *Reinvention of the Social Contract*. Keynote lecture at 23rd Nordic Sociological Congress, Turku, Finland.

Sundli, L. (2007). Mentoring – A new mantra for education. *Teaching and Teacher Education, 23*(2), 201–214.

Syrjälä, L. & Heikkinen, H. (eds) (2007). *Minussa elää monta tarinaa. Kirjoituksia opettajuudesta*. Helsinki: Kansanvalistusseura.

Syrjäläinen, E. (2002). *Eikö opettaja saisi opettaa? Koulun kehittämisen paradoksi ja opettajan työuupumus* (Tampereen opettajakoulutuksen julkaisuja No. A 25). Tampere: Tampereen yliopisto.

Tillman, L.C. (2003). Mentoring, reflection, and reciprocal journaling. *Theory into Practice, 42*(3), 226–233.

Training and Development Agency for Schools (TDA). (2011). *Induction Tutors*. Retrieved from http://www.tda.gov.uk/teacher/nqt-induction/what-is-nqt-induction/roles-responsibilities/induction-tutors.aspx.

Tuckman, B. (1965). Developmental sequence in small groups. *Psychological Bulletin, 63*, 384–399.

Tunkkari-Eskelinen, M. (2005). *Mentored to Feel Free: Exploring Family Business next Generation Members' Experiences of Non-Family Mentoring* (Jyväskylä studies in business and economics No. 44). Jyväskylä: University of Jyväskylä.

Tuomi, J. & Sarajärvi, A. (2009). *Laadullinen tutkimus ja sisällönanalyysi*. Helsinki: Tammi.

Tuschling, A. & Engemann, C. (2006). From education to lifelong learning: The emerging regime of learning in the European Union. *Educational Philosophy and Theory, 38*(4), 451–469.

Tynjälä, P. (2007). Integratiivinen pedagogiikka osaamisen kehittämisessä. In H. Kotila, A. Mutanen & M.V. Volanen (eds), *Taidon tieto* (pp. 11–36). Helsinki: Edita.

—— (2008). Perspectives into learning at the workplace. *Educational Research Review, 3*(2), 130–154.

—— (2009). Connectivity and transformation in work-related learning – Theoretical foundations. In M.-L. Stenström & P. Tynjälä (eds), *Towards Integration of Work and Learning. Strategies for Connectivity and Transformation* (pp. 11–37). Dordrecht: Springer.

Tynjälä, P. & Heikkinen, H.L.T. (2011). Beginning teachers' transition from pre-service education to working life. *Zeitschrift für Erziehungswissenschaft, 14*(1), 11–34.

Tynjälä, P. & Kallio, E. (2009). *Integrative Pedagogy for Developing Professional Expertise in Higher Education*. Paper presented at the biennial conference of EARLI, August 2011, Amsterdam, the Netherlands.

Tynjälä, P., Heikkinen, H.L.T. & Kiviniemi, U. (2006). Integratiivinen pedagogiikka opetusharjoittelussa opettajan autonomisuuden tukena. *Kasvatus, 42*(4), 302–315.

Tynjälä, P., Slotte, V., Nieminen, J., Lonka, K. & Olkinuora, E. (2006). From university to working life: Graduates' workplace skills in practice. In P. Tynjälä, J. Välimaa & G. Boulton-Lewis (eds), *Higher Education and Working Life – Collaborations, Confrontations and Challenges* (pp. 73–88). Oxford: Elsevier.

Välijärvi, J. (ed.). (2000). *Koulu maailmassa – maailma koulussa. Opettajien, kuntatyönantajien ja yrityselämän näkemyksiä yleissivistävän opetuksen ja opettajankoulutuksen tulevaisuudesta*. Helsinki: Opetushallitus.

—— (2005a). Muutoksen kohtaaminen opettajan työssä. In O. Luukkainen & R. Valli (eds), *Kaksitoista teesiä opettajalle* (pp. 105–120). Jyväskylä: PS-kustannus.

—— (2005b). Oppimisen ympäristöt ja opiskeluolosuhteet [Learning environments and conditions for learning; in Finnish]. In P. Kupari & J. Välijärvi (eds), *Osaaminen kestävällä pohjalla* [Learning on the solid basis; in Finnish] (pp. 182–222). Jyväskylä: Institute for Educational Research.

—— (2007). Mistä hyvät opettajat tulevat? In E. Estola, H. Heikkinen & R. Räsänen (eds), *Ihmisen näköinen opettaja* (Acta Universtitatis Ouluensis No. E92, pp. 59–74). Oulu: Oulun yliopisto.

Välijärvi, J., Heikkinen, H., Hansen, S.-E. & Aspfors J. (2011). Finländsk lärarutbildning som kontext för gruppmentorskap. In J. Aspfors & S.-E. Hansén (eds), *Gruppmentorskap för nya lärare* (pp. 42–53). Stockholm: Södeströms.

Välijärvi, J., Linnakylä, P., Kupari, P., Reinikainen, P. & Arffman, I. (2002). *The Finnish Success in PISA – and Some Reasons Behind It*. Jyväskylä: University of Jyväskylä, Institute for Educational Research. Retrieved from http://www.jyu.fi/ktl/pisa/publication1.pdf.

Valtonen, A. (2005). Ryhmäkeskustelut – millainen metodi? [Focus Groups – Which Method?; in Finnish]. In J. Ruusuvuori & L. Tiitula (eds), *Haastattelu – tutkimus, tilanteet ja vuorovaikutus* (pp. 223–241). Tampere: Vastapaino.

Virkkunen, J. (ed.). (2002). *Osaamisen johtaminen muutoksessa. Ideoita ja kokemuksia toisen sukupolven knowledge managementin kehittelyyn* (Työelämän kehittämisohjelma No. 20). Helsinki: Työministeriö.

Vulkko, E. (2001). *Opettajayhteisön kokema päätöksenteko kouluorganisaatiossa* (Joensuun yliopiston kasvatustieteellisiä julkaisuja No. 66). Joensuu: Joensuun yliopisto.

Vuorikoski, M. (2004). Opettajien heimokulttuurit ja opettajankoulutus. *Oppiva, 1*, 9.

Vuorinen, R. (2004). Mentorointi yleistyy. *Ekonomi, 69*(8), 19.

Wang, J. & Odell, S. (2002). Mentored learning to teach and standards-based teaching reform: A critical review. *Review of Educational Review, 7*(3), 481–546.

—— (2007). An alternative conception of mentor-novice relationships: Learning to teach in reform-minded ways of as a context. *Teaching and Teacher Education, 23*, 473–489.

Wei, R.C., Darling-Hammond, L., Andree, A., Richardson, N. & Orphanos, S. (2009). *Professional Learning in the Learning Profession. A Status Report on Teacher Development in the US and Abroad* (Technical report). Dallas TX: National Staff Development Council.

Wenger, E. (1998). *Communities of Practice. Learning, Meaning and Identity*. Cambridge: Cambridge University Press.

—— (2006). *Communities of Practice: A Brief Introduction*. Retrieved from http://www.ewenger.com/theory/index.htm.

Wheelan, S., Davidson, B. & Tilin, F. (2003). Group development across time. Reality or illusion? *Small Group Research, 34*(2), 223–245.

Whitaker, D.S. (1989). *Using Groups to Help People*. London: Tavistock.

Whitty, G. (2008). Marketization and post-marketization in contemporary education policy. A keynote lecture in the Finnish Conference on Educational Research University of Turku, Turku, Finland.

Williams, A. (2003). Informal learning in the workplace: A case study of new teachers. *Educational Studies, 29*(2/3), 207–219.

Willman, A. & Kumpulainen, K. (1998). Teachers' conceptions of their profession in Finland: An interpretative analysis of teacher job satisfaction. In R. Erkkilä, A. Willman & L. Syrjälä (eds), *Promoting Teachers' Personal and Professional Growth* (Acta Universitatis Ouluensis No. E32, pp. 148–164). Oulu: Oulun yliopisto.

Wittgenstein, L. (1953). *Philosophical Investigations*. (G.E.M. Anscombe trans.). Oxford: Basil Blackwell.

Wong, H. (2004). Induction programs that keep new teachers teaching and improving. *National Association of Secondary School Principals Bulletin, 88*(638), 41–58.

Index

Page numbers in **bold** refer to figures, page numbers in *italic* refer to tables